THE GOLD

COOKERY BOOK.

Price 2s.

*Obtainable from all principal European and
African Stores in the Gold Coast.*

First published February, 1933 as *The Gold Coast Cookery Book*, British Red Cross Society (Gold Coast Branch); Government Printing Office, Accra. Illustrations are from that work and from the 1922 *South and East African Year Book*.

This edition published by Jeppestown Press, 10A Scawfell St, London, E2 8NG, United Kingdom.

Editing, arrangement, notes and introduction copyright © David Saffery 2007

ISBN   0-9553936-6-3
ISBN-13 978-0-9553936-6-2

The Ghana Cookery Book

Originally compiled by the British Red Cross Society (Gold Coast Branch) in 1933

JEPPESTOWN

Contents

FISH

Contents

CONTENTS

CONTENTS

CONTENTS

CONTENTS

CONTENTS

CONTENTS

xvi

CONTENTS

Contents

CAKES

CONTENTS

Contents

CONTENTS

CONTENTS

CONTENTS

Contents

xxvii

INTRODUCTION TO 2007 EDITION

From okra stew to cassava cakes, the *Ghana Cookery Book*, first published in aid of the British Red Cross (Gold Coast branch) 1933 as *The Gold Coast Cookery Book*, presents a snapshot of West African colonial cuisine in the early twentieth century.

The contents of earlier West African cookery books, often compiled by the wives of white colonial government servants, basically differ little from British cookery books of the same period. At a time when most cooking in West Africa was done by black male servants whose social and professional prestige relied on their mastery of European dishes, there was little inducement to present indigenous cooking, and few opportunities for white women to master the traditional cuisines of the region.

This book, however, is notable for its wide and enthusiastic use of local West African foodstuffs such as millet, groundnut, palm oil, cassava, okra and tigernut. The yeasts in fermenting palm wine are suggested as raising agents for bread, and the presence of dozens of recipes for preserving tropical fruits like guava, grapefruit and pawpaw testify to the enthusiasm with which the few white women living in West Africa before the Second World War (preference in the civil service was given to unmarried men; and 'government wives' had to apply for official permission to join their husbands in West Africa) adapted to life in such an unfamiliar environment.

Who were the contributors to this book? Women like Una Keast, originally from Wentworth in Northumberland, who had served with distinction as a nurse in France during the First World War. In 1919 she married Major Sydney Banks Keast of the Royal Engineers, and the couple came to Accra (where Keast was Superintending Sanitary Engineer, eventually becoming Director of Public Works) later the same year, and remained there for 18 years.

Lady Thomas was the wife of Shenton Thomas, Governor of the Gold Coast, and later Governor of the Straits Settlements; Lady Thomas and her husband endured three years as prisoners of the Japanese following the fall of Singapore.

Edith Northcote, who wrote the original introduction to this volume, was the wife of the Colonial Secretary of the Gold Coast, and had spent many years in East and Central Africa. Mrs Biden was the wife of Claude Biden, Deputy Auditor of the Gold Coast, and Mrs Hemans the wife of the Harbour-Master of Takoradi.

Sister Angèle and Sister Antonia were almost certainly Sisters of Our Lady of Apostles, which opened a mission school for girls in Cape Coast in 1890. Sister Angèle appears to have been based at the school, while Sister Antonia was from Keta, where the Society of African Missions founded a station in 1890. Miss Lamont was the head of the Krobo Girls' School; and Miss Spears, head of the Methodist Girls' High School in Accra. Mrs Fraser was the wife of Alexander Fraser, the first head of Achimota School and former Principal of Trinity College in Kandy—which explains the preponderance of Sinhalese recipes submitted to the book by Mrs Fraser—while the collection of sculpture and other material culture amassed by Sister Evelyn Bellamy may still be seen at the University of Birmingham's Centre of West African Studies.

The recipes in this book will delight any cook with an interest in West Africa and the cultural histories of the region.

D.S. 2007

The Contributors

ACHIMOTA SCHOOL
MRS. ALLARD, Sekondi
SISTER ANGELE, Cape Coast
SISTER ANTONIA, Keta
MRS. AUCHINLECK, Accra
MISS BARCHI, Sekondi
MRS. BARTLETT, Accra
MRS. BARTON, Kumasi
MRS. BEACH JOHNSTONE, Accra
MRS. BECKETT, Accra
MISS EVELYN BELLAMY, Cape Coast
MRS. BEVERIDGE, Accra
MRS. C. E. DE B. BIDEN, Accra
MRS. BOOTH, Accra
MRS. BROWNING, Cape Coast
MRS. BUSH, Sekondi
MRS. BUTLER, Accra
MRS. CAPON, Winneba
MRS. V. R. COE, Wenchi
MISS COUTZ, Agogo
MRS. BRUCE CRABB, Accra
MRS. CRANSTON, Accra
MRS. CREWE, Accra
MRS. CUTHBERT, Koforidua
MRS. DE CARTERET, Kumasi
MRS. DEVEREAUX, Accra
MRS. DIXON, Salaga
MRS. DONNATT, Winneba
MRS. DOWLING, Cape Coast
MRS. DRAKE, Tamale
MRS. EGG, Accra
MRS. ELLIS, Kumasi
MRS. W. EMMETT, Accra
MRS. FIELDGATE, The Residency, Koforidua
MRS. FRASER, Achimota
MRS. FREELAWN, Asokore
MRS. GIDDINGS, Wenchi
MISS. GOETZ, Agogo
MRS. GROVER
MRS. HENDERSON, Accra

MRS. HEMANS, Takoradi
MRS. HENDRY, Accra
MRS. HEWITT, Takoradi
MRS. HILDITCH, Tarkwa
MRS. W. HILL, Accra
MRS. HOLLAND, Oda
MRS. HORSEY, Obuasi
MRS. HOWE, Nkawkaw
MRS. KEAST, Accra
MRS. KEEVIL, Sekondi
MRS. KELLY, Accra
MISS S. F. LAMONT, Krobo Girls' School
MRS. LLOYD WILLIAMS, Tamale
MRS. MILLER LOGAN, Accra
MRS. LOCKHART, Mfantsipim, Cape Coast
MRS. LYNCH, Cape Coast
MRS. E. McELROY, Accra
MRS. MACFARLANE, Tamale
MRS. MARTIN, Agogo
MRS. MILES, Accra
MRS. MILNE, Winneba
MRS. MOOR, Koforidua
MRS. NICHOLAS, Kumasi
MRS. NICHOLSON, Accra Ice Co.
MRS. NORTH
MRS. NORTHCOTE, Accra
MRS. OAKLEY, Accra
MRS. PANK, Cape Coast
MRS. PASSELLS, Accra
MRS. PUCKRIDGE, Accra
MRS. ROTHWELL, Koforidua
MRS. SAMPLES, Takoradi
MRS. SAMUEL, Accra
MRS. SHAW, Accra
MRS. SHIRER, Yendi
MRS. SILCOCK, Takoradi
MRS. SINCLAIR, Kumasi
MISS SPEARS, Methodist Girls' High School
MRS. STEELE, Tamale

CONTRIBUTORS

MRS. STRADLING, Accra
MRS. SUTHERLAND, Koforidua
MRS. SWAN, Tamale
MRS. TAYLOR, Cape Coast
LADY THOMAS
MRS. THOMAS, Cape Coast

MRS. WARRINGTON, Kumasi
MRS. WEBB, Accra
MRS. WILKINS, Kumasi
MRS. WILKINSON, Dunkwa
MISS. WOOD, Accra.

The Ghana
Cookery Book

WALKER, HARRISON & GARTHWAITES, LTD.

Established Nearly a Century.

MANUFACTURERS OF

SHIPS' & EXPEDITION BISCUITS

A Prisoner of War writes:
" The best Biscuits it is possible to send."

SHIPPERS OF

FLOUR ⋆ OATMEAL ⋆ RICE PEAS AND ALL CEREALS

Government Contractors

ADDRESS

PHŒNIX BISCUIT WORKS, RATCLIFF CROSS, LONDON, E. 14, and at GRIMSBY.

This cookery book contains recipes kindly contributed by residents in this country upon whom the sole condition was imposed that all the ingredients of every recipe should be easily obtainable in the Gold Coast.

No attempt has been made to edit the contributions.

SOUPS

Quickly made Asparagus Soup

1 tin asparagus
1 oz. butter
1 small tin Ideal milk
1 teacup water
½ oz. flour
White stock

Melt the butter in a saucepan, stir in the flour, add the milk and water and bring to the boil; add pepper and salt and simmer for 10 minutes. Meanwhile strain off the liquid from the asparagus, and rub through a sieve. Add the sieved asparagus to the contents of the pan and re-heat for a short time.

MRS. DRAKE, Tamale.

Bone Stock.

3d. bones
Salt
1½ pint water
A few peppercorns
½ oz. dripping

Break the bones into medium-sized pieces, wash and dry them. Melt the dripping, and when smoking hot add the bones and brown. Add the water gradually. Bring to the boil, and take off scum as it rises. Let the stock simmer all the morning, and from 5p.m. until late evening, strain, cool, and put in ice-chest. The fat the next morning can be taken off, and the stock which will measure ¾ pint is ready for use, and any recipe followed for soup that day. As no vegetables are added the stock will keep for a few days in a Frigidaire, but it should be re-heated each evening if put in an ice-chest.

MRS. KEAST, Accra.

Bouillabaisse Soup (Provençal).

Allow for each person 10 tablespoons water, 2 tablespoons oil and, according to taste, 2 or 3 onions and small portions of lemon peel, parsley, spice, salt and if liked saffron. Add as many kinds of fresh fish as possible in proportion to the water, cut into pieces, put on very fierce fire and cook for 15 or 20 minutes.

MRS. FRASER, Achimota.

Carrot Soup.

Cut into strips the red parts only of 2 lbs. carrots, and stew them in 2 ozs. margarine stirring now and then, add salt and 4 pints stock, white or brown, simmer till carrots are soft. Sieve and re-boil with ½ teaspoonful sugar, pepper and salt, and stir in ¼ pint milk.

MRS. W. HILL, Accra.

Celery Purée.

One lb. celery, 1 onion, 1 oz. butter, 1 pint white stock, ½ oz. corn flour, ½ gill milk, ½ gill cream, pepper and salt. Wash, scrape and blanch the celery. Melt the butter, and sauté the celery and onion in it without browning. Add the stock, and cook until celery is tender, from one to two hours. Rub through a sieve, add the cornflour broken with the milk, and cook for 10 minutes. Add the cream and seasonings.

MRS. HENDERSON, Accra.

Celery Soup.

Two ozs. of butter, one onion, two heads of celery, 2 quarts of stock, rind of half a lemon, a bunch of herbs. Cook vegetables for 10 minutes in butter, but do not brown them. Add stock, and boil for two or three hours, and thicken with corn flour and milk.

MRS. BUSH, Sekondi.

Cheese Soup.

1 pint milk
2 ozs. Kraft or cheddar cheese
Salt and pepper
½ oz. butter
½ oz. flour
1 yolk of egg

Grate cheese and melt it with a little milk, but do not boil. Heat remaining milk. Melt the butter, and mix well with the flour. Add the milk gradually and stir well until boiling. Add the cheese, salt and pepper, make very hot, but do not boil again. Put yolk of egg beaten into basin and pour soup over, stirring all the time, add to each plate some shredded lettuce just before serving. Sufficient for 2 persons.

MRS. KEAST, Accra,

Chicken Broth.

Cut up the chicken into small pieces. Scald and skin gizzard and feet, wash liver and bones and stew in 2 quarts cold water and teaspoonful salt. Boil, skim, and add 1 onion, minced mace and seasoning, cook gently 3 hours, strain, boil up, sprinkle in 1 tablespoonful rice and simmer 20 minutes. Add 1 teaspoonful chopped parsley and serve.

MRS. W. HILL, Accra.

Chestnut or Groundnut Soup.

1½ lb nuts
1 quart stock
Seasoning
½ pint milk
A few drops carmine, for chestnut soup.

1. Prick nuts and roast in a moderate oven until shells crack.
2. Remove shells and inner skin, and pound slightly.
3. Put into pan with stock, simmer about 1½ hours till tender,
4. Rub through a sieve, add milk and seasoning.
5. Re-heat but do not boil. Add colouring, if needed.

MRS. BEACH JOHNSTONE, Accra.

Clear Soup.

(Quantities for four.)

One lb. meat (lean), 1 turnip, 1 stick celery, 1 carrot, 1 onion, dried herbs, 6 cloves, shells of 2 eggs and beaten whites of eggs, pepper and salt.

Wash and cut up the meat and put in a saucepan with enough cold water to cover, put on fire, boil up quickly, and skim very carefully. Cut up all vegetables small and add seasoning, also herbs and cloves. Simmer slowly for about 2 hours, strain, return to saucepan and boil up again. Beat up whites of eggs and add, also the finely crushed shells and beat up well in the saucepan on the fire for 5 minutes. Strain again through a clean cloth and return to fire in a clean saucepan and add a glass of sherry. This can be used hot or cold, but if cold a little gelatine improves it.

MRS. NORTHCOTE, Accra.

Coconut Soup

Make ordinary stock with beef bones and vegetables, thicken with barley or cornflour, strain, and add the milk of a ripe coconut, obtained in the following way: grate the coconut into a bowl, and pour over it just enough water to cover it, let it steep for 10 minutes, then squeeze it through a clean cloth. Mix a teaspoonful of curry powder into a smooth paste with a little cold water, add to the stock, and boil for a few minutes. Remove to the side of the fire, and add the coconut milk, taking care that it does not boil, or it will curdle.

MISS BARCHI, Sekondi.

Coconut Soup.

2 oz. coconut (shredded)
2 oz. flour
1 qt. stock
½ pint milk.
Pinch of ground mace
Salt, pepper

The stock may be made beforehand by stewing a fowl to get a white stock. Simmer the coconut in the stock for one hour; then sieve it, thicken with the flour, and boil up, then add milk, seasoning and mace and re-heat before serving. Serve with fried bread.

MRS. OAKLEY, Accra.

Corn Soup.

Boil the corn till soft. Take off the stalks and rub through a sieve with a little onion, heat the purée in a double saucepan. Mix one dessertspoonful of corn flour with one pint of milk, add this to the purée and stir till boiling, season with pepper and salt.

MRS. PUCKRIDGE, Accra.

43

Corn Soup.

Six ears young corn, 1 quart water, milk and eggs if desired. Grate the corn, pour the water over and strain, add salt and pepper, cook, stirring constantly until the soup is thick. If desired the soup may be thinned with milk. Two eggs, beaten and added just before serving may be used if a richer soup is wanted.

MRS. NICHOLAS, Kumasi.

Cream of Corn Soup.

Two cups grated green corn, 1 tablespoonful corn cut from cob, 2 tablespoonfuls Ideal milk, and 2 small onions. These quantities are sufficient for two portions. Add 1 cup of cold water to the 2 cups of grated corn and boil. Skim off husk as it rises to the surface. Add 2 small onions, salt and pepper to taste and the corn cut from the cob. Boil for two hours, adding water to maintain original level. Take off the fire, add milk and keep hot until required. Do not boil again or the milk may curdle.

MRS. MOOR, Koforidua.

Fish Soup.

Take 1 pints fresh stock in which fish has been boiled, one large onion, half pint milk and pepper, thicken with one spoonful of corn flour.

MRS. BROWNING, Cape Coast.

Garden Egg Soup.

Meat or fish 1s., 5 onions, 2 tomatoes, pepper, 3 okras, garden eggs[1] 3d., salt. Boil the garden eggs, okras and pepper till tender. Clean and cut the meat into pieces, put on the fire until half cooked and add in some salt. Grind the boiled pepper and garden eggs. Add in when the meat is half-cooked, let it boil for 15 minutes, and simmer for five, serve hot.

SISTER ANGELE, Cape Coast.

---

[1] i.e. aubergine or eggplant. DS

44

Groundnut Soup.

Meat 2s., onions 1d., pepper, groundnuts 6d., 2 garden eggs, 1 tomato, salt, and a little flour. Roast the nuts until they are of a light-brown colour, place them on a sieve to cool, rub between the hands until all the brown covering comes off, then grind into a paste. Cut the meat into small pieces and dredge each piece with flour, fry in lard for about 10 minutes. Have one quart of boiling water and put in meat and salt, and boil for half hour. Next take some of the water and mix it with the groundnut paste, add the whole to the boiling water and meat. Crush the garden eggs, tomato and onion and add to the soup. Boil for another half hour.

SISTER ANGELE, Cape Coast.

Groundnut Soup.

1 pint good stock, 1 lb. groundnuts.

Bake groundnuts in oven and when cooked grind to a powder, mix into a paste with a little milk, then add to stock. Stir thoroughly before serving.

MRS. ROTHWELL, Koforidua.

Groundnut Soup.

3d. groundnuts, 9d. pork, onions, tomatoes, pepper and salt to taste.

1. Shell and fry groundnuts, remove the skin and grind.
2. Wash and cut the pork into chunks, put into a saucepan with a little water and salt. Bring to boil and allow to boil for 10 minutes. Take the saucepan from the fire and put the contents in a dish.
3. Wash the saucepan, put back the pork and fry with sliced onions and tomatoes.
4. Mix the groundnut with four cups of water, strain, and pour it on the fried pork. Allow to boil for 5 minutes, then add the ground pepper, stir and cover. Allow to cook slowly for 45 minutes.

SISTER ANTONIA, Keta.

Kidney Soup.

6 ozs. kidney
6 ozs. lean beef
2 tablespoons rice
1 onion
1 oz. butter
Pepper and salt.

Shred beef and kidney also onion and cook in a little butter for 10 minutes. Add stock, rice, pepper and pass through a sieve. Heat again and add parsley. Serve with fried bread.

MRS. BROWNING, Cape Coast.

Kidney Soup

Four Ice Co. kidneys, or 12 market kidneys, 4 pints stock, 2 large onions, 2 ozs. dripping, 2 ozs. flour. Cut up the kidneys and onions, fry all in the dripping. Take out the kidneys and onions and add the flour to the pan and brown. Put back the kidneys and onions, add the stock and mix well, bring to the boil, and skim. Simmer as long as possible, skimming frequently. Add one Oxo cube, strain, cool, and put in ice-chest.

The next day, take off the grease, and reheat for dinner. Add some thickening to the soup. A little kidney cut in pieces, may be added to each soup plate. Sufficient for 8 persons.

MRS. KEAST, Accra.

Lentil and Tomato Purée.

Half lb. lentils, 1 onion, 3 pints water or stock, small tin tomato purée, 1 teaspoonful sugar, pepper and salt. Wash lentils well in several waters. Put on to boil with cold water or stock. Add onion and cook from 4 to 2 hours. Rub through a sieve, return to pan, add tomato purée and bring all to boil. Add seasonings.

MRS. HENDERSON, Accra.

Lobster Soup.

One lobster, 1 quart milk, 1 pint water, 1 lb. butter, 1 tablespoon flour, salt, red pepper to taste. Chop lobster finely, scald milk and water, add lobster, butter, flour, salt and pepper, boil 10 minutes, serve hot.

MRS. BROWNING, Cape Coast.

Macaroni Soup.

Two ozs. macaroni, 3 breakfastcups water, 1 breakfastcup milk, 3 small onions, ½ oz. breadcrumbs, ½ oz. butter, seasoning. Soak macaroni for 2 hours. Bring milk and water to the boil, and when boiling, add macaroni. Add bread, onion and salt, boil all slowly till soft. Rub through a sieve, return to pan, add more seasoning and the butter, boil for a few minutes. Serve with toast. A little stock may be used instead of some of the water, if preferred.

MISS LAMONT, Krobo Girls' School.

Mulligatawny Soup (Ceylon).

Mix 3 onions—slice and fry in 1 tablespoon butter— 1 apple sliced, left on slow fire with onion till soft, 1 tablespoon curry powder, 1 tablespoon flour. Add 40 tablespoons any stock. Simmer for 1 hour and pass through sieve. Warm any remains of cold fowl and serve in the soup. Serve with rice and sliced lemon.

MRS. FRASER, Achimota.

Mutton Broth.

Cut up 1 lb. scrag end of mutton into small pieces, remove fat, and place with bones in 1 quart water and salt. Boil up and skim, add 1 turnip, 1 carrot, 1 onion, cut up in dice along with 1½ oz. pearl barley (washed), and boil for 2 hours. The mutton may either be cut smaller and put back in soup or served separately.

MRS. W. HILL, Accra.

Okra Soup.

1 pint good stock, 1 dozen okras.

Boil okras until soft, remove seeds from inside, mash into a pulp, then add to stock. Stir continuously while boiling.

MRS. ROTHWELL, Koforidua.

Okra Soup.

4d. lobster, 6d. meat, 5 cups water, 3 tomatoes, a little cold fish, 20 okras, pepper, onions and salt to taste.

1. Wash and clean the lobsters. Grind the heads, mix with a little water and strain.

2. Cut the meat, put in a saucepan, add four cups of water and a little salt, allow to boil for 10 minutes.

3. Strain the water and fry the meat until brown. Pour back the water on the fried meat and allow to boil for minutes. Add the lobsters, the strained water from heads, tomatoes, cold fish and pepper. Cover with a lid and cook for 20 minutes.

4. Clean and pound the okra, add to soup and cook for one hour.

SISTER ANTONIA, Keta.

Onion Soup.

1 pint good stock, 2 bunches local onions. Add finely chopped onions to the stock and simmer slowly. Thicken with flour and milk before serving.

MRS. ROTHWELL, Koforidua.

Oxtail Soup.

Cut the oxtail in small pieces, after washing well in cold water, put on with 2 quarts stock and boil quickly. Skim thoroughly, add salt, 1 teaspoonful peppercorns, and a few cloves tied in a muslin bag and boil for 3 hours. Cut into dice 1 carrot and 1 turnip and add to soup hour before serving. Remove the larger pieces of tail and serve for meat course.

MRS. W. HILL, Accra.

Oyster Soup.

1 tin oysters
1 pint milk
1 onion
1 tablespoon butter
1 tablespoon flour
Seasoning.

Melt the butter in an enamelled pan and mix the flour with it. Add the milk gradually, and the tin of oysters with the liquor, also the onion, and stir till it thickens, simmer gently for 10 minutes.

MISS BARCHI, Sekondi.

Packet Soup.—Two Uses.

I.—Take one pint soup cube—oxtail, vegetable, or mulligatawny—and make in accordance with the instructions on the packet. While it is cooking slowly, mince a pound of cold beef finely. Chop up one small onion, and fry in a little dripping in a saucepan to a pale brown, then stir in a teaspoon of flour. Pour this into the prepared soup, add the meat, a few chopped capers (if liked) and salt, and pepper to taste. Let the mince get thoroughly hot, but do not let it boil or it will be tough. Serve on a hot dish with a border of mashed potatoes.

II.—Prepare a tomato soup cube as directed, using rather less than the required amount of water. Cut cold lamb into neat cutlet-shaped pieces, brush them over with salad oil or melted dripping, and sprinkle with seasoned flour. Arrange them in a fireproof dish, and pour over the soup to just cover. Place in a cool oven and allow to simmer gently for 10 to 15 minutes. Do not boil. Serve on a hot dish garnished with fingers of dry toast dipped in chopped parsley, and rings of tomato. An extra soup should be served separately as gravy.

MRS. PASSELLS, Accra.

Palm Oil Chop.

(Some people find this indigestible owing to the amount of oil in it, this method of preparing it will be found much more digestible). One soup-plateful of oil nuts, 1 cup of ground nuts, 1 tin prawns or fresh when available, about a dozen okras, 4 or 5 garden eggs, 2 or 3 large green pepper, 3 plants of spinach, 4 hard boiled eggs, 1 chicken.

Wash the nuts and put in a saucepan and boil for an hour in enough cold water to cover them. Remove from fire and strain off the water, crush the nuts well and put in saucepan with enough fresh water to cover, mix well and strain carefully and put on fire. Boil about ½ hour, grind the groundnuts well and mix with a little water to make a paste, and add little by little to palmnut soup, taking care that it does not get too thick. Leave it to simmer slowly, cut the chicken into joints and add to the soup with onions and pepper and salt. When it is properly cooked the oil will be seen floating on the top, and all this can be skimmed off carefully. Replace near fire and simmer very slowly, meanwhile cook the spinach in another saucepan, strain when cooked and chop finely and add to soup. The prawns, okras and garden eggs are cooked each in a separate saucepan. When soup and chicken are ready, put them in a casserole or deep dish and add the prawns, okras, garden eggs and hard boiled eggs. Crush the green pepper well and serve in a separate dish.

Hand round coco-nut, fried bananas, pawpaw, pineapple, orange and ground native ginger.

MRS. NORTHCOTE.

Palmnut Soup.

Fish 1s., 10 onions, pepper, palmnuts 3d., 2 tomatoes, salt. Wash and boil the palmnuts, mix with water and strain. Clean the fish. Cut the onions and tomatoes into slices. Grind the pepper. Put the strained palmnut into a clean pot and add the other ingredients, boil for one hour.

SISTER ANGELE, Cape Coast.

Palmnut Soup with Fresh Fish.

Sixpence fish, 4d. palmnut, onions, pepper, tomatoes, one okra, salt to taste.

1. Cook and pound the nuts.
2. Mix with warm water and strain into a clean saucepan.
3. Clean the okra and add to strained palmnut. Bring to boil.
4. Clean the fish and grind the pepper, onions and tomatoes separately. Add one by one to boiling palmnut, add salt. Cover with a clean lid and allow to simmer gently for one hour.

SISTER ANTONIA, Keta.

Palmnut Soup with Fowl.

One fowl, 7 handfuls palmnuts, ½ teaspoonful pepper, 10 onions, a little ginger, 6 tomatoes, salt to taste.

1. Clean and cut fowl into pieces.
2. Cook nuts (30 minutes).
3. Pound, mix with boiling water and strain.
4. Grind tomatoes, ginger, pepper and four onions.
5. Cut remaining onions into slices.
6. Salt meat and fry for 20 minutes, add slices of onions and let them brown.
7. Add tomatoes, ground onions, pepper and ginger, and let it cook for 10 minutes.
8. Pour on the strained nuts and allow to cook slowly for 1 hours.

SISTER ANTONIA, Keta.

Potato Soup.

Pare and cut up a dozen potatoes and put them in sufficient boiling water with 3 or 4 sliced onions, a marrow bone or piece of dripping, boil for 2 or 3 hours. Add seasoning 10 minutes before serving.

MRS. W. HILL, Accra.

Potato Soup.

1 lb. potatoes
1½ pints stock or water
2 small onions
½ oz. dripping
½ oz. sago
½ pint milk
Seasoning.

1. Wash, peel and slice potatoes finely.
2. Cut onions into thin slices and cook in the fat, with the lid on the pan, for 10 minutes, with the potatoes.
3. Add stock, and simmer gently for one hour or until soft.
4. Rub through a sieve, return to pan and add sago and milk.
5. Cook until sago is transparent.
6. Season and serve. The soup should be the consistency of thick cream.

MRS. BEACH JOHNSTONE, Accra.

Pumpkin Soup.

Boil 1 small pumpkin with an onion in 4 pints of water. Strain through a sieve. Add pint of milk, salt and pepper to taste and a small lump of butter and bring to the boil.
Serve with crisp croutons of bread.

ACHIMOTA.

Pumpkin Soup.

A good piece of pumpkin
2 large onions
½ oz. butter
½ tablespoon corn flour or
1 tablespoon flour
1 tin milk
1½ pint water
Salt, pepper

Peel and cut up the pumpkin into pieces, peel and slice the onions, fry these in the margarine till soft but not coloured, then put the pumpkin and onions to cook in the water till soft. Strain out the vegetables, sieve these, make thickening with the liquid and corn flour or flour, put all together again, add the milk and seasoning and re-heat before serving. Cubes of fried bread may be served with this.

MRS. OAKLEY, Accra.

Scotch Broth.

Put 1½ to 2 lbs. beef or mutton into 3 quarts boiling water, also 1 teacupful pearl barley, 1 cupful of green peas, the same of carrot and turnip cut in dice, and 4 small onions cut up small. Boil for fully 3 hours, keeping the lid closed, and stirring occasionally. Season some time before serving.

MRS. W. HILL, Accra.

Soup Jelly.

(For eight persons.) One lb. lean beef, 1 onion, 1 large carrot, wine-glass sherry. Cut up beef, add vegetables and one quart water, (simmer for three hours, strain and cool. Skim off fat, re-heat to liquid state, add salt to taste, wine and eight sheets gelatine to one pint soup. Set on ice, chop up and serve in cups, very cold.

MRS. DEVEREAUX, Accra.

Spinach Soup.

(Cooked with salted meat.) Ingredients.—9d. salted meat, 12 onions, 3 big tomatoes, 5 teacupfuls of spinach leaves, ½ teaspoonful of pepper, 5 cloves, 30 caraway seeds, 7 peppercorns, a little cold fish; salt to taste.

Method—1. Wash and boil spinach, strain and beat well (with a wooden spoon. Put aside covered.

2. Wash salt from meat and cut into fairly big pieces.

3. Cut 6 onions into big slices and fry with meat, adding a dessert-spoonful of lard.

4. Chop the other 6 onions, tomatoes, cloves, peppercorns, pepper and caraway seeds separately and add to the meat on fire, add also the cold fish.

5. Cook on a moderate fire for 6 minutes, then add two cupfuls boiling water and allow to simmer for 10 minutes.

6. Add the prepared spinach, keep boiling until well cooked.

N.B.—Spinach soup may be cooked with fowl or smoked fish with crabs. Sometimes 3 tablespoonfuls of palm or kernel oil are added.

SISTER ANTONIA, Keta.

Thickening for Soups.

To thicken soup take 2 teaspoons of flour and add a little stock, mix well and strain into soup, stir continually for about five minutes over fire, and strain soup before serving.

MRS. KEAST, Accra.

Tomato Soup.

1 pint tinned or 1 lb. fresh tomatoes
1 pint white stock
1 gill milk
1½ ozs. margarine
1½ ozs. flour
1 teaspoon sugar
1 small onion
Bouquet garni
A few drops carmine
Seasoning.

1. Put tomatoes, onions and flavouring in a pan,
2. Simmer till tender, about hour,
3. Rub through a sieve.
4. Mix fat and flour in a pan over small heat till bubbling,
5. Add purée gradually and stir till boiling,
6. Add seasoning, sugar and colouring.

MRS. BEACH JOHNSTONE, Accra.

Tomato and Barley Soup.

Six large tomatoes, 3 onions, 1 teacup barley, 3 teacups milk, 12 teacups hot water. Put tomatoes, onions and water in pot and boil for 2 hours. Strain, and add milk. Boil up, and add pepper, and salt to taste.

MRS. SWAN, Tamale.

Tomato and Rice Soup.

1 pint of tinned tomatoes or 1 lb. fresh
½ oz. margarine
1 quart stock or water
1 oz. rice
1 onion
Pinch of sugar
Seasoning.

1. Chop onion finely and cook in fat.
2. Remove skins from tomatoes and cut into dice.
3. Add to the onion with the stock and washed rice.
4. Simmer gently till cooked, to of an hour.
5. Season, colour and serve.

MRS. BEACH JOHNSTONE, Accra.

Vegetable Soup.

Cut up very small 2 potatoes, 1 turnip, 1 carrot, 1 onion, and add to 4 oz. margarine melted in pan. Stir the vegetables but do not brown, add 4 pints water and simmer until the vegetables are soft. Skim, season with salt, pepper and nutmeg. Mix 1 oz. flour with 1 gill milk till smooth, add to soup and boil 10 minutes.

MRS. W. HILL.

Vegetable Soups.

Any vegetable—carrots, onions, turnips, potatoes, tomatoes, etc. 1½ pints fresh milk (or equivalent in tinned milk), 1½ pints water, 1 tablespoon butter, 2 tablespoons flour.

Boil the selected vegetable and put it through a sieve. Tinned vegetables do not require cooking and potatoes should be carefully mashed. Rub flour and butter together, add milk and pepper and salt to taste. Stir over the fire until thick and smooth and no lumps remain. Add the water, preferably that in which the vegetable was boiled, and finally the vegetables. Heat but do not bring to the boil. Serve with fried sippets of bread.

MRS. MOOR, Koforidua.

Vegetable Soup (White)

1 carrot
1 small turnip
1 small onion
1 stick celery
1 bay leaf
½ oz. dripping
1½ pints stock or water
½ pint milk
1 oz. flour
Seasoning.

1. Prepare vegetables, cut into inch-long blocks, then into strips, the thickness of a match.
2. Chop onion finely
3. Put vegetables and fat in pan and cook a few minutes with lid on the pan.
4. Add stock and flavouring, simmer till tender about one hour.
5. Mix flour and milk smoothly, add to soup and stir till boiling.
6. Simmer for five minutes, remove bay leaf, season, and serve.

MRS. BEACH JOHNSTONE, Accra.

White Sauce or Dry Soup.

Two tablespoons coconut oil, 3 small onions, 7 red peppers, 2 tomatoes, 1 teaspoon salt, 1 okra, ½d. cold fish, 8 cups water, 6d. or 9d. smoked fish, 4 tablespoons baked corn flour

Grease a pan with oil. Slice the onions, tomatoes, add salt, put into pan with ground pepper and fry for 5 minutes. Mix the baked cornflour with the 8 cups of water, pour into the saucepan. When boiling add the fish which has been broken into small pieces, then add the okra. Keep well stirred and allow to cook for 45 minutes.

SISTER ANTONIA, Keta.

Vegetable Soup (Brown).

2 small carrots
2 small onions
2 small turnips
2 ozs. flour
2 ozs. dripping
1 quart stock or water
Seasoning
1 bouquet garni.

1. Peel and cut vegetable in pieces.
2. Fry sliced onion in fat till just brown.
3. Add flour and cook till brown.
4. Add stock and vegetables and stir till boiling.
5. Simmer till tender, one to two hours.
6. Sieve if required, re-heat. Season and serve.

MRS. BEACH JOHNSTONE, Accra.

FISH

Baked Fillets or Cutlets (any white fish).

Four cutlets or fillets, 1 tablespoon tomato sauce, 1 tablespoon Worcester sauce, ½ cup of stock or meat extract mixed with water, ½ oz. of butter, a few chopped capers.

Place the fillets or cutlets of fish in an enamel baking tin or pie dish, with a knob of butter on each fillet or cutlet. Mix sauces and stock and chopped capers together, pour over the fish, Cover with grease-proof paper. Cook in the oven for about 20 minutes, according to size of cutlets or fillets. Baste well.

Place fish on a deep dish or entree dish, pour sauce over, serve very hot.

MRS. DONNATT, Winneba.

Baked Fish.

One lb. fish, 1 oz. butter or margarine, 1 tablespoonful flour, ½ pint milk, 1 egg, 1 tablespoonful breadcrumbs, 1 dessertspoonful grated cheese, pepper and salt, 1 onion and parsley.

Steam fish 25 minutes, remove skin and bone and break into flakes. Melt butter in saucepan, make a thin paste of flour with a little milk, boil remains of milk with butter then pour on flour, return to saucepan, boil for two minutes; stir in fish, salt, pepper, onion, parsley, let cool. Whip yolk of egg, stir in, and last white whipped to froth. Turn into pie dish, sprinkle with cheese and brown breadcrumbs, slightly brown in oven.

MRS. DOWLING, Cape Coast.

Baked Halibut.

Few people realize how economical halibut is, Take 1 lb. halibut, onions, tomatoes, butter, pepper and salt. Slice the halibut into ½ inch slices, put a small piece of butter into a fireproof dish, then slices of tomatoes and onions, pepper and salt, then a slice of fish well seasoned, a small piece of butter, continue so, keeping tomatoes for the top, add a very little drop of water, cook until tender, but do not let the fish break.

MRS. NICHOLSON, Accra.

59

Baked Salmon Pudding.

Pick and bone one tin of salmon, and beat well with some butter and plenty of pepper. Put into a well greased pie dish and make the following sauce and pour over the top.

One cupful of milk, heated to boiling point and thickened with cornflour. Strain some liquid taken from the fish into this. Add 1 oz. butter, a teaspoonful of tomato sauce, pepper and one well beaten egg. Bake for half an hour.

MRS. HOWE, Nkawkaw.

Cold Fish Piquant.

One tin of salmon (or other fish), 1 lettuce, slices of cucumbers, the yolks of 2 eggs, the juice of half a lemon (or lime), a seasoning of salt and pepper (cayenne), 1 oz butter, 4 tablespoons of water. Skin and bone the fish and place it on a dish, whip the yolks of eggs, mix with them salt, pepper, butter (melted) and the lemon juice and water, stir over gentle heat, beat until the mixture is quite thick, cool and pour it gently over the fish, garnish, when cold, with lettuce and cucumber.

MRS. HOLLAND, Oda.

Cold Fish Mayonnaise.

Half lb. of any cold boiled fish, ½ lb. cold cooked potatoes, ½ lb. tomatoes, a few olives, a bottle of mayonnaise and, where obtainable, a cucumber. Flake the fish, cut potatoes into dice, slice the tomatoes thickly and the cucumber thinly, arrange in a glass dish alternate layers of the vegetables, making a slight hollow in the centre, in which pile the flaked fish. Pour on the mayonnaise sauce, and decorate with the olives, halved and stoned.

MRS. HEWITT, Takoradi.

Crab Scallops.

One cup crab meat (contents of one tin of "My Lady" dressed crab, boned and flaked, was found just right), 1 tablespoon butter, ¼ teaspoon salt, ¼ cup breadcrumbs, ⅓ cup milk, ¼ teaspoon minced parsley, pepper to taste. Melt the butter in a saucepan, add the flaked crab meat, and cook for three minutes. Now stir in the milk, crumbs, salt, pepper and parsley, also a dash of grated nutmeg, if liked. Make piping hot; pile into buttered scallop-shells or ramekin cases, sprinkle with crumbs, dab with tiny bits of butter, and bake for 10 minutes in a hot oven.

MRS. WILKINSON, Dunkwa.

Creamed Fish.

White boiled fish, salad oil, hot milk, onion, seasoning. Warm a spoonful of oil, add a little onion, fry slightly (but not brown); add the flaked boiled fish, and beat up adding alternately a little hot milk and a little oil, until the mixture is the consistency of creamy mashed potatoes. Serve hot with fried croutons.

ACHIMOTA.

Creamed Lobster.

2 lb. tinned lobster
½ oz. butter
½ oz. flour
½ pint milk
Lemon juice
One or two tablespoonfuls cream
Salt and pepper

Cut lobster into small pieces; melt butter, stir in flour and add milk. When boiling, add lobster, salt, pepper and cream; add lemon juice just before serving.

Note—Prawns or shrimps may be substituted for lobster.

MRS. CUTHBERT, Koforidua.

Creamed Prawns.

One tin prawns, ½ tin ideal milk, 1½ tablespoons flour, 1 tablespoon butter. Melt butter in saucepan and add a little water to make a paste, then pour in milk. Add the prawns, half of which should be chopped and the remainder put in whole, season to taste. Boil for about five minutes. Put the mixture into scallop shells and finish with breadcrumbs and butter, place in oven to brown. Decorate with parsley.

MRS. SUTHERLAND, Koforidua.

Creamed Prawns.

Allow 1 pint fresh prawns, or 1 large tin prawns for four persons. Melt a tablespoonful of butter in a saucepan, add a tablespoonful flour, blend well and add gradually ¾ pint hot milk, taking care to get the mixture really creamy. Heat the prawns for a few minutes in the sauce, turn all into a casserole and keep hot in the oven while dishing up.

MRS. LLOYD WILLIAMS, Tamale.

Creamed Salmon.

1 tin salmon (1 lb.)
2 tablespoons flour
2 boiled and chopped egg whites
1 pint hot milk
1 tablespoonful butter
1 cup chopped groundnuts
Salt and cayenne pepper

Melt butter and flour together and season with salt and cayenne. Add hot milk, cook until quite smooth. Add salmon, free from bones and skin, groundnuts and chopped hard boiled whites of eggs. Serve on rounds of buttered toast or fried bread. Enough for four or five people.

MRS LLOYD WILLIAMS, Tamale.

Dublin Lawyer.

(A favourite bachelor breakfast dish in Ceylon.)[2]

One tin lobster, 2 tablespoons butter, 5 tablespoons sherry, red pepper and salt to taste and a squeeze of lemon, cook if possible at table on small spirit lamp or stove.

MRS. FRASER, Achimota.

East India Fish.

Half lb. cooked fish, 2 ozs. butter or margarine, 2 small onions, 1 tablespoon flour or rice flour, I dessertspoonful curry powder, 2 tablespoons coconut, 2 hard-boiled eggs, 1 pint milk, lemon or lime juice, pepper and salt. Melt the fat in a frying pan, add the onions finely chopped and cook until they become yellow. Stir in the rice flour and curry powder mixing them until smooth. Then pour in the milk and stir until boiling.

Draw the pan to the side of the fire and add the eggs cut in small pieces, the fish flaked and free from bone and the grated coconut. Season to taste with pepper and salt and allow to become thoroughly hot. Garnish with slices of lemon and serve boiled rice separately. Can be served hot or cold.

MRS. PUCKRIDGE, Accra.

Fillets of Fish.

(Very digestible for invalids.) One fish (filleted), 1 piece butter, size of an egg, 1 lime, pepper and salt. Cut filleted fish in pieces and lay in pie dish. Season with pepper and salt. Put butter on top in small pieces. Squeeze juice of lime over. Cover with buttered paper. Bake in a moderate oven for 10 minutes.

MRS. SWAN, Tamale.

---

[2] Mrs Fraser and her husband had lived for some time in Kandy, Ceylon, where Rev. Fraser was Principal of Trinity College. DS

Fillets of Fish (whitebait style).

Skin and fillet a sole, cut into strips 2 inches long, thicker fish can be used and cut into strips as above. Roll the strips in flour, toss on a coarse sieve and fry in very hot fat, drain well, sprinkle with salt and cayenne mixed and serve with cut lemon and brown bread and butter.

MRS. OAKLEY, Accra.

Fillets of Sole and Mushrooms.

One sole (filleted), 4 large mushrooms, 1 oz. butter, ½ gill water, ½ gill milk, 1 teaspoonful mushroom ketchup (juice from tin of mushrooms will do), a few drops cochineal, salt and pepper, ¾ oz. flour.

Place the mushrooms in a steamer, under-side up with a piece of butter in each. Wash the fillets and roll them up tightly with the skin inside, lay the fillets in a tin plate on top of the steamer. Pour in half a gill of water, and put on the lid. Steam till the mushrooms are tender and the fish is white and soft (about 20 minutes), place the mushrooms on a hot dish with a fillet of sole standing in each one. Use the liquid from the fish and mushrooms to make the sauce.

Sauce.—Mix the flour smoothly with the milk and pour the hot stock on to it, stirring well. Stir till it boils, add the ketchup and a few drops of cochineal, and season to taste. Strain the sauce round the fish.

MRS. DONNATT, Winneba.

Fish

Fillets of sole, milk, tomatoes, Scoop inside of tomatoes, season and make into batter with milk, lay fillets in greased dish, cover with mixture, bake slowly 15 minutes, sprinkle with breadcrumbs and bake a further 15 minutes to brown.

MRS. DEVEREUX, Accra.

Fish

One lb. cooked white fish, 3 tablespoons grated cheese, 4 tomatoes, ½ pint thick white sauce. Grease dish, lay in pulp of two tomatoes, lay in fish, cover with cheese, then layer thinly sliced skinned tomatoes and cover with sauce and bake 15 minutes.

MRS. DEVEREUX, Accra.

Fish Croquettes (with gravy).

Three-quarter lb. fish (uncooked), 1 egg, 1 onion, ½ teaspoon salt, $\frac{1}{8}$ teaspoon pepper, 1 dessertspoon Worcestershire sauce, 1 dessertspoon of butter. Mince fish and onion together, beat egg, add same and all other ingredients, also a little breadcrumbs, shape as for croquettes. Roll in breadcrumbs and fry in hot fat until brown.

To make Gravy.

Fry a tomato and a few slices of an onion; add pepper, Worcestershire sauce, butter and 2 cloves with water to cover contents ; let it all simmer for 15 to 20 and serve hot.

MRS. EGG, Accra.

Fish and Tomatoes.

One lb. fish, 2 or 3 large tomatoes, 2 to 3 ozs. rice, 1 oz. butter, seasoning, 1 small onion.

1. Cook the rice and dry it.
2. Chop the onion.
3. Melt the butter and lightly fry the onion in it.
4. Skin the tomatoes and cut them up.
5. Cook them for a few minutes with the onion.
6. Wash the fish and cut it into small pieces.
7. Add it to the tomato and onion and cook all together, very gently, for about 10 minutes.
8. Season well.
9. Make a border of the rice on a hot dish.
10. Put the fish mixture into the middle. Serve very hot.

ACHIMOTA.

Fish Cakes.

Skin and bone 1 lb. cooked fish, and mix with 1 lb. mashed potatoes, cold, some chopped parsley, pepper and salt. Form into small cakes, cover with egg and breadcrumbs (4 tablespoonfuls), and fry in hot fat to a golden brown.

MRS. W. HILL, Accra.

Fish Creams.

1lb. fish
3 eggs
1 tin cream
2 tablespoonfuls breadcrumbs.
Pepper and salt

Wash and skin the fish and remove the bones, pass it through the mincing machine (raw). Mix in the breadcrumbs and 1 tin cream (well whipped), beat the eggs well and add them to the mixture with the seasoning, pour into ramekin cases or dariole moulds and steam for 1 hour. Turn out, cover the top of each with sauce and decorate with a small sprig parsley. Sufficient for 8 or 10 persons according to size of moulds, can be served hot or cold.

Sauce for Fish Cream.

One large tin cream, 3 tablepoonfuls Heinz mayonnaise, 1 tablespoonful tinned spinach, salt and pepper. Whip all well together. If it is to be served hot, do not bring to the boil.

MRS. HEMANS, Takoradi.

Fish Custard.

One fish (haddock or sole), 1 dessertspoon flour, 1 teaspoon butter, 1 egg, 1 teacup milk, salt and pepper. Cut fish in pieces and place in pie dish, sprinkle well with pepper and salt. Mix in a bowl 1 dessertspoon flour, 1 teaspoon butter (melted), 1 egg (well beaten),

1 teacup milk. Pour this mixture over fish and cook in moderate oven for half an hour.

MRS. SWAN, Tamale.

Fish Moli.

(Ceylon)—very good.

Soak 4 tablespoons grated coconut for 12 hours in 8 tablespoons water. Boil for 1 hour and strain. 1 onion cut into rings, fried in 2 tablespoons butter. Add 3 bay leaves, ½ tablespoon tarragon vinegar and the coconut liquor. Boil 1 hour, strain, and add a small tin unsweetened milk. Thicken with flour and add remains of boiled fish.

MRS. FRASER, Achimota.

Fish Patties or Fish Flan.

Any kind of cooked fish will do—tinned salmon or lobster is excellent. One tin of salmon or lobster, tin of peas, 1 oz. butter, 1 oz. flour, 1 gill milk or cream, and the liquid from the fish, salt and pepper.

For the Pastry case or Patties.

Half lb. flour, 6 ozs. lard or butter, teaspoonful salt, 1 teaspoonful baking powder, cold water. Make rich short pastry and roll out to medium thickness, and line patty tins, about 6 or 8, or a medium-size sandwich tin, and bake until golden brown. Make a thick white sauce with flour, butter and milk or cream and then add fish and peas. Fill the flan case or patty cases with the mixture and serve either cold or reheated.

A little anchovy essence may be put on the top or they may be garnished with parsley. Very useful where fresh fish is unobtainable, and excellent for using up left-over peas and fish.

MRS. HORSEY, Obuasi.

Fish Pie.

Cut up some fillets of white fish in neat pieces and flour and season each piece in pepper and salt. Put a layer of these pieces in a pie dish and on this arrange a layer of strips or dice of cold fried bacon, cover with slices of skinned tomatoes, season with pepper and salt. A little chopped onion and parsley may be added, repeat until the dish is full, pack closely, pour over all a very little cold water to moisten the ingredients and cover with a good pie crust. Bake for about one hour, can be eaten hot or cold. Finnan haddock (tinned) can be used.

MRS. HOLLAND, Oda.

Fish Pie.

The remains of cold boiled fish (boned and flaked). Put into pie dish together with finely chopped onion, tomatoes (skinned), and chopped parsley. Cover with breadcrumbs, pour over beaten eggs and milk and bake in moderate oven for about half an hour.

MRS. HOLLAND, Oda.

Fish Pudding.

One lb. of cold fish free from bones and skin, ½ lb. mashed potatoes, pepper and salt, 1 oz. flour, ½ pint of milk, (Ideal diluted), put fish into a well greased dish, add seasoning, chopped parsley (if liked) add sprinkle of lime juice, make a sauce of flour and milk and pour over the fish. Cover with potatoes mashed with milk and butter, ruffle top with a fork, bake one hour, decorate with parsley. Sufficient for two or three persons. (Tinned salmon may be used.)

MRS. FIELDGATE, Koforidua.

Fish Salad *à la* Njala.

Half to ¾ lb. of cold boiled fish, 2 or 3 hard boiled eggs, 2 or 3 cold boiled potatoes, a small quantity of cold green peas and/or asparagus, 2 or 3 avocado pears, uncooked, salad oil, lemon juice or vinegar. Flake the fish, cut up the eggs, potatoes and avocado pears, mix together and arrange in a dish, garnishing with egg and peas. Mix a sufficient quantity of oil with the pounded yolk of a hard-boiled egg and flavour either with lemon juice or vinegar, according to taste. Place in Frigidaire before serving.

MRS. SAMUEL, Accra.

Fish Shape.

Three-quarter lb. cooked salmon, or other cooked fish, ¾ oz. gelatine (8 sheets), 1 small tin green peas, pint water, 2 hard-boiled eggs, shred of onion. Soak gelatine in water. Boil eggs hard. Bone and skin fish, mix with peas, onion and seasoning, add gelatine when soaked to mixture. Cut up eggs into rounds, line sides of basin with egg, previously seasoning basin with a little of the fluid gelatine. Fill up with the mixture carefully. Turn out when set and cold.

MISS BARCHI, Sekondi.

Fish with Macaroni (Hot).

1 lb. cold fish, flaked
2 ozs. macaroni
5 hard boiled eggs
1 tin of oysters
¾ pint white sauce
Champignons
Sherry
Chopped parsley.

Flavour the sauce with a little sherry and add the champignons, and oysters. Make hot but do not boil. Surround a dish with some cooked macaroni, preferably milkaroni. Turn the sauce and fish into this. Sprinkle some chopped parsley, cut the eggs in half, coat with a little sauce and sprinkle with parsley. Place pointed upwards on the top of the fish. Suitable for eight persons.

MRS. KEAST, Accra.

Fish Soufflé.

Take some boiled and boned white fish, mix and pound with 1 oz. margarine, and stir in the yolks of 2 well-beaten eggs. Whip the whites to a stiff froth with pepper and salt. Mix and bake in a soufflé mould for 10 minutes in a moderate oven.

MRS. W. HILL, Accra.

Fish Soufflé.

One and a half teacups fish, cooked and chopped, 1 teacupful breadcrumbs, 1 tablespoonful melted butter, 1 tablespoonful Yorkshire relish, 2 eggs, half a teacupful milk, pepper and salt. Mix all together, pour into greased mould. Cover with greased paper and steam one hour. Turn on to a hot dish and serve with white parsley sauce.

MISS SUTHERLAND, Aburi.

Fish and Tomato Pie.

Fish, tomatoes, breadcrumbs, pepper and salt, butter, gravy. Put a little gravy in a pie dish. Lay in dish layers of flaked fish, sliced tomatoes and breadcrumbs, seasoned with pepper and salt, till pie dish is full. Cover well with breadcrumbs and small pats of butter. Bake in a moderate oven until browned.

MRS. SWAN, Tamale.

Fish with a Mexican Sauce.

Two slices of cod, turbot or any large white fish, 1 oz. butter, or good margarine, 2 tablespoons olive oil, 3 or 4 onions, 6 small tomatoes, 2 or 3 red peppers, salt and pepper. Wash the tomatoes, peel them and cut them up. Peel and chop the onions, heat the olive oil and the butter or margarine in the frying pan. Put in the tomatoes, onions, peppers, salt and pepper, and fry together gently until they are all well blended.

70

Put the slices of fish in the hot sauce, and cook until ready, turning the fish over once. When done place the fish on a hot dish, with the sauce poured over and round it.

MRS. CREWE, Accra.

Fresh Herrings for Breakfast.

Split three or four herrings, remove the heads, tails and back bones. Place overnight in a pie dish, with a tablespoonful of oil, the same of vinegar, a small onion cut in pieces, a little parsley, pepper and salt. In the morning drain them, roll in breadcrumbs—or, preferably, in fine oatmeal—and fry them. Serve very hot.

MRS. CREWE, Accra.

Fricassée of Fish.

1 lb. of cooked fish
1 hard boiled egg
1 pint white sauce
1 teaspoonful of lemon juice
Parsley

Ingredients for white sauce—1 oz. of flour, 1 pint milk or ½ pint milk and ½ pint water, or ½ pint milk and ½ pint fish stock, 2 ozs. butter, salt and pepper. Divide the fish into flakes, chop the white of egg, and put the yolk through a sieve, wash and chop the parsley, melt the butter, stir in the flour, remove from fire and add all the milk and stir till it boils, season with salt and pepper, simmer for five minutes. When cooked add fish, leave until thoroughly hot through, add lemon juice and parsley, turn on to a hot dish, decorate with a border of yolk of egg, and put little heaps of white here and there.

MRS. EMMETT, Accra.

71

Fricassée of Fish.

Half lb. cooked white fish, broken into flakes, one or two hard-boiled eggs, seasoning of salt, pepper and a squeeze of lemon juice, ¾ milk, 1 oz. flour, 1 oz. butter. Make a sauce with the milk, flour and butter. Add to this the flaked fish, seasoning and the roughly chopped white of egg, and stir this in a saucepan over the fire, until thoroughly hot, then serve, decorating the fricassee with the yolk of egg put through a sieve, and garnish with slices of cooked tomato.

MRS. McELROY, Accra.

Garden Eggs Stew.

Curved fish 1., garden eggs 3d., herrings 3d., salt, palm oil, pepper ¼d., salt and onions.

Clean the garden eggs, put them to boil together with some pepper. Then take from the fire and grind. Put some palm oil in a saucepan and put on fire to boil. When boiling, add in the sliced onions, pepper, and curved fish stirring all the time until cooked. Then add a little water and let it boil for five minutes. Lastly, add the salt and stir until well cooked.

SISTER ANGELE, Cape Coast.

Haddock with Tomatoes.

Break some cooked haddock into small pieces, moisten with white sauce, season to taste, pile on slices of dry toast, cover with slices of skinned tomatoes and bake in a moderate oven for 10 minutes. Bacon may be served if liked. This makes a good breakfast dish and is an excellent way of using up "left-overs".

Haddock (Another way to cook).

Skin and fillet a haddock, cut each fillet in half, arrange a greased fireproof dish, mix 3 ozs. of grated cheese with ½ gill milk, teaspoonful of made mustard, pepper and salt, one beaten egg, cover the fish with this mixture, cook in a hot oven until the fish is cooked and the cheese nicely browned. Serve very hot.

All fish and game are improved in flavour if rubbed over with lemon or lime before cooking.

MRS. NICHOLSON, Accra Ice Co.

Jellied Salmon.

One tin salmon, ½ oz. leaf gelatine, 3 tablespoonfuls of water, 2 tablespoonfuls of vinegar, little powdered mace, 1 pepper, salt, and cayenne. Dissolve gelatine in water, stirring over a gentle heat. When melted add mace, pepper, salt, cayenne and vinegar. Remove skin and bone from salmon, then flake it and add to the seasoned liquid. Stir well and when nearly cold turn into a wet mould until set, turn out and serve on lettuce leaves.

MRS. HENDRY, Accra.

Jellied Salmon.

Flake a pint of salmon, mix with ½ pint of mayonnaise, melt ¼ oz. gelatine in cold water. Stir all together until the mixture begins to set, then pour into a mould. Serve with a border of cucumber and a green salad, white fish can be used in the same way. Sweet peppers make a good border.

MRS. NICHOLSON, Accra.

Lobster Cocktail.

1 small tin lobster
Tomato sauce
Lemon juice
Worcester sauce
White vinegar
Salt

Cut the lobster into small pieces. Blend the other ingredients to taste, and pour over the lobster. Mix well together, place in cocktail glasses and chill before serving.

MRS. DRAKE, Tamale.

Lobster Cream.

Four small crayfish, 1 teaspoon butter, glass sherry, 1 tin cream. Cut a lime in three and use juice of one part, salt and pepper. Boil the crayfish and remove from shell taking care not to break shell. Wash the shells thoroughly and drain well. Mince the meat, put it into a small basin and add all the other ingredients and mix well.

Stuff the shells with the mixture and put dried breadcrumbs on the top and warm up carefully in the oven taking care that it does not get too brown. Dish on a bed of finely chopped lettuce.

MRS. NORTHCOTE.

Lobster *à la* Newburg.

One tin lobster, 1 tin prawns, 3 hard boiled eggs cut in halves, yolks taken out, mixed with a little butter, pinch of salt, pinch of mustard, and a few drops of Worcester sauce. Pack this back in the whites, cut small pieces off ends so that the eggs stand firmly, toasted bread. If poached eggs are preferred, poach them in milk before the sauce is made, I moisten the toast with a little hot milk before pouring the sauce over all.

74

Newburg sauce for above:—

½ teaspoon mustard
2 tablespoons butter (measure before melting)
Salt to taste
Red pepper (very few grains)
Pinch of grated nutmeg
1 teacup milk (Ideal and water)
2 yolks eggs
2 tablespoons sherry.

Put lobster in a soup-plate and sprinkle with the pepper, salt and nutmeg, pour the sherry over it and let stand for quite an hour. Melt butter in saucepan, beat yolks of eggs, add milk to them, then add slowly to melted butter with mustard, stirring and beating all the time. Let sauce thicken, but do not really boil it or eggs will curdle. Put in lobster and allow to get hot, but do not boil. You may add a few chopped mushrooms or olives or truffles. When lobster is hot, pour over the moistened toast and serve at once.

If poached eggs are served (instead of stuffed) place them on the soft toast and keep hot in oven until sauce and lobster are ready.

MRS. DONNATT, Winneba.

Lobster Newburg.

One lb. lobster meat, 1 teaspoon flour, ½ teaspoon salt, ½ tablespoon butter, cup of milk, 2 egg yolks, a good pinch paprika. Melt butter in the top of a double boiler. Stir in the flour and cook till smooth and creamy, add salt and milk, stirring all the time, then stir in yolks, paprika and the lobster in small pieces. Keep stirring until the mixture is smooth but on no account boil. When blended, flavour with sherry and serve in lobster shells or on buttered toast.

MRS. LYNCH, Cape Coast.

Lobster Salad.

5 large lobsters
8 hard-boiled eggs
1 lb. grapes
Mustard and cress
2 cucumbers
Mayonnaise.

Boil the lobsters. Split them and take out the meat, mix with a little mayonnaise sauce and put in entree dish. Add alternate layers of minced cucumber, the grapes which have been peeled, seeded and cut in half, and an egg mixture; the yolks having been pounded with a little ideal milk, and the whites chopped and folded in. Decorate with lobster coral, the claws, and mustard and cress at the corners of the dish. Tie two of the empty shells together and place tails uppermost in the centre of the dish. Bend back the tails and fill with mustard and cress or parsley. If lobsters are unobtainable use cold fish and prawns. Sufficient for eight persons.

MRS. KEAST, Accra.

Mock Whitebait (Hot).

One large sole, fried parsley, brown bread and butter. Fillet the sole, dry and cut into neat strips, toss in seasoned flour, fry, drain well and serve hot with fried parsley.

Fried parsley: Wash the parsley in cold water, dry well, then place it in a wire frying basket, fry in hot fat for about two minutes until it stiffens. There must be enough fat to completely cover the parsley. Remove and drain thoroughly, hand brown bread and butter with this dish.

MRS. BUTLER, Accra.

Prawns and Eggs Dish.

Make pint white sauce adding a little anchovy essence if possible, put into the sauce some shrimps or prawns, pour into a shallow glass dish, and then break on top of this the) number of eggs required, put into the oven at once for 10 minutes, sprinkle if possible with parsley.

MRS. DIXON, Salaga.

Prawns Pastry.

Take one tin of prawns, one tablespoonful of butter, 4 tablespoonful of breadcrumbs, four skinned mashed tomatoes. Wash the prawns and shred finely. Brown the breadcrumbs lightly in the butter add tomatoes and a very little water to prevent sticking. Pour the mixture when hot over the prawns, mix well and turn into a buttered pie-dish. Cover with short pastry, brush the tops with beaten yolk of egg, and bake in a hot oven for 20 minutes.

MRS. PASSELLS, Accra.

A Salmon Cream.

One large tin salmon, 2 oz. butter, 2 eggs, onions and tomatoes. Cream the salmon with the butter, add grated onion and tomato to taste, beat in the two eggs, then steam for half an hour, allow to go cold and serve with garnishing of salad.

MRS. ROTHWELL, Koforidua.

Salmon Loaf.

One tin salmon, breadcrumbs, 2 tomatoes, butter. Remove all skin and bones from salmon and pour off any oil. Put into a bowl and mix with breadcrumbs till dry. Place on ashet and form into a loaf. Sprinkle with melted butter. Garnish with slices of tomato.

MRS. SWAN, Tamale.

Salmon Mould.

One large tin salmon, 2 oz. cooked rice, 2 hard boiled eggs. Mix the cooked rice thoroughly into the salmon, then steam for half an hour. Lime the bottom of a basin or mould with slices of hard boiled egg and place the cooked mixture inside. Serve hot or cold.

MRS. ROTHWELL, Koforidua.

Salmon Pie.

One tin salmon, mashed potatoes, hot milk. Pick the salmon free of skin and bones, and cut up small. Grease a pie dish, put in a layer of mashed potatoes, a layer of salmon, and another layer of potatoes, pour over a little hot milk to moisten and brown in oven.

MRS. HILDITCH, Tarkwa.

Salmon Pudding.

One tin salmon, ½ lb. breadcrumbs, ½ pint milk, salt and pepper, 3 eggs. Soak the bread in the milk and beat it well with a fork. Add salt and pepper, and the salmon flaked and boned, and finally the beaten eggs. Turn into a buttered mould and steam for one hour. Serve with white or parsley sauce.

MISS BARCHI, Sekondi.

Salmon Rissoles.

(Sufficient for six people.)

One small tin of red salmon or ½ lb. fresh salmon (boiled), 5 tablespoonfuls breadcrumbs, about 8 ozs. of boiled potatoes (mashed), 1 egg, teaspoonful of salt and peppers to taste. Remove all bone and skin from the salmon, and pound thoroughly, adding salt and peppers, then gradually mix the breadcrumbs and mashed (dry) potatoes alternately. Next, mix in the egg. stirring well. Mould into shapes (a heaped tablespoonful of the mixture for each rissole), roll in flour, or egg and dried breadcrumbs, and fry in deep boiling lard or dripping for 10 minutes; serve hot.

MRS. WEBB, Accra.

Salmon Tarts.

Make some pastry cases with good short crust and let them get cold. Break some cold cooked salmon into flakes and fill the cases three-quarters full. Sprinkle a little salt, pepper, and lemon juice on top; fill up the cases with prepared aspic jelly and scatter chopped capers over.

MRS. LYNCH, Cape Coast.

Shrimps or Prawns and Egg Dish.

Make pint of white sauce, add a little anchovy essence. Put shrimps into sauce and then in a shallow casserole breaking on top the number of eggs required (1 per person). Put into the oven for about 10 minutes. If possible, sprinkle with a little chopped parsley round the edge.

MRS. DE CARTERET, Kumasi.

Shrimps or Prawns and Macaroni au gratin.

Boil 3 ozs. macaroni for 20 minutes, pour off the water and dry the macaroni. Butter a casserole or entree dish and arrange the macaroni in it, put ½ pint picked shrimps over cover with a thick white sauce made with 4 ozs. flour, ½ pint macaroni water, ½ pint milk and 4 ozs. margarine or butter and to which 2 ozs. of grated cheese has been added. Sprinkle breadcrumbs and grated cheese on the top, also small pieces of butter, and brown in the oven.

MRS. OAKLEY, Accra

Sole and Grated Cheese.

1 sole
1 onion chopped
2 oz. butter
2 tomatoes
Chopped parsley
Grated cheese
Teaspoon of anchovy essence
Breadcrumbs.

Mix the butter, parsley, anchovy essence, and a little onion, cut the sole down the centre, and separate the fish from the backbone. Stuff the butter, etc., mixture in this place. Grease a baking dish, lay the fish on it, scatter on it a little chopped onion and cover with sliced tomatoes, sprinkle the top with grated cheese and breadcrumbs. Add a few dabs of butter, and bake for about 20 minutes in a moderate oven.

MRS. HILDITCH, Tarkwa.

"Sole à la Simon."

Wash, skin and fillet sole and place fillets in a Pyrex or baking dish. Prepare a mixture of nearly equal parts of vinegar and olive oil, a little salt and pepper, a small chopped onion, and a lime leaf. Put this over fish and let all stand for 10 minutes. Then put in oven, which should be very hot, for 10 minutes; remove dish, then mix chutney and curry powder and put on top of fish. Return dish to oven and bake for 20 minutes.

For, say, four portions of fish, the quantities are:—
1½ dessertspoonfuls of chutney.
1½ dessertspoonfuls of olive oil.
2 dessertspoonfuls of vinegar.
1 teaspoonful of curry powder.

MRS. GROVER.

Spiced Fresh Fish.

One lb. fresh fish, ½ pint vinegar, 6 cloves, 6 peppercorns. Put the fish in a deep dish and bake until cooked through. Put vinegar in a saucepan, add cloves, peppercorns and salt to taste and boil for 10 minutes. Pour the liquid over the baked fish and allow to cool. Serve cold with salad garnishing.

MRS. ROTHWELL, Koforidua.

Sole (Stuffed).

One medium-sized sole, stuffing, 3 tablespoonful bread-crumbs, 1 oz. dripping, 1 teaspoonful chopped parsley, ½ teaspoonful mixed herbs, 1 teaspoonful of grated lemon rind, squeeze of lemon juice, salt and pepper. Wash and skin the sole, cut off the fins and dry well, cut four fillets, make the stuffing by mixing the breadcrumbs, parsley, dripping, grated lemon rind, salt and pepper together, moisten with a little milk, if necessary only, squeeze a little lime juice over the stuffing, rub the fillets into flour, put some stuffing inside each fillet and then roll and tie. Roll in fine crumbs and fry a golden brown in deep very hot fat. Take out and drain on a paper and serve on a dish garnished with slices of lime and a little parsley.

MRS. FIELDGATE, The Residency, Koforidua.

MEAT DISHES

Bacon and Potato Rolls.

½ lb. bacon in rashers
6 tablespoons of flour
Water
2 ozs. lard or margarine.
1 teaspoonful baking powder
6 tablespoons of mashed potatoes

Make some pastry by mixing flour, lard, baking powder, salt and mashed potatoes, and bind with a little water. Roll out thinly on a board, cut the pastry into as many strips or rolls as required, and on each strip lay a rasher of bacon, without rind. Fold up into rolls; lay on a greased tin, and bake in a quick oven for 20 minutes.

MRS. HILDITCH, Tarkwa.

Banana Steak (Baked).

Half to ¾ lb. beefsteak, 2 bananas, 2 or 3 slices bacon, 1 teaspoonful sugar, seasoning, a little water. Choose a tender piece of steak 1 inch in thickness, wipe it and split it open leaving one end uncut like a book. Season with pepper and salt and a little grated nutmeg. Cut the bananas in pieces, lay them on one side of the steak, sprinkle with sugar and cover with the other. Place thin slices of bacon on the top and fasten together with a small skewer. Place in a baking dish with a little water, and bake in the oven for about half an hour, basting occasionally. Serve garnished with parsley.

MRS. PUCKRIDGE, Accra.

Beef and Ham Mould. (A Breakfast or Cold Dish.)

One lb. shin beef, ½ lb. lean ham, 2 ozs. breadcrumbs, salt, pepper, 1 egg, a little nutmeg. Mince the meat, add the other ingredients and bind all together with the beaten egg. Put the mixture in a lightly greased basin, cover tightly with greaseproof paper and steam about 2 hours. Let the water reach about half the side of the basin and keep lid of pan closed. When quite cold turn out on meat dish, cut in slices.

MRS. BOOTH, Accra.

Beef Birds.

Thin steak is wiped with a damp cloth, rubbed with lemon and a garlic clove, and cut in pieces about four by six inches. After each piece has been flattened with a knife, a half slice bacon is laid over it and covered with soft buttered crumbs and minced parsley, and a piece of celery on top of all. Each piece is then rolled and tied both ways, seared in hot dripping and steamed for two hours with a brown sauce covering the birds; can also be roasted or fried.

MRS. BARTON, Kumasi.

Beef Olives.

4 lb. of fillet of beef or rump steak
½ teaspoonful of mixed herbs
3 ozs. breadcrumbs
1 egg
2 ozs. beef suet
Salt and pepper
1 teaspoonful of chopped parsley
1 pint brown sauce

Cut the beef into thin slices about 4 inches long. Chop up the trimmings of the beef, the suet, parsley, and mixed herbs and mix them in a basin with the breadcrumbs, salt, pepper, and the egg. Stuff each piece of beef with this mixture, roll it up and tie it round with a piece of string.

82

Place these stuffed rolls of beef in a stewpan with 1 pint of brown sauce and stew gently for of an hour. For serving take off the string and dish up with mashed potato or spinach with the sauce poured round.

This dish is often made from cold lean beef, and is an excellent way of using up cold meat.

MRS. W. EMMETT, Accra.

Beef Roll (Cold).

1 lb. raw beef
½ lb. ham
2 eggs
¼ lb. suet
4 ozs. breadcrumbs
½ a nutmeg
Salt
Pepper
2 hard boiled eggs for the centre.

Glaze or brown crumbs to coat. Mince the meat and ham, chop the suet, mix all the ingredients together with the beaten eggs. Mould the mixture round the hard boiled eggs, tie in a floured cloth and boil for two hours. Turn out and coat with glaze or brown crumbs. This makes a good breakfast or luncheon dish, also uses up remains of ham.

Beef Sausage.

Take some left-over meat from a joint, mince, adding odd bits of bacon or ham, season well, add enough egg and breadcrumbs to form into a solid roll. Roll very tightly in a cloth and boil for two hours, remove from the cloth, coat with breadcrumbs and allow to cool.

MRS. HOWE, Nkawkaw.

Beefsteak en Casserole.

1 to 2 lbs. steak
Carrot
Dripping
Turnip
2 potatoes
Onion
1 teaspoonful chopped parsley
1 tablespoonful pickles or chutney
1 pint weak stock
1 tablespoon cut-up bacon.

Fry the meat quickly in the dripping, slice the vegetables, put into the casserole, sprinkle over the parsley, put the meat on the top. Pour away the fat, make the stock hot in the frying pan, put the bacon on the meat and add the stock. Put on the lid and cook in a moderate oven for 2 to 3 hours, put the meat on a dish and wash the casserole, if necessary, add pickles cut up or chutney, salt and pepper, if necessary, return all to the casserole, re-heat before serving. This can be altered to Jugged Beefsteak, by omitting the pickles and bacon and substituting forcemeat balls, made and fried separately and put in just before serving.

MRS. OAKLEY, Accra.

Brain Cutlets.

Blanch the brains in cold water for hour and remove skin. Boil slowly in a little vinegar and water with seasonings, when cold cut into cutlets, dip in batter or egg and breadcrumbs, fry in deep boiling fat, drain and serve with tomato sauce.

MRS. FRASER, Achimota.

Braised Local Beef.

Melt one ounce of dripping or butter in stewpan and brown about 1 lbs. of market fillet beef all over in it. Lift out the meat, and fry two carrots, two onions, and an equal quantity of turnip (all sliced) in the fat, and then add half a pint of stock. Season and place the meat on top of the vegetables, cover closely, and simmer gently for about ¾ of an hour.

Place the meat on a hot dish and arrange the vegetables around it. Thicken the remaining stock with one teaspoonful of flour, adding a little Worcestershire sauce, and pour over meat and vegetables.

MRS. MILES, Accra.

Burton Sausage.

(If served cold, this makes a capital Sunday breakfast or supper dish.) Half a pound of raw, lean beef, half a pound of chopped or grated nuts (any kind), half a pound of breadcrumbs, four ounces of bacon pieces, half a pound of mashed potato, two tablespoonfuls of finely chopped onion, one raw egg, one gill of stock, salt and pepper. Chop the beef and finely, or pass it through a mincing machine. Mix the meats, nuts, crumbs, potato, and onion thoroughly, adding a good seasoning. Beat up the egg, mix it with the stock, and work it well in; shape the mixture like a roly poly pudding. Tie it up in a clean, dry cloth, and boil it gently in the stock-pot for two hours.

Then remove the cloth, lay the roll on a hot dish, and strain all over it a nice hot tomato or brown sauce. Or, if you prefer it cold, let it cool and then brush it over with little warmed glaze or gelatine dissolved in brown stock and garnish it with parsley or salad.

MRS. BARTLETT, Accra.

Gateau of Cold Meat.

One breakfast cup cold minced meat (or chicken), 1 breakfast cup breadcrumbs, 1 onion, 1 dessertspoon Worcestershire sauce, 1 teaspoon chopped parsley, 2 tomatoes, 1 large egg, salt and pepper, ¾ gill stock, 1 oz. good dripping or butter. Chop the onion and fry it in the dripping, heat the stock and pour it on the breadcrumbs. Add to this, the onion well chopped, a tomato, the parsley and the Worcester sauce with the minced meat. Mix with well beaten egg; grease a small round cake tin or pie dish, line it with slices of tomato, fill with mixture and bake in moderate oven 40 minutes or till set, turn out and decorate with parsley. Can be eaten hot or cold. Sufficient for three persons.

MRS. KEEVIL, Sekondi.

Cervelles à la Mornay.

Calf's brains, ½ pint Mornay sauce, Parmesan cheese, 1 oz. butter or margarine, pepper and salt. Take the skin off the brains and soak them in cold water until they are quite white. Put them in a saucepan, cover them with boiling stock or water, adding a sprig of parsley, an onion, a teaspoonful of vinegar, pepper and salt, cook for 30 minutes. Remove from the saucepan, drain, and cut in fairly thick slices.

Put a layer of Mornay sauce at the bottom of a fireproof dish, place the sliced brains on this, then another layer of sauce. Sprinkle the grated Parmesan cheese on top, put tiny pieces of butter over the cheese, and bake until brown.

MRS. CREWE, Accra.

Chicken Maryland.

2 young chickens
2 eggs
¼ lb. soft sugar
1 small tin milk
Vanilla essence
Flour, egg and crumbs for coating.

Dress and clean the chickens, cut up, sprinkle with salt and pepper, dip in flour, egg and breadcrumbs. Place in a well greased dripping tin and bake 30 minutes in a hot oven, basting occasionally. Arrange on a plate and pour over a cream sauce made by beating the white of the eggs until stiff, adding the well beaten yolks and the sugar. Beat the milk (or cream if available) add to the egg mixture and flavour with vanilla.

MRS. DRAKE, Tamale.

Chicken Croquettes.

Any minced chicken, 1 cup soft boiled rice, parsley and seasoning. Mix well with a little milk, form into balls, dip in beaten egg, then in breadcrumbs and fry a golden brown.

MISS BARCHI, Sekondi.

Chicken en Casserole.

1 chicken
1 oz. butter
½ pint milk
Salt and pepper
1 small onion
1 oz. flour
½ pint water
Small tin of mushrooms.

Skin the chicken, cut it into portions. Fry lightly in butter. Put the chicken in casserole with onion, salt, pepper and water, and stew very gently for an hour, add mushrooms. Blend flour with the milk and add to the chicken, stir the gravy to prevent it being lumpy and stew again very gently for hour. The goodness depends on the gentle cooking, boiling spoils the chicken. Always add the milk and flour just hour before serving. Fried bacon or sausages can be served with the dish.

MRS. DE CARTERET, Kumasi.

Chicken en Casserole.

One chicken, a little flour, seasoning, fat for frying, 12 small onions, 2 stalks of celery, 2 or 3 carrots, pint tomato purée. Cut the chicken into pieces. Dredge with well seasoned flour, fry in hot fat till brown. Lay the pieces in a casserole with onions, celery and carrots. Sprinkle with salt and pepper and pour on pint of tomato puree (fresh or tinned tomatoes sieved). Put small pieces of butter on the top; put on the lid and cook in a moderate oven for 2 to 3 hours. Remove fat from the top. Serve boiled rice separately.

Chicken Galantine (Economical).

One chicken, breadcrumbs, 3 eggs, salt and pepper. Take all the meat off a chicken, and put through the mincer. Scald in milk 4 to 6 tablespoonfuls of breadcrumbs. When cool, mix with chicken, add some chopped parsley, salt, pepper and a little powdered mace. Mix with well beaten eggs to a fairly moist consistency. Put into a well-greased basin and steam from 1 to 4 hours. Can be eaten hot or cold.

MRS. C. E. DE B. BIDEN, Accra.

Chicken Pancakes.

Chop some cooked chicken and a little lean ham. Bind with a thick white sauce. Add some chopped black mushrooms. Make some small pancakes, substituting a little salt instead of the usual sugar. Brown the pan-cakes well, Put a thick layer of the mixture on each and roll. Serve with slices of fried bacon.

MRS. KEAST, Accra.

Chicken Cassolettes.

Make a Yorkshire pudding mixture. Put some dripping in some deep wide patty cases. Make very hot and pour in the Yorkshire pudding. Bake until the mixture is brown and crisp. Take out the soft centres, reserving the tops for lids, and fill with a mixture similar to that used for the chicken pancakes. Pile high and put on the lids. Serve very hot in a dish, and surround with French beans.

MRS. KEAST, Accra.

Chicken Pie (Raised).

3 Chickens
1 lb. sausage
1 lb. bacon
2 hard boiled eggs.
Salt and pepper
Pastry.

Take the meat off the chickens, and cu in pieces about 1 inches long. Skin the sausages and cut the bacon, which should be lean, into small pieces. Grease a raised pie mould with clarified butter. Line the three pieces with pastry and clip together with the metal skewers. Press the pastry carefully into the shape of the mould. Cut a strip of pastry ¾-inch wide, wet with water the edge of the mould and lay round the pastry.

Fill the mould with alternate layers of chicken, bacon, and sausage, seasoning every third layer with a little salt and a generous supply of pepper. When the mould is half- full, put in the hard-boiled eggs whole. As the meat is being put in, it must be well pressed down and to the sides, otherwise there will be a space between the pastry and the meat due to shrinkage in the cooking. Pile the meat high in the centre of the mould, so that it looks well arched when covered.

Cover with pastry and knock up the sides with a knife. Brush over with a beaten yolk of egg and decorate with pastry leaves. Make a hole in the top to let the steam escape, and tie a band of greased paper round the outside of the mould and standing 2 inches above the top of the pie.

Place mould on a tin and bake in a moderate oven for 3 hours. After the pie is cold, carefully take off the mould, and pour through the hole some liquid jelly stock. Garnish with parsley, and the feet of the birds can be scalded and glazed and stuck in the hole at the top of the pie, or else it may be filled with a bunch of parsley. Serve the pie with slices of cold ham and a plate of thin brown bread and butter. The length of the mould measures 7 inches, and is suitable for eight persons.

The Pastry: One and a half lbs. self-raising flour, 12 ozs. Butter, 5 tablespoons of iced water, mixed with 1 yolk of egg, 1 spoon salt.

The Liquid Jelly Stock: Cover the bones of the chickens with water and to the boil. Simmer and skim well, measure pint of liquid, and add to it 8 sheets of gelatine. Pour in the pie and put on ice. The pie should be eaten the day it is and must be started very early in the morning if wanted for cold supper dish.

MRS. KEAST, Accra.

Chicken Pie (Cold).

1 chicken, boned and cut in pieces
Any vegetables such as potatoes, carrots, peas, beans,
A few mushrooms either fresh or tinned
1 onion or shallot, chopped
8 ozs. pastry
½ oz. aspic powder
Stock
1 yolk of egg or milk
Seasoning

1. Put chicken and vegetables in alternate layers in dish with plenty of salt and pepper.
2. Melt aspic powder in half pint stock and pour over mixture.
3. Cover with pastry about inch thick, decorate and brush over with beaten egg or milk.
4. Bake first in hot oven till pastry browning, then in moderate oven, altogether about two hours.
5. Serve cold.

NB—If stock used has formed a jelly when cold, the aspic powder is not necessary.

MRS. BEACH JOHNSTONE, Accra.

Chicken Pie.

One chicken, some slices of bacon, 1 onion, stock, 2 hard-boiled eggs, 1 yolk of egg, chopped parsley, if possible, pastry, salt and pepper.

Cut the chicken into neat joints, boil the backbone, gizzard and neck for about 2 hours to make the stock, cut the bacon into small pieces and roll, slice the egg. Place the chicken and bacon in alternate layers in the pie dish and fill the dish three-quarter full with the stock, season carefully and add chopped parsley. Cover with a pie dish and cook in a moderate oven for 1 hours, then take out and put the sliced eggs on the top and cover with pastry, and bake for about hour. Brushing the pastry with the yolk of an egg greatly improves the appearance of the pie. Sufficient for four persons.

MRS. FIELDGATE, Koforidua.

Chicken Pilau (India).

Wash 4 tablespoons rice and fry in butter, boil in chicken stock, drain, add a little butter, groundnuts or almonds, sultana raisins (washed and steeped in warm water) let it dry and serve round and over a chicken which has first been boiled (hence the stock) and then cut into portions and fried butter together with sliced onions and sliced green mangoes. The drained off stock can be served as gravy, if liked, and the whole garnished with hard-boiled eggs.

MRS. FRASER, Achimota.

Chicken Mousse.

One cup hot chicken stock, ½ cup blanched almonds, 1 teaspoonful salt, 1 teaspoonful pepper, yolks of 3 eggs, cayenne, ½ cup cold cooked chicken, 1 cup cream (white sauce replaces), 1 tablespoonful gelatine, 1 tablespoonful cold water.

Beat eggs slightly, add salt and pepper, and gradually chicken stock. Cook over hot water until mixture thickens, add gelatine soaked in cold water and when dissolved, strain and add to chicken and almonds finely minced. Season highly with salt and cayenne, put in ice water and stir mixture thickens, then fold in cream beaten until stiff. Turn into mould and chill. Turn out and serve.

MRS. FRASER, Achimota.

Chicken Stewed.

Cut a chicken into small parts. Put a Spanish onion into a stewpan, cut up very small, with 2 ozs. butter, a little cayenne and salt, and let it stew for about an hour till it is a complete pulp. Half an hour before you want it put in the pieces of chicken and let them gently stew for ½ hour and when done put into a deep dish (such as fireproof or one that it can be served up in) with a teaspoon of garlic vinegar, if not liked, the juice of ½ lemon. It requires no water, the fowl will be done in its own gravy.

MRS. EMMETT, Accra.

Stewed Chicken in Red Wine.

One chicken, 1 large Spanish onion (or 2 small), 6 cloves, 1 ripe lime, ¼ lb. margarine, ¼ lb. flour, 1 pint of stock made from the chicken head, neck, and feet, 1 tumblerful of red wine and a little mixed herbs. Pluck and clean your chicken thoroughly and cut into small pieces (at the joints), peel your lime and cut into halves, have ready on a plate flour seasoned with pepper and salt, dip the pieces of chicken into this and fry with margarine until brown, then put into a stew jar with the onion stuck with cloves, lime rind, salt, herbs, stock and half the wine, and cover and stew for about an hour, then add the remainder of the wine, thicken with a little flour and cook for an hour.

MRS. MILNE, Winneba.

Chicken with Macaroni.

Boil a few sticks of macaroni together with one or two onions till quite tender, adding salt to taste. Drain it, saving some of the water (about a pint), put this back in the saucepan again, then put in the pieces of chicken (removing all skin and bone) a little pepper, and herbs if liked.

Make a little thick sauce with flour or corn flour and milk, adding this to the other things in the saucepan, and simmer or boil very gently for half an hour, stirring occasionally or it will burn; or use a double saucepan, it will then be quite safe.

MRS. KEEVIL, Sekondi.

To "Devil" Cold Chicken.

Make a paste of: one dessertspoonful curry powder, 1 teaspoon made mustard, ½ teaspoon sugar, 4 teaspoons flour, 1 teaspoon vinegar, salt and pepper. Mix thoroughly. Then gash the meat and insert the mixture and fry.

MRS. NORTHCOTE, Accra.

Corned Beef.

One tin "Fray Bentos" corned beef, 6 or 7 cold cooked potatoes, ¾ pint white sauce, 3 ozs. cheese (grated), pepper, salt and mustard.

Prepare white sauce in usual way, when boiled for eight minutes stir in cheese and add salt, pepper and made mustard. Line a pie dish with sliced cold potatoes.

Mince the beef and arrange in dish on top of potatoes, pour over half the sauce, cover with remainder of potatoes and add remainder of sauce. Put in a moderate oven for 30 minutes and then brown in a very hot oven.

MRS. CUTHBERT, Koforidua.

Curry of Fowl.

(One can do Mutton like this as well.) One fowl, 2 ozs. of ghee or butter, ½ lb. of Kabool chennah or Indian corn, a lb. of onions sliced, ½ an oz. of green ginger, ½ an oz. of coriander seeds, ½ of a teaspoonful each of black pepper, ground cinnamon, clove and cardamoms, salt.

Cut the fowl into neat joints, place them in a stewpan barely covered with cold water, add the sliced onions, coriander seeds, green ginger, pepper, 1 dessert-spoonful of salt and the Kabool chennah previously well washed, and cook until the fowl is tender.

Mix the ground cinnamon, cloves and cardamoms together, moisten with a little cold stock or water, add the strained liquor from the fowl, stir until it boils and simmer gently for about 20 minutes. Fry the fowl in hot ghee until nicely browned, put it into the stewpan containing the sauce and let it stand for about 20 minutes where it will keep hot, serve with plainly boiled rice. Sufficient for three or four persons.

MRS. NORTH.

Custard Meat Pie.

1 lb. beefsteak
2 slices white bread
Salt and pepper.

For Custard.

1 pint milk
4 eggs
2 tablespoonfuls flour
1 tablespoonful butter

Mince the beefsteak, mix with the bread soaked in a little milk, salt and pepper to taste. Butter a pie dish, put the mixture in and place in a hot oven for ¼ of an hour. Pour over the custard which has been mixed the following way: Beat together the yolks, butter flour, then add the milk and lastly the whisked whites of eggs. Flavour with salt. Bake for another 1 hour.

MRS. LLOYD WILLIAMS, Tamale.

Egg Mince.

Cold meat. Chopped onion, herbs, pepper and salt, stock, toast, poached eggs. Mince the meat finely, add the chopped onion, herbs and seasoning. Cover with stock and simmer in a saucepan for 20 minutes; poach the required number of eggs and arrange them on rounds of toast. Pour the mince when cooked on to a dish and surround with the poached eggs.

SISTER ANTONIA, Keta.

Fillet of Beef with Yam and Bananas.

Cut four or five round fillets of beef, fry them in butter for six minutes, or longer if desired, and season with pepper and salt. Place them on yam cakes of the same size, and on the top lay a section of banana that has been fried in the butter. Add two or three tablespoonfuls of water, and a teaspoonful of Bisto to the pan in which the meat was cooked. Stir until boiling and pour round the dish.

MRS. MILES, Accra.

94

Fricassée of Chicken.

(For using cooked meat.) Take flesh from the bones and dice together with a few vegetables. Carrots, onions or peas and mushrooms. Simmer the carcase until sufficient stock is made. Put meat and vegetables in a saucepan with a little butter or dripping and when smoking hot add a tablespoonful of flour, mix thoroughly and add the stock slowly till it thickens. Draw from the fire, add pepper and salt and sufficient condensed milk to whiten the stew, pour into a double boiler, simmer for one hour, being careful not to let the mixture boil. Remains of turkey and duck can be used up in the same way and any stuffing over added to it for flavouring.

MRS. SHAW, Accra.

Fricassée of Veal.

Three-quarter lb. cooked veal, 1 oz. butter, 1 oz. flour, ½ pint veal stock, seasoning, a pinch of nutmeg, 1 dessertspoonful chopped parsley, 1 or 2 egg yolks, a squeeze of lemon juice, a garnish.

Remove all skin and gristle and cut the meat into small neat pieces. Make a sauce with the butter flour and stock and season it with pepper, salt and a pinch of nutmeg. Put in the veal and let it warm thoroughly without boiling. Just before serving stir in the chopped parsley and the yolk of the egg beaten with a little lemon juice. Serve in a hot dish and garnish with rolls of bacon, croutons of toast or pastry or a few small baked tomatoes. A few champignons cut in halves or some cooked green peas may be added to the fricassee to give flavour.

MRS. PUCKRIDGE, Accra.

Galantine or Meat Cake.

Six ozs. of minced cooked beef and ham, some onions, 2 ozs. breadcrumbs, 2 large mushrooms (if chopped, seasoning, and 1 egg. Mix the ingredients with the egg, tie the mixture up in a cloth and boil 1½ hours. Then re-roll, tie tightly and press till cold. If preferred mixture may be pressed well into a mould, baked for one hour; turned out and eaten cold.

MRS. HOLLAND, Oda.

Gammon Rasher of Ham (Baked).

Gammon rasher about ¾ to 1 inch in thickness, 2 tablespoons brown sugar, 1 teaspoon unmade mustard, vinegar and cloves. Remove the rind from the rasher, a little of the fat. Cut the fat into small pieces.

Mix together the brown sugar and the mustard, and rub well into both sides of the ham, shake off any surplus. With a sharp knife make lines across the ham, about ¼ inch deep and an inch or so apart. Insert about a dozen cloves into the top of the ham at equal distances apart.

Place the ham in a baking dish, scatter the chopped fat over it, and bake in a hot oven for 20 minutes. Then pour over it ½ gill of vinegar and ½ gill water, and bake slowly until tender—about 1½ to 2 hours according to the thickness of the ham. Serve with tomato sauce and mashed potatoes.

MRS. CREWE, Accra.

Giblet Pie.

2 sets poultry giblets
1 lb. flaky pastry
1 small onion
1 egg
1 lb. rump steak
Cold water
6 peppercorns
A little seasoned flour
Salt and pepper
1 sprig parsley.

Prepare, clean, and wash giblets and place in a saucepan. Add peeled onion, 6 peppercorns and a sprig of parsley. Cover with cold water. Bring to the boil, add a pinch of salt and then skim. Cover and simmer gently for 2 hours. Then remove and allow to cool. Line the bottom of a buttered pie dish with steak cut in small pieces and dipped in seasoned flour. Cover with chopped giblets and then with another layer of seasoned steak. Add giblet stock and season highly.

Cover pie dish with pastry in the usual way, and brush top with beaten egg. Bake in a quick oven for 1½ hours. If pastry shows signs of scorching during that time cover with a sheet of grease-proof paper. Enough for five people.

MRS. LLOYD WILLIAMS, Tamale.

Golden Stew.

One chicken, carrots and turnips, potatoes, and ½ lb. groundnuts. Joint the chicken and stew together with carrots, turnips and potatoes. Ten minutes before serving thicken with groundnut paste and stir thoroughly, serve hot.

MRS. ROTHWELL, Koforidua.

Goulash of Livers.

3 or 4 chicken or other bird livers
½ cup strong stock
1 minced onion
½ teaspoon paprika
1 teaspoon salt
1 tablespoon butter
Flour.
Boiled rice.

Slice the livers and dredge well with flour. Fry the onion in butter until light brown. Put in the liver and shake pan over fire to sear all contents. Add seasoning and stock. Allow it to boil up at once. Serve immediately with boiled rice for supper or luncheon. Enough for four persons.

MRS. LLOYD WILLIAMS, Tamale.

Ham Cake

Take the remains of a cold ham—about 1½ lbs. fat and lean together—and pass through the mincing machine. Soak a large slice of bread in ½ pint of milk and beat it and the ham well together, and add 1 well beaten egg. Put the whole into a mould and bake a rich brown. To be eaten cold, cut like a cake.

MRS. NORTHCOTE, Accra.

Ham or Egg Mould.

Instead of mincing the meat, cut it into pieces and dissolve a ¼ of an oz. of gelatine in a gill and a half of stock and mix all together. Arrange some slices of hard-boiled egg and tomato on the bottom of a well wetted mould; put in the mixture, press it down firmly and leave till cold.

MRS. HOLLAND, Oda.

Ham Fritters.

Slices of ham
1 egg
Cayenne pepper
1 tablespoon flour
1 teacup milk
Parsley.

Cut the ham and dust with pepper, prepare a batter of egg, milk and flour. Beat it well before dipping the slices of ham into it, then fry in boiling fat, drain and serve on a dish with parsley.

MRS. HILDITCH, Tarkwa.

Ham and Pineapple Hot Pot.

This is a good variation of the ordinary hot pot.

About 1 lb. potatoes, ¼ lb. sliced cooked ham, some slices of pineapple previously stewed, 1 onion finely chopped, brown sugar, pepper, salt. Arrange in layers, in a greased dish, with a very little brown sugar on the pineapple. Add enough stock or water to keep it moist, and bake in a moderate oven from 1¼ to 1½ hours. Remove the lid for the last half hour of baking in order to brown the potatoes.

ACHIMOTA.

Indian Curry.

Two ozs. butter or dripping, put in stewpan with one large onion sliced thinly, put on slow fire and when nicely brown, add two dessertspoonful of curry powder, stir quickly for five minutes. Then add chicken meat or rabbit, cut into small pieces, stir and simmer for 10 minutes, add pint stock or gravy, two apples peeled and cored, one tomato, a little salt and juice of one lime, steam gently for 4 hours, if veal or rabbit, two hours.

MRS. BROWNING, Cape Coast.

Italia's Pride.

One large cup chopped meat, 2 onions minced and fried brown, 1 pint cold boiled macaroni, 1 pint fresh or cold stewed tomatoes, 1 teaspoonful salt, ½ teaspoonful white pepper. Butter a pudding-dish and put first a layer of macaroni, then tomato, then meat and some onion and seasoning till dish is full. Cover with breadcrumbs, dot bits of butter over and bake ½ hour.

MRS. THOMAS, Cape Coast.

Jellied Lamb.

1 packet aspic jelly
1 gill mint sauce
1 cupful peas
1 cup cold lamb (chopped)
Salt and pepper to taste.

Dissolve the jelly in pint of hot water, add the mint sauce. Chop the meat, season with salt and pepper. Oil a mould, and strain into it a little of the jelly, and when this has almost set, put in a row of peas with two tablespoons of jelly. Let this almost set, and put in the chopped meat and more peas, keep a few peas back for garnishing. Fill up the mould with jelly, and when set, turn out on to a dish and decorate with little heaps of peas.

MRS. E. McELROY, Accra.

Jellied Mixed Grill.

Half a pound of lean ham, 2 sheep's kidneys, 2 pork sausages, 2 tomatoes, 1 tablespoon of chopped parsley, an oz. of powdered gelatine (Cox's powdered gelatine).

Cut the ham into small pieces, halve the kidneys and roll them with the sausages in pepper, salt and slice the tomatoes and place with the meat in a casserole. Cover and cook slowly for 3 hours. Dissolve the gelatine in a little water, add it to the contents of the casserole and let it stand over night to set firm. When required turn out on to a dish and garnish with fresh parsley.

MRS. HOLLAND, Oda.

Jelly Pie.

Take 1½ lbs. steak, cut into small pieces and freed from all fat and gristle, and half as much cooked macaroni as you have meat. Mix together and put in a casserole with salt, pepper, chopped parsley, a pinch of dried herbs, a little grated lemon (or lime) peel and 2 hard-boiled eggs sliced.

Pour in a teacupful of stock, cover, and bake very gently for 3 hours. Leave to get quite cold, and remove any grease that may have formed. Mix a dessertspoonful of marmite, a teaspoonful of vinegar, salt, pepper, a pinch of sugar and ½ oz. gelatine in ½ pint of hot water. Mix well with the meat, etc., in the casserole, and when quite cold sieve a little hard-boiled egg yolk on the top and serve in the casserole.

MRS. NORTHCOTE, Accra.

Jugged Game.

Cut your game into neat joints (either birds of any kind, or hare, or buck-meat) flour, and fry them slightly till just brown. Arrange a layer of thin slices of fat bacon at the bottom of the casserole, fit the meat in closely and cover with another layer of bacon. Add a few cloves (and if you can get them) a bay leaf and a few peppercorns, a pinch of salt, ½ pint claret and ½ pint good gravy or stock. Set it to simmer very gently till done.

A young hare will take about an hour and a half, a wild goose, 3 to 4 hours. When tender take out the meat and bacon and keep them warm while the gravy is prepared. Strain it and let it boil down a little; then mix it with a glass of port wine (or more claret) a tablespoonful red jelly, and thicken with butter and flour and season with cayenne pepper. When the gravy is ready put the meat back into it and heat all thoroughly together. This can be eaten hot or cold. If cold, a little gelatine added to the gravy is an improvement, and all fat should be carefully removed before serving.

MRS. NORTHCOTE, Accra.

Kidney.

Six ozs. kidney, 6 ozs. lean beef, 1 onion, stock, 2 tablespoons rice, 1 oz. butter, pepper and salt. Shred beef and kidney also onion, cook in butter 10 minutes, add stock, rice, pepper and salt; pass through sieve, heat again, add parsley, serve with fried bread.

Kidney Batter.

Make an ordinary Yorkshire pudding with flour and eggs and milk. Put the mixture into a well-greased pie dish. Take as many kidneys as required and cut them into thin slices and lay in the batter. Bake in a hot oven and when cooked slip out of pie dish and serve on a large flat dish with fried tomatoes.

MRS. LLOYD WILLIAMS, Tamale.

Lamb and Vegetables.

Prepare 2 lbs. potatoes, 1 lb. green peas, 3 carrots, 3 turnips, 3 young onions, all cut up, 1 teaspoonful mint, and a tablespoonful parsley. Cut 2 lbs. lamb in neat pieces. Place a layer of vegetables in the bottom of a saucepan, then the lamb, another layer of vegetables, and potatoes on the top, add sufficient water and simmer for 2 hours.

MRS. W. HILL, Accra.

Liver and Bacon (Baked).

Half lb. calf's liver, ¼ lb. bacon, fresh breadcrumbs, ¼ oz. butter or margarine, ½ gill gravy. Cut the liver into slices about ¼ inch thick. Slice the bacon very thinly, and remove the rind. Butter a fireproof dish. Place a layer of breadcrumbs, then a layer of liver, then a layer of bacon in the dish, and repeat, finishing with a final layer of breadcrumbs. Heat the gravy (or use marmite, if none is available), pour into the dish, and bake for about an hour.

MRS. CREWE, Accra.

Liver in Cups.

Liver, boiled and grated, bacon, breadcrumbs, 2 yolks of eggs, and seasoning. Steam in buttered moulds or cups. French beans or tails of leeks round the mould make a pretty garnishing.

MRS. THOMAS, Cape Coast.

Liver Hot Pot.

(Cold meat may be used instead.) About ¾ lb. liver, 2 onions, 4 large potatoes, a slightly thickened gravy, ½ teaspoonful of mixed pepper and salt.

Grease a small pie dish. Cut the liver in rather thin slices and put in sufficient slices to cover the bottom of dish. Sprinkle the mixed herbs, add pepper and salt and gravy. Slice the onions and potatoes and put a layer of onions and then potatoes, continue with a layer of onions and potatoes until the top of the dish is reached, put a little dripping or margarine on the top layer of potatoes and cover with a pie dish.

Bake in a moderate oven for about 1¼ hours and then remove the pie dish and allow the potatoes to become brown and crisp. Sufficient for two persons.

MRS. FIELDGATE, Koforidua.

Meat and Macaroni Pudding.

Three-quarter lb. cold meat or corned beef, 4 ozs. breadcrumbs, pinch dried herbs, pinch grated lemon or lime rind, 2 ozs. suet or dripping, 2 ozs. cooked macaroni, 1 tablespoonful flour, 1 egg.

Mince meat mix with breadcrumbs and half macaroni finely chopped, add herbs, lime rind, fat and flour, mix with well beaten egg, turn into greased basin, cover with cloth or paper, steam gently half an hour. Turn out carefully, surround with remainder of macaroni. Serve with tomato sauce or brown gravy.

N.B.—Baked beans in tomato sauce can be substituted for macaroni.

MRS. DOWLING, Cape Coast.

Meat Cake (Cold)

Half lb. of any cold meat, minced, 2 cooked potatoes, 1 onion chopped small, 2 eggs, baked breadcrumbs. Mix the minced meat, the potatoes mashed, the onion chopped, and the eggs, with a good seasoning of salt and pepper. Grease a cake tin and sprinkle with the breadcrumbs, put the mixture in it and bake for 45 minutes, turn out on to a dish and serve hot or cold.

MRS. HEWITT, Takoradi.

Meat Mould.

Mince some cold meat and add onion and tomato to taste, beat in two eggs and steam for half an hour in a basin. Turn out on to dish and serve very hot with brown gravy.

MRS. ROTHWELL, Koforidua.

Meat Roll.

Half lb. cold beef, ¼ lb. cooked ham, 2 tumblersful of breadcrumbs, 1 egg, salt, pepper, a little stock or water.

Mince meat and ham, mix well with breadcrumbs, add beaten egg, moisten with stock or water, season, and tie tightly in larded pudding cloth. Put in boiling water, and boil fast for five minutes, then draw to side and let simmer gently for 35 minutes. When cold roll in brown breadcrumbs.

MRS. WARRINGTON, Kumasi.

Minced Meat and Garden Eggs (A way of serving).

One large garden egg and sufficient meat for each person. Salt and pepper, a little onion and tomatoes, small amount of breadcrumbs.

Mince meat or cut into very small pieces. Boil the garden eggs whole, when cooked cut lengthwise and remove seeds. Next take out pulp without destroying the skin— mix pulp, meat, a little chopped onion and tomato, season to taste and steam till cooked. When done return to the skins of the garden eggs, sprinkle with a little breadcrumbs and brown in oven. Serve hot, with a little gravy if desired.

MRS. SILCOCK, Takoradi.

Mock Goose with Minced Meat.

One medium-sized marrow (or slightly ripe pawpaw would do), ½ lb. of minced meat, 1 grated carrot, 1 grated onion, 2 or 3 rashers of fat bacon, a little sage. Peel and cut the marrow in half, take out the seeds. Mix well together the minced meat, carrot, onion and pepper and salt to taste, stuff both halves of the marrow and tie together; place in a baking tin with plenty of dripping and roast in a moderate oven, keeping it well basted.

When half baked, place the fat bacon over the top and roast until well browned. Serve very hot with vegetables.

MRS. HOLLAND, Oda.

Okra Stew.

Thirty okras, 3 tomatoes, 7 onions, 6d. salted pork, palm oil, pepper and salt.

1. Wash and cut the okras into slices, put in a saucepan, cover with water and allow to cook until half done. Then drain off water and put okras aside covered.

2. Slice tomatoes and onions and grind the pepper.

3. Cut the meat, wash and then fry in oil, add tomatoes, half the onions and salt. Cook until brown. Make a pulp of the okras, add to meat with remaining onions, pepper and salt. Stir with a wooden spoon, allow to cook for an hour.

SISTER ANTONIA, Keta.

Palmnut Hash.

Forty palmnuts (about), 1 lb. stewing steak, onions, carrots, turnips, tomatoes and potatoes. Boil the palmnuts until cooked, strain off the water and beat the palmnuts. Add water, strain through a sieve several times, and put into saucepan. Take the meat and vegetables, fry a golden brown. Add this to the palmnuts, simmer gently for two hours, skimming off any grease that rises to the top, adding the potatoes half an hour before serving. A chicken can be used instead of meat.

MRS. HOWE, Nkawkaw

Pawpaw (Stuffed).

Cut small unripe pawpaw in two; boil till tender, scoop out the inner portion of the pulp, mash, and mix with any kind of minced meat and season to taste. Fill the halved pawpaws with the mixture; sprinkle with breadcrumbs and dab with butter. Bake for a few minutes.

ACHIMOTA.

Pawpaw (Stuffed.)

(Makes a nice dish for using up Cold Meat). Boil an unripe pawpaw until soft, slice in half and remove seeds. Fill the cavities with minced cold meat which has been seasoned to taste with grated onion and tomato, then bake in the oven until brown on top.

MRS. ROTHWELL, Koforidua.

Pawpaw Stuffed.

One unripe pawpaw (medium size), 8 ozs. minced beef, 1 large onion, 1 large tomato, ¼ teaspoonful salt, peppers to taste. Peel the pawpaw and take out the seeds, boil for about 10 minutes. Mince the onion and cut up tomato, add these to the minced beef with salt and peppers. Stuff the pawpaw with this mixture and cook in a casserole for 45 minutes in very hot oven, and serve with "chip" potatoes, or crisps. Sufficient for two to three people.

MRS. WEBB, Accra.

Pawpaw (Stuffed).

One green pawpaw, ½ lb. cold meat or corned beef minced, 4 tablespoonful breadcrumbs, 2 onions, mixed herbs, 1 egg, pepper, salt, and dripping. Peel pawpaw, cut in two, remove seeds, boil 10 minutes in salt water.

Mix other ingredients together, fill pawpaw, put the two halves together, tie firmly with string, bake with hot fat, bake in moderate oven until brown, sprinkle with browned breadcrumbs before baking, serve with a brown sauce.

MRS. DOWLING, Cape Coast.

Pigeons (Stewed).

Choose small plump birds, sprinkle them with pepper, salt and flour and fry in hot butter for a few minutes before adding 1 breakfastcup stock and a little chopped onion. Parboil 2 ozs. macaroni, drain it, and add it to the pigeons with a gill of cider (if procurable) and a tablespoon finely chopped parsley and thyme. Simmer for 30 or 40 minutes.

MRS. LLOYD WILLIAMS, Tamale.

Pork Chops (Dressed).

Half cup breadcrumbs, 2 tablespoons butter, salt and pepper, powdered sage and sliced apple. Grease tin, lay in chops, cover each with dressing, pour small water around, bake slowly. Do not turn or baste.

MRS. DEVEREUX, Accra.

Rice *Ménagère*.

One lb. rice, 3 rashers bacon, onions and tomatoes, sausage, steak, ham, or chops. Boil 1 lb. rice for 10 minutes, strain and allow to cool. Cut the bacon into dice and fry with onions and tomatoes and when cooked mix it into the rice. Place the mixture in the oven and heat thoroughly add tomato sauce if desired.

Grill or fry either sausage, steak, ham or chops and when cooked place on the rice and serve hot.

MRS. ROTHWELL, Koforidua.

Roast Fowl (Cold) — Use of Remains.

Two or 3 small onions sliced, 1 oz. of butter, 1 oz. of clarified dripping, 1 tablespoonful of curry powder, 1 lemon and a few raisins. Divide the fowl into neat joints, score them, spread on a little butter, sprinkle on a little salt and the curry powder, and let stand for about one hour.

Heat the dripping, fry the onions brown, then remove and keep hot, now fry the pieces of fowl, and when nicely browned, pile them on the onions, and serve garnished with lemon. To fry, about 30 minutes.

MRS. NORTH.

Sausage and Bacon Pie.

Sausages, sliced bacon, sage, onions and pie crust. Put the sausages and bacon together with the sage and onions, and a little gravy into a pie dish. Cover with a good short pie crust and bake.

MRS. HOLLAND, Oda.

Sausage and Tomato Pie.

1 lb. pork sausages
2 large tomatoes
1 small onion
½ pint stock
1 lb. cooked potatoes
Salt and pepper.

Peel, slice and fry the onion, skin sausages, cut into half lengthwise and lay half of them in a pie dish. Cover with the onion rings and peeled and sliced tomatoes, add pepper and salt. Place remaining sausages in dish, pour over the stock and cover with a thick layer of mashed potatoes, smooth with knife and decorate with fork markings. Place small pieces of butter on top and cook in a hot oven.

MRS. CUTHBERT, Koforidua.

Savoury Batter.

Four tablespoonful of finely minced cooked meat, 1 teaspoonful of finely chopped parsley, ½ teaspoonful of mixed herbs, 1 salt-spoonful of salt, ½ salt-spoonful of pepper, 4 ozs. of flour, 2 eggs (West African), ½ pint of diluted Ideal milk.

Mix the flour, eggs, milk, salt and pepper into a smooth batter, let it stand for half an hour, then add the meat, parsley and herbs. Melt a little dripping in a tin and pour into the batter and bake for 20 to 30 minutes in a moderately hot oven. Sufficient for two or three persons.

MRS. FIELDGATE, The Residency, Koforidua.

Scotch Eggs.

Three hard boiled eggs, 4 ozs. cold meat, 1 gill stock, 1 oz. flour, 1 oz. butter, seasoning. Make a panada by melting butter in pan, adding flour and liquid, stir briskly until smooth and in a ball, add meat and seasoning. Shell the eggs, rub with a little flour and coat in the mixture. Egg and crumb, and fry in hot fat. Cut into halves, arrange on a dish and garnish with parsley, serve with or without sauce. Instead of the meat mixture sausage may be used in which case the Scotch eggs must be fried longer to thoroughly cook the sausage meat.

MRS. HENDRY, Accra.

Sheep Bag Dish.

1 sheep's bag and pluck
2 teacups oatmeal
2 onions
1 clove garlic
1 teaspoon mixed herbs
Pepper and salt.

(One sheep's bag and pluck, i.e. large and small heart, and liver. Discard lungs and wind-pipe.)

Clean bag, and pluck thoroughly in cold water and salt. Leave steeping in salt and water for 2 hours. Boil liver, heart, and any tripe not being used as bag until tender, in salted water.

When the meat is cooked remove and pass through mincer, add finely chopped onions, garlic, herbs, salt, pepper, and 2 teacups of Scotch oatmeal, mix all together in a bowl adding as much water from the meat boiling as will bring a to plum-pudding mixture consistency.

Turn this mixture into the uncooked bags, filling bags to not more than three-quarter capacity. Sew up apertures of the bags with a darning needle and strong cotton, cast back into the water of the original boiling, adding more if necessary, and boil for half an hour. Dry off for 5 minutes in the oven.

MRS. MACFARLANE, Tamale.

Smothered Sausages.

One lb. sausages, 1 lb. tomatoes, and spring onions or sliced onions. Put sausages into a shallow saucepan with cold water to half-cover them and onion. Cook for 10 minutes, add sliced tomatoes and two teaspoons of mixed flour. Cook altogether for another 10 minutes and season, serve hot.

MISS. WOOD, Accra.

Soufflé of Fish or Meat or Chicken.

Take any pieces of the above left over from a meal. Mince the meat. Fish must be pounded or well mashed. Make sufficient good white sauce to make a moist mixture of the ingredients, add pepper, salt and suitable flavouring.

Take 1 egg for each person. Separate the whites, add yolks to mixture and beat. Beat whites to a stiff froth, and fold into the mixture. Put into a well-oiled soufflé dish and bake for hour or longer according to size of soufflé.

MRS. C. E. de B. BIDEN.

Steak and Kidney (Curried).

Fry 3 onions sliced, in hot dripping, and put in ¾ lb. steak and ½ lb. kidney cut up small, 4 teacupfuls water. Simmer for 5 minutes, then cover the meat with water and cook slowly for 1 hour, then add 1 dessertspoonful curry powder, 1 tablespoonful flour, and a little browning mixed to a smooth paste. Boil till thick and smooth. Serve with boiled rice.

MRS. W. HILL.

Steak and Macaroni.

½ lb. steak
3 ozs. macaroni
Mushrooms
Tomato sauce
½ pint stock
1 oz. grated cheese
Seasoning.

1. Cut the steak into small pieces and stew with the mushrooms in the stock till very soft.
2. Rub the mixture through a sieve, add some tomato sauce and seasoning to taste.
3. Boil the macaroni in salt water and put in a fireproof dish.
4. Cover macaroni with layer of purée and sprinkle with cheese, bake in quick oven till cheese browns.
5. Garnish with a few mushrooms stewed in butter.

6. Serve very hot.

MRS. BEACH JOHNSTONE, Accra.

Steak and Macaroni.

½ lb. steak
2 ozs. grated cheese
1 beaten egg
1 lb. macaroni
3 ozs. breadcrumbs
Stewed tomatoes.

Cut the meat into small squares, dip it in the cheese, breadcrumbs, and egg. Fry in boiling fat for one minute, boil the macaroni, broken into small lengths, in boiling water, salted, for 20 minutes; drain it, spread it on a hot dish, sprinkle with salt, pepper and grated cheese. Lay the steak on top, and serve it with the stewed tomatoes.

MRS. HILDITCH, Tarkwa.

Tomato Braidee[3].

Best end of neck of mutton or lamb, according to number of people. Cut up into smallish joints, leaving plenty of fat. Brown 2 or 3 onions, add meat and brown it. Then add lots of tomatoes and a sprinkling of flour, pepper and salt, cayenne or cut-up chili. Let all cook slowly together, no water is required. Serve with boiled rice.

MRS. C. E. DE B. BIDEN.

---

[3] i.e. the South African Cape Muslim dish *bredie*. DS

Tongue with Mushrooms.

Boil a tongue, and let it simmer all day until tender. Cut in slices, and place in a deep casserole dish. Cover with a good brown sauce. Add some cooked kidneys, tinned black mushrooms or champignons, some small pieces of cooked carrots and turnips, and a few tinned peas. Let all simmer for about half an hour, taking care to remove grease. Serve a dish of fried bacon with it.

MRS. KEAST, Accra.

Timbales of Cold Meat.

½ lb. cold meat
2 tablespoon breadcrumbs
1 egg and 1 yolk
2 teaspoon chopped parsley
½ oz. butter
2 teaspoon chopped onion
½ gill stock
3 ozs. boiled macaroni
Seasoning.

Thickly butter some dariole moulds or small cups, cut the macaroni into thin rings, line moulds evenly with the rings. Mince the meat, mix with the crumbs and parsley, brown the onion in the butter, add to the meat, bind with the beaten eggs and stock, mix and season well. Press the mixture carefully into the moulds, cover with greased paper, steam gently for hour till firm. Turn out carefully and pour some good sauce round.

MRS. OAKLEY, Accra.

Timbale de Macaroni (Chicken).

A handful straight macaroni, 2 teacups of chicken minced with a little ham and six mushrooms, salt, pepper, cayenne, 1 teaspoonful finely chopped onion, little grated lemon peel, 2 eggs, cup milk or cream, 1 tablespoonful grated Parmesan cheese.

Boil macaroni, taking care it does not break and line a well-buttered basin or mould with it. Mince up 2 teacups chicken with a little ham and 6 mushrooms. Season with salt, pepper and cayenne, a little grated lemon peel, and a teaspoonful of finely chopped onion, mix all well together with 2 eggs well beaten in cup milk or cream, and 1 tablespoonful of grated Parmesan cheese.

Put this mixture into the middle of the macaroni, lined basin, cover with greased paper and steam for one hour; turn out. If desired hot serve with white sauce. If cold garnish with hard boiled egg, 7 tomatoes and mayonnaise dressing.

MRS. SINCLAIR, Kumasi.

Veal and Ham Pie.

One and a half lbs. veal, flour, salt, pepper, lemon rind, parsley, ¼ lb. ham or fat bacon, two hard boiled eggs, pastry, 6 ozs. flour, 1 oz. lard and 3 ozs. butter.

Cut up veal into small squares. Mix together with flour and seasoning and dip each piece of veal into it, put a layer of meat in the bottom of the dish then a layer of ham or bacon, cut in thin slices until the dish is full; chop up fine parsley and sprinkle, more than half-fill with stock, whisk up an egg and stir in, then lay sliced hard boiled eggs and cover with pastry.

MRS. BROWNING, Cape Coast.

Veal Cake.

1 lb. veal
¼ oz. Swinborne's isinglass or 3 leaves gelatine
¼ lb. bacon
1 gill stock
3 eggs
Grated lemon rind
Pepper and salt.

Boil the eggs for 12 minutes. Cut the veal into dice, bacon into small strips, and the shelled eggs into round slices. Decorate the bottom and sides of a plain cake tin or mould with slices of egg and strips of bacon. Mix the rest of bacon with the veal, the rest of the eggs (cut small) and the seasonings. Put this mixture into the mould.

Dissolve gelatine in the stock. Pour into mould adding more stock or water if necessary to cover the meat, Cover the top with greased paper. Put the mould in a baking tin half-filled with water, bake in a moderate oven for 4 to hours.

MRS. SINCLAIR, Kumasi.

Vegetable Marrow or Pawpaw (Stuffed).

One marrow, minced meat, small cup of breadcrumbs, one onion, a little parsley, all mixed together, add salt and pepper, one egg. Peel and cut in half lengthways, remove seeds, stuff with mince, put halves together, tie with string, bake 4 hours. Serve with nice brown gravy.

MRS. BROWNING, Cape Coast

Hot Sweets

Apple Amber.

3 ozs. short pastry
A little water
1½ lbs. apples or 1 large tin
2 ozs. margarine
2 or 3 eggs.
¼ lb. sugar.

1. Stew apples with margarine, sugar and water till tender.
2. Rub through a sieve.
3. Add beaten yolks.
4. Line sides of dish with pastry.
5. Pour mixture into dish.
6. Bake till firm in moderate oven.
7. Make meringue with whites and pile on the mixture.
8. Bake in cool oven till set.

MRS. BEACH JOHNSTONE, Accra.

Apple Charlotte.

Peel, core, and slice some apples and fill a buttered pie dish with alternate layers of apple—sprinkled with lemon juice and sugar—and thin slices of bread and butter, the last layer being bread and butter.

Cover with greased paper and bake in a moderate oven for just under an hour. Serve with custard sauce or cream.

MRS. LYNCH, Cape Coast.

Apple and Rice Surprise.

Apple rings, ¼ lb. rice, 1 pint milk, lemon rind (if obtainable), 2 egg whites, 2 tablespoons castor sugar. Stew the soaked and cored apple rings with 3 cloves and sugar to taste. Bring the milk to the boil with the lemon rind; stir in the rice and simmer till the rice is soft and has absorbed the milk; remove the lemon rind. Make a border of the rice round a hot dish, then pour the apples into the centre, and cover them with stiffly whipped egg whites mixed with the castor sugar. Dust thickly with castor sugar, and place in a moderate oven to set and delicately brown.

MRS. WILKINSON, Dunkwa.

Adjustable Puddings.

Aunt Margaret.

Eight ozs. flour, 4 ozs. sugar, 1 teaspoon baking powder, salt, 4 ozs. butter (rubbed into flour), 1 egg, milk to mix to a batter.
Steam 1 hours.

Variations.

1. Two tablespoons jam at the bottom, steam this.
2. The same baked for 1½ hours.
3. "Canary" lemon rind flavour.
4. "Cake" the same, add ¼ lb. raisins, currants and steam.
5. As 4 but baked. Serve sauce.
6. "Castle" made in small moulds.

MRS. OAKLEY, Accra.

Bachelor's Pudding.

2 ozs. flour
2 ozs. suet
2 ozs. breadcrumbs
2 ozs. apple
2 ozs. sugar

116

2 ozs. carrots
1 egg
2 tablespoons milk.

Mix all the dry ingredients together, and add the egg, well beaten in milk, pour into a greased mould, and boil for two hours.

MRS. HILDITCH, Tarkwa.

Baked Bananas.

Peel 6 ripe bananas and lay in a pie dish; cover with a syrup made of 3 tablespoonfuls of sugar, the juice of a lime and water, bake in a slow oven. Serve with coconut cream.

ACHIMOTA.

Baked Bananas.

6 bananas
1 cup tinned cherries
3 tablespoons butter
1 tablespoon lemon juice.
2 tablespoons castor sugar.

Peel the bananas and halve lengthwise, arrange in a shallow baking dish. Sprinkle with lemon juice and sugar. Cover with cherries, dot with pats of butter. Bake in a hot oven, basting occasionally with cherry syrup until the bananas are soft. Serve with cream. Enough for six persons.

MRS. NICHOLAS, Kumasi.

Banana Fritters.

Four bananas, 1 egg, 2 tablespoonfuls flour, 4 ozs. sugar. Peel and mash the bananas, beat the egg, add in the beaten egg and sugar. Heat the pan and put in about 2 tablespoonfuls of the batter at a time; fry it until a nice brown and then sprinkle castor sugar over. Serve hot.

SISTER ANGELE, Cape Coast.

117

Banana Pudding.

Six bananas, 4 ozs. breadcrumbs, 4 ozs. sugar, 2 eggs, grated rind or juice of lemon. Mash bananas, add crumbs, sugar, lemon rind or juice and eggs well beaten; mix thoroughly and steam for 2 hours, serve with white sauce.

MRS. BROWNING, Cape Coast.

Banana Pudding.

Two bananas, 4 ozs. sugar, 4 ozs. flour, 10 ozs. butter, gill milk, 2 eggs. Cream the butter and sugar well together. Beat in the yolks of the eggs separately. Stir in the flour and add the milk, and the bananas thinly sliced. Whisk the whites of the eggs to a stiff froth and add them lightly to the ingredients, pour the mixture into a well-greased mould, steam or, bake for about 1½ hours.

SISTER ANGELE, Cape Coast.

Banana Pudding.

2 or 3 bananas
2 ozs. butter
2 ozs. sugar
2 ozs. flour
2 eggs
½ teaspoon baking powder
2 tablespoon milk
A few drops of lemon or other flavouring.

1. Peel bananas and cut in thin slices.
2. Put butter, sugar and flavouring into basin and cream together.
3. Add eggs and flour by degrees and beat well.
4. Add milk and bananas.
5. Mix very lightly so as not to break bananas, stir in baking powder.
6. Put into greased basin and steam until well risen firm to the touch. Time 1 hour.

7. Serve with lemon sauce.

MISS SPEARS.

Banana Soufflé.

Rub 4 or 5 bananas through a sieve and mix into purée 1 tablespoon of castor sugar and the grated rind and juice of 1 orange. Separate the whites from the yolks of 4 eggs, beat yolks one by one into the purée, then fold in lightly the stiffly beaten whites. Pour into a well-buttered soufflé dish and bake in a hot oven until lightly browned and well risen. Serve at once with or without cream.

MRS. BRUCE CRABB, Accra.

Barley Pudding.

(Enough for three persons.)

One level tablespoonful of pearl barley, 1 pint milk (evaporated milk and water) 8 lumps of sugar. Dissolve sugar in the milk, put into baking dish, add the barley put into oven. Do not cover the dish.

The pudding is to be stirred occasionally to prevent barley sticking. Bake for 1½ hours, in a slow oven.

Stewed fruit may be cooked in it, or served with it.

MRS. BECKETT, Accra

Bread and Jam Pudding.

Some slices of bread and butter, a little jam, 2 ozs. sugar, ½ pint milk, 2 eggs, nutmeg and raisins. In a greased pie dish place a layer of bread and butter, spread some jam on each slice of bread, add some raisins. Beat the eggs well, add milk and sugar. Pour over sufficient custard to soak the bread. Continue the layers of bread, raisins and custard until the dish is half full. Sprinkle with nutmeg, and bake for about twenty minutes.

MRS. LYNCH, Cape Coast.

Bread and Marmalade Pudding.

Half pint milk, 4 tablespoons marmalade, 1 oz. currants, 2 eggs, 1 tablespoon sugar, pinch nutmeg, pinch ground ginger, 2 or 3 slices of bread. Heat the milk and add it to the well beaten eggs, the ginger and nutmeg.

Spread the bread with marmalade and place the slices in a well-greased pie dish, adding the currants and sugar. Pour the eggs and milk over the bread and bake in a moderate oven until the custard is set.

MRS. LYNCH, Cape Coast.

Biscuit Pudding.

Eight ozs. flour, 4 ozs. beef dripping or butter or margarine, 3 ozs. brown sugar, 2 ozs. currants or sultanas, teaspoonful baking powder, 1 egg, salt, nutmeg, a small cup of milk. Mix flour, dripping, baking powder, sugar, salt and nutmeg; add egg, milk and currants. Put in hot oven, allowing it to become moderate shortly; bake 1½ hours.

ACHIMOTA.

Castle Puddings.

Two eggs and their weight in butter, sugar and flour, ¼ oz. baking powder. Cream the butter and sugar together, beat in the eggs alternately with a little flour, add the rest of the flour and baking powder well mixed, half fill greased tins and bake 20 minutes; serve with custard or jam sauce.

Castle Pudding.

The weight of 2 eggs in butter, self-raising flour and castor sugar. Cream the butter, add the sugar, and beat until white. Add the flour, pour into greased pudding moulds, and bake in a quick oven. Just before serving pour 1 teaspoonful of sherry on to each pudding and surround with jam sauce.

This quantity makes four puddings.

MRS. KEAST, Accra.

Chocolate Custard (Baked).

Three ozs. grated chocolate, 2 tablespoons sugar, 3 eggs well beaten, 1 pint milk. Boil milk, add chocolate and boil 2 or 3 minutes; pour in gradually on eggs, pour into pie dish and bake in moderate oven about 15 or 20 minutes until set at the top.

MRS. BROWNING, Cape Coast.

Christmas Pudding

1½ lbs. raisins
½ lb. sultanas
1 lb. kidney suet
1 teaspoon cinnamon
1 teaspoon mixed spices
1 lb. breadcrumbs
1 breakfastcupful flour
1 lb. sugar
1 lb. currants
½ lb. mixed peel
¼ lb. sweet almonds
A pinch salt
A little milk.
I nutmeg grated
Juice and rind of a lemon
6 eggs (or 9 local ones)
1 wineglassful brandy.

Mix all very well together. Put in well-buttered basins allowing room for swelling. Tie up in floured cloths and boil for four hours or steam for five. Serve with brandy butter.

Brandy Butter.

Eight ozs. fresh butter, 4 ozs. sugar (castor if possible) 2 wineglasses brandy, 1 teacupful whipped cream. Beat the butter to a smooth white cream. Add sugar and brandy and finally whipped cream. Put on ice.

MRS. NORTHCOTE, Accra.

Coconut Cream.

Grate one coconut and pour on a teacup of boiling water, stir well and strain through muslin. Let stand for one hour and skim off the cream.

ACHIMOTA.

Coconut Pudding.

One coconut (grated), teaspoon baking powder, 2 eggs, 1 tin milk, 1 dessertspoon sugar. Mix together coconut and baking powder, beat together eggs, milk and sugar. Add coconut to beaten mixture and beat all together. Put in pie dish and bake ¼ hour.

MRS. SWAN, Tamale,

Coconut Pudding.

Half lb. grated coconut, whites of 4 eggs, 1 oz. butter, 1 lb. sifted sugar, juice of lemon and rind. Mix the coconut, butter, sugar and lemon juice, add the grated rind. Whisk the whites of eggs stiffly, fold into the mixture, put into a greased dish or cup and bake till risen and set.

MRS. OAKLEY, Accra.

Corn Pudding (Steamed).

One cup ground corn, 1 cup grated coconut, ½ cup grated pumpkin and ½ cup grated sweet potato, or 1 cup grated pumpkin, half cup cane sugar or ¾ cup beet sugar, grated rind of 1 orange, half teaspoon ground cinnamon, 1 egg well beaten, 2 tablespoonfuls butter or margarine.

Stir well together and steam in a covered pudding bowl for 2 hours. Serve with sweet custard or syrup.

MRS. MOOR, Koforidua.

Date Pudding.

Half lb. dates, 3 oz. suet, 2 tablespoons sugar (not heaped), 4 heaped tablespoons flour, 1 teaspoon baking powder, 1 egg, little milk.

Shred the suet, stone the dates and cut in half, mix the sugar, flour, baking powder, suet and dates together. Add the egg and then some milk until a fairly firm mixture is obtained. Grease basin well. Pour in the mixture and steam for at least 2 hours.

MRS. STRADLING, Accra.

Dough Nuts.

Four ozs. flour, ½ oz. butter, 1 oz. sugar, 1 egg, milk, salt, ½ teaspoonful baking powder. Put baking powder and salt into flour, beat butter and sugar to a cream, and add in egg and flour. Add milk to make the batter stiff and knead with the hands. Turn on a board and roll it; divide into rounds and fry in dripping (the fat must not be too hot).

SISTER ANGELE, Cape Coast.

Eve's Pudding.

Apples, 3 pieces butter (size of eggs), 3 level tablespoons sugar, 3 heaped tablespoons flour, 2 eggs, ½ teaspoon baking powder. Beat butter and sugar till creamy. Add eggs, beat, and stir in flour and baking powder. Cut up apples and put in a pie dish. Cover with batter and bake in moderate oven 25 to 30 minutes.

MRS. SWAN, Tamale.

Five Cup Pudding.

One cup flour, 1 cup breadcrumbs, 1 cup suet, 1 cup jam, 1 cup milk.

Mix all ingredients together, an egg and a little sugar can be added (but is not absolutely necessary). Boil or steam for about 2 hours.

MRS. TAYLOR, Cape Coast.

Ginger Pudding.

Half lb. flour, ¼ lb. suet, ¼ lb. sugar, 2 large tablespoonfuls of grated ginger. Shred suet very finely, mix with flour, sugar and ginger, stir well together, butter a basin and put in mixture, place basin in hot water and boil for three hours. Serve either hot or cold.

SISTER ANGELE, Cape Coast.

Ginger Pudding.

(Sufficient for six people). Five tablespoonfuls of flour, 3 tablespoonfuls shredded suet (2 of tinned suet), 1 tablespoonful sugar, 2 tablespoonfuls treacle or golden syrup, 1 dessertspoonful of ground ginger, ½ teaspoonful baking powder, 1 egg (or little milk). Mix all dry ingredients together, add treacle or syrup, stir well, gradually adding the egg (well beaten), put into well-greased basin, then put into boiling water up to rim of basin, and boil for 1¼ hours. A little mixed spice may be added if desired.

Serve hot.

MRS. WEBB, Accra.

Ground Rice Pudding (Baked).

The weight of 3 eggs in flour, ground rice, castor sugar and butter, 3 teaspoons baking powder. Cream, butter, and sugar together, add eggs, etc., alternately. Make into thick batter and bake one hour.

Hong Kong Pudding.

One tablespoon flour, 2 oz. butter, 2 eggs, pinch of salt, ¼ teaspoon baking powder, 4 oz. preserved ginger, 2 oz. sugar, 1 tea cup milk, 4 oz. breadcrumbs. Beat butter and sugar to a cream, separate whites from yolks of eggs. Beat yolks with a little milk until creamy, add crumbs to creamed butter and sugar. Then add egg and milk, beat well. Add salt and baking powder and chopped ginger and flour. Reserve some ginger for ornamenting. Pour mixture into a pudding dish lined with short crust, bake in a moderate oven until set.

Whip whites of eggs until stiff, sweeten with 2 oz. castor sugar and vanilla flavouring. Pile roughly over pudding. Decorate with diamonds of ginger, brown meringue in oven.

MRS. HOLLAND, Oda.

Lemon or Orange Sponge Pudding.

Weight of 2 eggs in butter, sugar, flour, juice of 1 orange, lemon or lime. Cream sugar and butter, stir in eggs and flour alternately, add fruit juice. Steam in basin in a saucepan of boiling water until cooked. Serve with jam or white sauce if liked. Do not allow the water to get into the pudding.

MRS. STEELE, Tamale.

Lemon Tarts.

Pastry 8 ozs., flour 4 ozs., lard or butter 1 teaspoon, baking powder, pinch of salt. Lemon mixture, 1 teacup boiling water, 1 teacup white sugar, 1 tablespoon corn flour, juice and grated rind of 1 lemon, 2 eggs. Make short crust in usual way, bake before putting in the mixture. Mix corn flour with a little cold water then add boiling water and sugar and boil for 10 minutes, when this has cooled add lemon also yolk of eggs, put a spoonful into each tartlet. Whisk whites of eggs to stiff froth and put a little on each mixture, put in oven for each to set.

MRS. BROWNING, Cape Coast.

Lime Cheese Tartlets

Short crust pastry, 2 eggs, 2 limes (juice of), castor sugar 1 tablespoonful, ½ tin Ideal milk, small walnut, butter. Melt butter in double saucepan, add beaten yolk and lime juice and sugar and milk, stir until thick but do boil. Make six tartlet cakes from the short crust pastry cook slightly, add the lime cheese filling and return to oven till thoroughly hot and browned. Ten minutes before serving beat whites of egg till quite stiff and place on top of tartlets and return to oven till slightly browned.

MRS. SHAW, Accra.

Lemon Pie.

3 ozs. short crust pastry
1 dessertspoon corn flour
3 eggs
1½ tablespoons sugar
2 lemons
¼ tablespoon cinnamon
3 tablespoons castor sugar
½ pint milk.

1. Blend the corn flour with a little of the milk.
2. Bring remainder of milk to boil with grated lemon rind.
3. Pour milk over the blended corn flour, stirring all the time.
4. Boil, stirring well, till it thickens.
5. Add sugar and cinnamon to corn flour and allow to cool.
6. Make pastry and line sides (not bottom) of pie dish.
7. Separate yolks from whites, add yolks and lemon juice to corn flour mixture and pour into prepared dish.
8. Bake in moderate oven till set.
9. Beat whites till stiff and add 3 tablespoons castor sugar.
10. Heap beaten white on mixture and put all into cool oven till set and dry.

N.B. Six limes may be substituted for lemons if necessary.

MRS. BEACH JOHNSTONE, Accra.

Margaret Soufflés.

One-quarter lb. butter, 1 pint water, 1 grated lemon, 2 oz. castor sugar, 4 ozs. dried flour, 2 eggs, vanilla flavouring. Place the butter and water in pan over fire, add lemon rind, sugar and pinch of salt, stir until it boils, add enough flour to make a stiff paste, it may take more or less than the given quantity, beat up the eggs and when the mixture has cooled, slightly beat them well in; add a few drops of vanilla essence. Have ready a pan of boiling fat, shape the mixture into neat balls with two dessertspoons and when a smoke rises from the fat drop in some of the balls, fry a golden brown, drain well on paper, dredge with castor sugar.

MRS. BROWNING, Cape Coast.

Marmalade Pudding.

4 ozs. sugar
4 ozs. breadcrumbs
4 eggs
4 ozs. marmalade
4 ozs. minced suet

Mix, beating the eggs well, boil in a mould for at least two hours. These proportions of suet, breadcrumbs, are the foundation of several puddings: Treacle, preserved ginger, raisins, figs, etc., may be substituted for the marmalade, butter for the suet, and flour for the bread.

MRS. LYNCH, Cape Coast.

Mince-meat Roly-poly.

Make a roly-poly in the usual way, and spread with a thick layer of mince-meat. Serve a little brandy with it.

MRS. KEAST, Accra.

Mônch-Kappe.

Beat up 1 egg with 5 tablespoons milk, ¼ tablespoon sugar and a squeeze of lemon. Cut slices of bread, 2 inches thick into 2 inch cubes, divide each cube lengthwise into 2 pieces, soak in the custard for a few minutes and fry in egg and bread-crumb to a light golden brown.
Serve with a white wine sauce or custard.

MRS. FRASER, Achimota.

Mysterious Pudding.

Two eggs, their weight in butter, flour, sugar, 1 teaspoon baking powder, 2 tablespoons marmalade. Mix all together and pour into a well-greased basin, steam for 2 hours.

MRS. BROWNING, Cape Coast.

Orange Pulp Fritters.

Much appreciated—prepare as much orange pulp as required, flavour with lemon juice and sugar as liked. Mix into a frying batter to which an extra egg or two is added and fry.

MRS. FRASER, Achimota.

Orange and Raisins Pudding.

Two ozs. raisins (stoned and chopped), if not obtainable, sultanas, 1 oz. butter, 1 oz. flour, 1 oz. sugar, 1 egg (2 if very small), grated rind of an orange. Grease some small moulds (or 1 large), cream the butter and sugar, add the egg and beat well. Add the flour, raisins, and orange rind to the mixture and fill the moulds (or mould) three parts full. Bake in a hot oven for 20 minutes, turn out, and pour orange sauce round.

MRS. DONNATT, Winneba.

Orange Sauce.

One large juicy orange, 2 ozs. sugar, 6 drops cochineal (this can be omitted if not obtainable), Squeeze the orange juice on to the sugar. Dissolve the sugar slowly, and boil it for 8 minutes. Add the cochineal.

MRS. DONNATT, Winneba.

Pears and Rice.

To ¼ lb. rice add 1 pint of milk, 2 ozs. castor sugar, a pat of butter, a pinch of salt, and the grated rind of half a lemon. Cook slowly until the rice is tender, cool slightly and stir in the previously beaten yolks of two eggs.

Complete the cooking and press the mixture into a flat-topped round mould and turn out on to a hot dish. Rapidly boil the syrup from a tin of preserved pears until ½ remains and add ½ teaspoon angostura bitters. Put in the pears and let them become thoroughly heated, then arrange them in a heap on top and around the rice adding syrup as desired.

Sprinkle with castor sugar and cover with the stiffly whipped whites of the eggs. Sprinkle heavily with castor sugar and bake in moderate oven until the meringue is set.

MRS. LYNCH, Cape Coast.

Pine-apple Fritters.

Three slices pineapple, milk, sugar, 1 egg. Mash the pineapple, add the milk and sugar, then the egg (beaten), fry in hot fat until a golden brown. Serve hot.

SISTER ANGELE, Cape Coast.

Pine-apple Pie.

One pineapple, 4 ozs. flour, I egg, 1 tablespoon sugar, 4 spoons milk (Ideal will do), half a cup of water, a little salt. Mix flour, sugar, egg and salt with the milk and water. Divide the paste in two portions and roll out. Cover a greased enamelled dish inside with the paste, fill the dish with thinly sliced pineapple, cover with rolled paste.

If paste is left, cut in strips and trim the upper side. Cover these with a little milk, butter or the yolk of an egg to make them shining; bake in a hot oven.

SISTER ANTONIA, Keta.

Pine-apple Pudding.

1 pine-apple
Margarine the size of half an egg
2 cups milk
½ cup flour
2 eggs
1 tablespoon sugar.

1. Stew pine-apple, dice and then stew with a little sugar.
2. Boil butter and milk.
3. Mix flour and sugar with cold pine-apple juice.
4. Add yolks of eggs, mix with the boiling milk and boil three minutes, stirring well.
5. Pour over the pine-apple.
6. When cold decorate with whipped white of egg.
7. Serve hot or cold.

MISS. SPEARS.

Queen Pudding.

One pint boiling milk, ½ lb. breadcrumbs, 1 oz. margarine, some sugar, vanilla essence, 2 eggs and jam. Pour the boiling milk over the breadcrumbs, add the margarine, 2 ozs. of sugar and a few drops of vanilla essence, then the yolks of eggs. Grease a pie dish, put in a layer of jam and pour in the mixture, bake till set. Beat up the whites of the eggs with a teaspoon of sugar, pile in heaps on the top of the pudding and return to the oven to brown slightly.

MRS. LYNCH, Cape Coast.

Queen of Puddings.

Half breakfast-cup of Ideal milk fill up with water to make ½ a pint, ½ pint of breadcrumbs, ½ oz. of butter, 3 eggs, grated rind of 1 lime, 2 oz. sugar, 2 tablespoonfuls of jam available. Boil the milk and sugar, put the bread-crumbs into a buttered pie dish and pour the milk over the crumbs.

Add the yolks of the eggs and grated rind and stir into the milk and breadcrumbs. Bake until set, spread on jam or, if not available, squeeze the juice of one lime over the pudding. Whip up the whites, sweetened, to a stiff froth, put on top of the pudding in little heaps and brown in the oven. Sufficient for four or five people.

MRS. FIELDGATE, The Residency, .

Railway Pudding.

Three ozs. butter or margarine, 2 ozs. flour, ¼ teaspoon baking powder, some jam, 2 ozs. sugar, 1 egg, a little milk. Beat the butter and sugar to a cream, add egg well beaten, and a little milk. Then flour and baking powder, put into grease-lined pie dish and bake in quick oven, when browned cut through and spread each piece with jam. Put together again and serve hot.

MRS. HOLLAND, Oda.

Raspberry Charlotte.

(Tinned or bottled may be used.)

Breadcrumbs, raspberries, sugar and butter. Well butter a dish and sprinkle with fine breadcrumbs then a layer of raspberries, sprinkle with sugar, repeat until the dish is full, place small pieces of butter on top, bake in moderate oven, serve with cream or custard.

MRS. BROWNING, Cape Coast.

Rice Custard.

One cup cooked rice, 1 pint hot milk, 3 eggs, ½ cup sugar, little butter, salt and flavouring. Heat the rice in the milk, add eggs slightly beaten, sugar and flavouring. Bake in a moderate oven till set.

SISTER ANTONIA, Keta.

Rice with Chocolate Nut Sauce.

Cook ½ cup rice in 1 quart of skimmed milk until the rice is soft. Turn into baking dish, stir in 1 cup of raisins or stoned dates and bake 30 minutes, adding more milk if necessary. Serve with nut sauce, made as follows :—

Two tablespoons cocoa, 2 tablespoons corn flour, teaspoonful salt, 1 cup milk, 1 cup syrup, 1 cup nuts and vanilla. Warm the milk, add syrup and salt, thicken with corn flour and cook until the starchy taste is removed, stir in the cocoa and the nuts and flavouring.

MRS. FRASER, Achimota.

Richmond Pudding.

One teacupful flour, 1 teacupful jam, 1 teacupful suet, 1 teaspoonful bicarbonate soda, 1 egg. Mix all together and steam for 2 hours, and serve with custard or sweet sauce.

MRS. W. EMMETT, Accra.

Scalloped Bananas.

Cover a buttered dish with a thick layer of sliced bananas, sprinkle over 2 tablespoons sugar and moisten with lemon juice. Then put a layer of breadcrumbs, repeat the process till the dish is full, pour a little melted butter over and bake till lightly browned.

MRS. OAKLEY, Accra.

Simple Pudding.

½ lb. flour
1 oz. breadcrumbs
2 ozs. margarine
1 egg
1 oz. sugar
1 little milk
Baking powder
1 tablespoonful syrup.

Rub the margarine into the flour; add sugar, baking powder, breadcrumbs, and the egg well beaten, and enough milk to form a stiff batter. Put a tablespoon of syrup in the bottom of a greased basin, pour in the mixture, cover with a greased paper and floured cloth, and steam for 2 hours.

MRS. HILDITCH, Tarkwa.

Sponge Pudding.

Jam or marmalade, 2 ozs. butter, 2 ozs. sugar, ½ gill milk, 2 eggs, 4 ozs. flour, 1 teaspoon baking powder. Grease a mould or basin, put in a thick layer of jam or marmalade. Cream together butter, sugar and eggs well beaten, stir in 4 ozs. of flour and baking powder, add milk, turn mixture into mould covered with buttered paper, steam 4 hours.

MRS. BROWNING, Cape Coast.

Sponge Pudding.

Take 1 oz. butter and mix with 2 oz. sugar. Beat in 2 eggs, then 2 oz. flour and a pinch of baking powder. Add flavouring to taste and steam for half an hour. Serve hot with syrup, jam, or stewed fruit.

MRS. ROTHWELL, Koforidua

Sweet Potato Pie.

Boiled and mashed sweet potatoes
3 beaten eggs
Milk to form into a batter
3 tablespoons sugar
Grated nutmeg or spice
Grated lemon or lime rind
1 tablespoon margarine.

1. Line a dish with pastry.
3. Mix all the ingredients together and form into batter.
3. Pour into pie dish, bake with a covering of pastry.

MISS SPEARS.

Sweet Potato Pudding.

1 lb. steamed potatoes
6 eggs
2 tablespoons sugar
1 lb. margarine.
Flavouring.

1. Mash potatoes until free from lumps.
2. Mix with the margarine.
3. Beat eggs and add gradually.
4. Bake until firm, this burns easily.

MISS. SPEARS.

Sweet Potato Pudding (as a Sweet).

Eight tablespoonfuls of boiled mashed sweet potatoes (sweet potatoes take 30 minutes boiling). One dessertspoonful of sugar, 2 tablespoonfuls of evaporated milk (not diluted). Beat up the potatoes and add the sugar and milk. Put into greased dish and bake for 20 minutes. Sufficient for six people.

MRS. WEBB, Accra.

Sweet Potato Pudding.

Make the same as Yam pudding, only different flavourings, etc.

Sweet Yam Pudding.

1 cup of grated cooked yam
1 cup breadcrumbs.
½ cup currants
Spice to taste
1 tablespoon sugar
1 tablespoon margarine.
Bananas or raisins or dates will substitute currants.

1. Beat sugar and margarine together.
2. Add all ingredients and yam last.
3. Bake in a hot oven for 15-20 minutes.

Sweet Yam Pudding. (Another method)

½ lb yam
2 ozs. margarine
1 lemon
2 eggs
2 ozs. sugar.

1. Cook yam and sieve whilst hot.
2. Beat yam and margarine together and allow to cool.
3. Beat yolks of eggs and add to sugar and yam.
4. Beat whites stiffly, stir in lightly.
5. Bake in greased dish in hot oven for 20 minutes.

MISS. SPEARS.

Tapioca Cream.

Boil together 15 minutes, 1 quart milk, 3 heaping tablespoons fine tapioca and a little salt, stirring frequently. Beat together the yolk of 1 egg and ½ cup sugar, and at the end of 15 minutes stir into the tapioca and milk. Boil until it begins to thicken like custard.

Remove from fire and, when partially cooled, add any flavouring desired. Pour into pudding dish. Cover with stiffly beaten white of egg and brown in oven. Serve hot or cold.

MRS. FRASER, Achimota.

Toffee Pudding.

Cut some neat squares white bread, soak them in milk to moisten, Make a good liquid toffee, ¼ lb butter, 2 oz. brown sugar, 2 tablespoonfuls golden syrup, generous squeeze of lemon juice. When the mixture is turning brown, put the bread squares into the toffee and allow to cook for a minute or two, pile them neatly onto a hot dish, pour over them the rest of the toffee, serve very hot with whipped cream.

MRS. C. E. DE B. BIDEN.

Treacle Roll (Baked).

Half lb. flour, 2 ozs. lard or margarine, 1 teaspoon baking powder, pinch of salt, water to mix, 2 tablespoons treacle, 2 ozs. breadcrumbs, 1 lemon. Sieve the flour, baking powder and salt. Rub in the fat, mix with sufficient water to make a stiffish dough. It takes about 1 gill of water but as some flours absorb more than others the exact quantity cannot be given.

The water should be added gradually until the mixture forms a pliable dough which, however, should not be sticky. Roll out on to a floured board into a long strip. Mix the breadcrumbs, grated rind and juice of the lemon and spread it over the pastry. Roll it up, seal the edges well, place on a greased baking sheet and bake in a moderate oven for ¾ to 1 hour.

MRS. LYNCH, Cape Coast.

Treacle Sponge.

Half lb. flour, salt, 1 teaspoon baking powder (large), ¼ lb. suet (chopped), 1 tablespoon sugar, 1 teacup milk, 1 teacup treacle. Warm milk and treacle together, add to ingredients, mix thoroughly and steam 2 hours.

Variations.
1. "Ginger" the same and 1 teaspoon ground ginger.
2. "Golden" no ginger but lb. raisins.
3. "Birthday" chopped preserved ginger, and cherries

MRS. OAKLEY, Accra.

Victoria Pudding.

One lb. smoothly mashed potatoes, 1 lb. carrots, chopped, 1 lb. flour, 1 lb. suet, 1 lb. sugar, 1 lb. currants, ½ lb. apples, chopped, teaspoonful mixed spice. Mix all the ingredients together and boil for 3 hours. This makes a good family Christmas pudding.

MRS. ROTHWELL, Koforidua.

Viennese Pudding.

2 ozs. bread (without crusts)
1½ eggs
1½ ozs. sultanas
1½ ozs. sugar
1 oz. candied peel
¼ pint and a good tablespoon milk
½ lemon rind (grated)
3 tablespoons sherry.

Cut the bread into small squares and place in a basin with finely-chopped peel, half the sugar, the raisins, rind and sherry. Place the extra sugar in an old pan and brown it a good dark brown, add the milk to this and stir till the is sugar melted and the milk a good brown colour. Pour on to the beaten eggs and strain on to the bread, etc., mixing well. Turn into a greased mould, cover with greased paper and steam 35 minutes. Turn out and serve with custard or Sabayon sauce.

MRS. OAKLEY, Accra.

Wafer Pudding.

One tablespoon flour, 2 ozs. butter (oiled), 2 eggs beaten. Blend these with ½ pint of milk, powdered sugar and lemon rind grated. Pour very little of the mixture into well-buttered saucers and bake in a quick oven. This quantity makes 6 puddings.

MRS. OAKLEY, Accra.

COLD SWEETS

America Ice Pudding

One pint milk, 6 teaspoons castor sugar, 7 or 8 leaves of gelatine, and yolks of two eggs. Put into saucepan and stir over fire until thickened. Beat up whites of eggs until stiff and pour hot mixture on them, stirring all the time, put into a mould and turn out when cold.

(Should be like jelly at the top and spongy underneath when turned out.)

MISS WOOD, Accra.

Apple Foam.

Four large apples, 3 tablespoonfuls sugar, white of 2 eggs. Cook apples in as little water as possible with sugar, when soft, pass through sieve. Whip white of 2 eggs till frothy. Stir in when apple pulp is cool. Serve in custard glass or dish. Cream may be added if desired.

MRS. CRANSTON, Accra.

Apples in Jelly.

Stew an apple for each person slowly and carefully keep whole in water and with sugar to sweeten. Place in a glass dish when partly cool, make a raspberry or lemon jelly, using the liquid in which the apples were cooked to melt it and adding enough water to make up the right amount. Pour this round the apples after it has cooled a little and allow it to set. Top the apples with a spoonful of whipped cream before serving. This makes a delicious sweet.

MRS. BUSH, Sekondi.

Apple Snow.

6 apples
5 whites of eggs
The juice of 1 lime
3 tablespoonful sugar.

Stew the apples with the juice of the lime and tablespoonful sugar. When quite soft pass through wire sieve. Beat the whites of eggs thoroughly with 2 tablespoonfuls sugar, and beat in the apple pulp. Serve in custard glasses. The mixture should be given a final beat just before serving. If cooking apples should be obtainable more sugar will be required. Sufficient for 4 people.

MRS. HEMANS, Takoradi.

Apple Tart without Apples.

Pastry, green pawpaw, lime or lemon juice and sugar. Cut up a green pawpaw into slices, add a little lime or lemon juice, a very little water and sugar, and boil until tender. When cold put into a pie dish and cover with a crust of short or puff pastry; bake in a hot oven. This tart may be served hot or cold.

Green pawpaw boiled with a little lime juice—makes an excellent substitute for a number of apple dishes where the latter are unobtainable.

MRS. GIDDINGS, Wenchi.

Apricot Soufflé.

One tin apricots, 2 ozs. castor sugar, 3 eggs, 1 tin cream, ½ an oz. of gelatine, ¼ breakfastcup of water, 1 tablespoon of lemon juice (or lime).

Dissolve the gelatine in water, rub apricots through a sieve (enough for about 1 breakfastcup), beat the yolks of the eggs with the sugar, add the fruit puree. Stand the basin over boiling water (or a double saucepan will do) and stir mixture until it thickens; set until cold. Whip the whites of the eggs until stiff, also the cream. Strain the gelatine into the fruit mixture, add the juice, mix well. Then very lightly stir in the whites of egg and cream. Pour into prepared soufflé cases, serve cold.

MRS.HOLLAND, Oda.

Apricot Shape.

One tin apricots, ¾ oz. leaf gelatine, ¼ lb. castor sugar, 1 glass maraschino (or sherry).

Rub enough apricots through a hair-sieve to make 1 pint of puree. Stir in the gelatine, dissolved in a little of the apricot syrup, then add sugar and maraschino. Mix well, then gently pile into a wet mould. Turn out when set, and decorate with minced almonds.

MRS. WILKINSON, Dunkwa.

Banana Blancmange.

Two bananas, 1 quart of milk, 2 ozs. of corn flour, 2 ozs. of castor sugar, 2 yolks of eggs, ½ a teaspoonful of vanilla essence. Mix the corn flour smoothly with a little milk, boil the remainder, add the sugar and blended corn flour, and simmer gently for 5 minutes. Let it cool, add the beaten yolks of eggs and stir by the side of fire until they thicken. Now put in the bananas thinly sliced, the vanilla essence and pour the preparation into a wetted mould. Time from 30 to 35 minutes and enough for 6 or 7 persons.

MRS. NORTH.

Banana Blancmange.

1½ pints milk
2 ozs. castor sugar
2 egg yolks
2 large bananas
3 ozs. corn flour
Vanilla essence.

Stir the corn flour with a little milk into a smooth paste. Pour the rest of milk into a pan and add sugar and boil. Stir in corn flour, as soon as thick, take off and stir in well-beaten yolk of eggs. Keep stirring until eggs are cooked and then stir in the bananas, rubbed through a hair sieve. Flavour with vanilla. Pour into a wet mould and chill. When set serve with custard.

MRS. COE, Wenchi.

Banana Chartreuse.

Six bananas, 1 pint Chivers' lemon jelly, whipped cream or custard if desired, a few chopped nuts (baked groundnut would do). Peel the bananas and cut them into thin dices. Line a plain mould thinly with jelly and decorate it with the banana and nuts. Whip the rest of the jelly until it is on the point of setting. Add the rest of the bananas. Pour into the mould. Place in a cool place to set. Turn out, decorate with whipped cream, or serve with custard.

MRS. HOLLAND, Oda.

Banana Cream.

Four bananas, coconut, pineapple, castor or crushed sugar, Ideal milk. Beat the bananas with a fork until they are quite creamy and without lumps. Take a large slice of fresh pineapple and pound and mix all the juice and a spoonful of the pulp with the banana cream. Mix a level dessertspoonful of sugar with a tablespoonful of undiluted Ideal milk. Add this to the banana and pineapple and beat well in a basin. Grate some coconut and put about a dessertspoonful (finely grated) inside the mixture. Then pile into four fruit or wine

142

glasses and put some grated coconut on the top, chill if possible. Sufficient for 4 persons.

MRS. FIELDGATE, Koforidu.

Banana Cream.

Mash bananas, add 2 ozs. castor sugar and ½ gill of cream. Beat thoroughly and place in a glass dish, sprinkle with lemon juice. Whip the whites of 2 eggs to a stiff froth, heap on top of bananas and garnish with cherries.

MRS. LYNCH, Cape Coast.

Banana Cream.

Make a thick custard of three yolks of eggs, 4 ozs. sugar, and sufficient milk with a flavouring of vanilla. Slice three or four bananas in a glass dish, spread with strawberry jam, pour the custard over, cover lightly with the whipped whites or cream, and decorate with mounds of red currant jelly.

MRS. CAPON, Winneba.

Banana Custard.

Six ripe bananas, 1 pint of custard, some raspberry jam. Peel bananas and cut into thin slices lengthwise. Spread jam on the slices and put together as sandwiches. Place in a glass dish and pour over the hot custard. Stand in a cool place.

MRS. LYNCH, Cape Coast.

Banana Custard.

Two bananas, 3 thin slices stale bread and butter, 2 eggs (native), ½ tin milk and 1 teacup water, 1 oz. sugar, grated lemon rind, a little nutmeg. Slice the bananas into a greased pie dish, put alternately slices of bread and butter, and bananas, and sprinkle a little grated lemon rind throughout.

Beat the eggs and sugar, add the milk and water, and pour it over the bread and butter and bananas in the pie dish. Grate a little nutmeg over the pudding and bake in a moderate oven for about 45 minutes.

MRS. DRAKE, Tamale.

Banana Custard.

Peel 5 or 6 bananas, cut lengthwise into thin slices, spread some jam between each two slices. Place these in glass dish pour over them 1 pint hot custard. Stand till cool.

MRS. BEVERIDGE, Accra.

Banana Meringue Custard.

Six bananas, juice of grape-fruit, 2 egg yolks and 3 whites, 5 sponge cakes, ½ pint milk, 2 dessertspoons corn flour, 1 teaspoonful granulated sugar, ¼ lb. castor sugar. Mix the flour to a smooth paste with a little milk, heat the remainder and stir on to it. Then return to the saucepan and bring to the boil, keeping it stirred all the time. Let this cook slowly for a few minutes, then draw aside. Add the granulated sugar and cool slightly. Beat up the yolk and add, stir over a low burner for a few minutes to cook the eggs, but be careful not to let it boil. Add a few drops of vanilla flavouring. Peel the bananas and mash to a pulp. crumble up the sponge cakes and add to the banana pulp with the strained juice of grape-fruit. Mix these together, turn into a dish, add the corn flour custard, and leave until cold. Whisk the egg whites to a stiff froth and fold in the castor sugar. Heap this on the top, then put into a cool oven to set the meringue. Serve cold.

MRS. W. EMMETT, Accra.

A Banana Dish.

Four bananas, 1 dessertspoon jam or lemon curd, a little milk or cream, and plain chocolate. Beat up the banana to a pulp, then add the jam or lemon curd and mix all well together. Place the mixture in individual glasses and pour over a little tinned milk or cream; sprinkle grated chocolate over the top and serve. Allow about 2 bananas per person.

MRS. GIDDINGS, Wenchi.

Banana Rolls.

Roll out short pastry thinly and cut into oblong pieces about 3 x 4 inches. Spread red jam all over them except for about ½ inch round the edges. Cut canary bananas into 2-inch pieces and place them on the pastry oblongs. Damp the edges and fold over like sausage rolls. Knock up the edges neatly, place on a baking sheet and bake in a hot oven until golden brown. Sprinkle with castor sugar when cold.

MRS. PASSELLS, Accra.

Banana Sponge.

Six or 8 bananas, 1 pint of made lemon jelly, 1 gill whipped cream, sugar to taste, a little cochineal, ½ teaspoon vanilla essence, some desiccated coconut, a few glace cherries. Peel the bananas and mash them with a fork until they are creamy, then beat in the lemon jelly and whisk together; add cream, sugar to taste and vanilla essence; then colour with cochineal and whisk again. Pile high on a glass dish, sprinkle with desiccated coconut and decorate with a few glace cherries.

MRS. LYNCH, Cape Coast.

Banana Sweet.

Mash 4 or 5 bananas and beat to a froth, add dessertspoonful of sugar, juice of an orange and tablespoonful of a sweet wine or liqueur, serve very cold.

This can be coloured with cochineal and garnished with almonds and cherries or whipped cream piled on the top.

MRS. DOWLING, Winneba.

Banana Sweet.

Mash 4 bananas with a fork and add the juice of 3 oranges, decorate with Caledonian cream and serve very cold.

MRS. LOCKHART, Mfantsipim, Cape Coast.

Banana Tart.

Pastry
Golden syrup
Banana
Coconut.

Line a sandwich tin or flan case with puff or short pastry. Put a layer of golden syrup at the bottom, then a layer of sliced banana followed by another layer of golden syrup. Sprinkle breadcrumbs or coconut over the top and bake in a hot oven. This may be served either hot or cold.

MRS. GIDDINGS, Wenchi.

Blancmange.

¼ pint milk
½ pint cream
1 oz. gelatine
Rind of lemon
2 tablespoon brandy
2 ozs. sugar.

Soak the gelatine in a little extra milk, put the milk cream, rind and sugar into a pan, stir occasionally over the fire until well

146

flavoured, then put in the gelatine and stir over gentle heat till dissolved. Strain, add the brandy when cooled, stir occasionally till beginning to thicken, then mould and set.

MRS. OAKLEY, Accra.

Boston Cup Pudding.

One teacupful of flour, 1 teacupful of brown moist sugar, ½ a teacupful of milk, 1 teaspoonful of baking powder, ½ teaspoonful of grated lemon rind, 1 ozs. of butter, 1 egg, raspberry jam. Cream the butter, sugar well together, then beat the egg in, add the lemon rind and flour, stir in the milk, and lastly the baking powder. Have ready a greased Yorkshire pudding tin, pour in the preparation and bake from 20 to 25 minutes in a moderately hot oven. When cold split and spread a good layer of jam between.

MRS. NORTH

Bufflote.*

Flour, sugar, currants, eggs, nutmeg, palm wine, dripping. Method and measurements are the same as for bread.

SISTER ANGELE, Cape Coast.

Claret Jelly.

Half pint claret, pint water, the rind and juice of 1 lime, 1 tablespoon red currant jelly, 2 tablespoons Nelson's gelatine, 3 tablespoons castor sugar. Put into a small saucepan the water, sugar and red currant jelly. Add the gelatine with the lime rind peeled off very thinly and the strained juice. Stir over the fire until the gelatine is quite dissolved. Simmer for a few minutes and add the wine. Do not boil again. Strain through a piece of muslin and if necessary add a few drops of cochineal. When nearly cold pour into one large or several small moulds that have been rinsed out with cold water. Set aside in a cool place until cold and firm. Turn out when required and if wished decorate with whipped and sweetened cream. Sufficient for 6 people.

MRS. HEMANS, Takoradi.

---

* See also Floats.

Coconut Cream.

Grate a coconut and extract the milk. Add 3 teaspoons castor sugar, 1 tablespoon gelatine and beat for a few minutes. Beat the whites of 3 eggs with a tin of cream; when this is done, whisk the whole together. Place on ice or in a Frigidaire until set and thoroughly chilled.

MRS. CAPON, Winneba.

Coconut Cream.

Grate 1 coconut, then sieve. Add the coconut milk and beat in the white of an egg. This makes an excellent accompaniment for sweets.

MRS. ROTHWELL, Koforidua

Coconut Cream.

Grate 2 or 3 ripe coconuts, moisten with a very little boiling water, squeeze through a piece of cloth. This cream is nearly as good as ordinary cream for all fruit dishes.

To make coconut ice cream prepare as above and add to one small tin milk and sugar to taste, freeze in usual way.

MISS BARCHI, Sekondi.

Coffee Cream.

Two tins Ideal milk, 1 milk tin water, 1 milk tin strong coffee (strained), 12 pieces lump sugar, 5 sheets gelatine, 1 teaspoonful vanilla essence, cream and almonds. Put milk, coffee, water, sugar and gelatine into a saucepan. Stir until gelatine and sugar are dissolved. When hot, not boiling, add the vanilla flavouring then turn into a mould. When set, turn into a dish and decorate with cream and almonds.

MRS. SUTHERLAND, Koforidua.

Coffee Cream Ice.

Pour half pint of very strong clear coffee (well sweetened) into a pint of good custard, mixing well; then add a quarter pint of whipped cream and freeze. Serve in glasses with a little whipped cream on top and ice wafers.

MRS. PASSELLS.

Coffee Mould.

2 ozs. sugar
1 pint milk
1 oz. cornflour
½ oz. custard powder
¼ oz. butter
3 teaspoonfuls coffee essence.

Place corn flour and custard in a lined pan, add milk slowly, stir till boiling, add sugar and coffee. Cook slowly, seven minutes, stirring all the time. Turn into mould, cover with paper and when set, turn out and decorate.

EVELYN BELLAMY, Cape Coast.

Cold Chocolate Sweet.

Two or 3 ozs. chocolate, ½ oz. gelatine, vanilla, ½ oz. butter, custard.

Make a pint of egg custard, melt the chocolate and butter and stir into custard, mixing thoroughly, dissolve the gelatine in 3 tablespoonfuls of water and add with vanilla, some cream may be added, and the custard should have a little extra sugar.

Before the mixture is set, drop into it some lumps of liquid toffee.

MRS. C. E. DE B. BIDEN.

Cold Guava Pastry.

6 oz. short crust pastry
3 eggs
½ lb. guavas
3 oz. sugar
1 lime
1 tin milk.

1. Line a flat dish with pastry and decorate the edge.
2. Stew guavas with 1 oz. of the sugar.
3. Make a custard with the eggs, milk and rest of sugar.
4. Add juice and grated rind of lime to custard when cool.
5. Pass the guavas through hair sieve to remove pips.
6. Put guavas on pastry and cover with custard.
7. Bake in moderate oven for half an hour.

MRS. BEACH JOHNSTONE, Accra.

Cold Orange Soufflé.

Three eggs, (4 if African eggs), 2 oz. castor sugar, ½ oz. gelatine, 1 gill milk, 4 gills orange juice (3 or 4 oranges), juice of ½ lemon, or 1 lime. Heat milk and sugar over water in double-saucepan till all the sugar is dissolved. Beat the yolks of eggs, add hot milk, and return to the saucepan; cook, stirring constantly, till it thickens. Strain mixture into basin; add strained fruit juice and gelatine dissolved in a little warm water. Beat whites of eggs till stiff, and fold into other ingredients, very gently. Stand the basin in cold water, or in a cool place, and stir the mixture till it is just beginning to set; then turn into a soufflé dish and leave in the ice-box to set. Serve in the dish, decorated with glace cherries, almonds, or slices of orange.

MRS. WILKINSON, Dunkwa.

Cold Strawberry Soufflé.

Three eggs, 1 oz. corn flour, ¾ pint milk, 2 oz. sugar, 2 oz. butter, ½ oz. gelatine, ¼ pint cream, 1 tablespoon red currant jelly, ½ lb strawberries or tin, vanilla essence. Mix corn flour to a cream with a little cold milk, put rest of milk in a pan with vanilla flavouring, heat, add corn flour and sugar, stir until it boils and thickens, then take off the fire. Mash the berries and rub through a sieve and stir into the

150

corn flour with butter, stir in yolks of eggs and cream and whisk over a very gentle heat for about ten minutes. Dissolve gelatine and red currant jelly, strain in mixture and add stiffly whipped whites of eggs. Pour in soufflé dish with a paper jacket tied round and put in refrigerator until set.

MRS. ELLIS, Kumasi.

Cold Sweets.

One and a half pints of custard, whites of three eggs, 3 tablespoons each of red jam, jelly, and icing sugar. Put the whites of eggs into a basin with the jam, jelly, and icing sugar, and stir with a wooden spoon for about 20 minutes, until the mixture is thick enough for the spoon to stand in it. Put a layer of custard in a glass dish, then a layer of the pink mixture and continue until the dish is full, having a pink layer on top.

MRS. LYNCH, Cape Coast.

Cold Sweet.

Six eggs, 2 tablespoonfuls sugar, 2 ozs. gelatine, 1 cup milk, vanilla flavouring, strawberry jam, cream. Beat eggs and sugar, then add gelatine melted in the milk and beat all till creamy. Spread jam on top and cover with whipped cream.

MISS SUTHERLAND, Aburi.

Crème Brulée.

Make one pint of custard without sugar and keep hot on the side of the fire. Put three tablespoonfuls of granulated sugar and one oz. of margarine or butter in an old saucepan. Cook, stirring all the time until it boils and slightly burns. Pour the hot toffee slowly into the custard and stir well until it becomes thoroughly mixed. Then pour into custard glasses and leave until cold.

MRS. PUCKRIDGE, Accra.

Cream Jelly

One packet jelly, 1 small tin Ideal milk, pint of water. Dissolve the jelly in the hot water and, when cold but not set, well stir in the undiluted milk. Pour into a wetted mould and leave to set.

MRS. LYNCH, Cape Coast.

Cream Jelly Sponge.

Follow the above directions, but when the jelly is half- set, whisk well for 10 minutes until it is light and spongy, then pour into mould and finish setting.

MRS. LYNCH, Cape Coast.

Caledonian Cream.

Whites of 2 eggs, 2 tablespoons sugar, 2 tablespoon strawberry or raspberry jam, 2 tablespoons red currant jelly. Beat all together with wooden spoon until thick, use for cakes or trifles.

MRS. LOCKHART, Mfantsipim, Cape Coast.

Caramel Custard Apples.

Five good-sized apples, 6 ozs. castor sugar, ¾ pint water and a few cloves, 2 eggs, ¾ pint milk—diluted Ideal milk, and almonds.

For the Caramel—3 ozs. lump sugar and ½ gill water.

To make the Caramel—Put the lump sugar and water into a saucepan and dissolve it slowly. Bring to the boil and boil until a rich golden brown. Take off and let it get cold; add the milk to the caramel and warm very slowly until caramel dissolves. Do not allow it to become too hot.

To make the Caramel Custard—Beat up eggs and stir caramel milk on to them. Then turn it into top of a double boiler and cook the custard over hot water until it thickens. Strain into a basin and leave it to get cold.

To prepare Apples—Peel apples and remove cores, then stick a few cloves into each. Put castor sugar into a pan with pint of water and let it dissolve. Bring sugar and water to the boil; add apples and cook them carefully until tender without letting them break. They should be turned over occasionally. It is advisable not to cook more than two or three apples at once, then they are less likely to break. When they are tender, take out and leave to get cold; arrange them in a dish and coat them with the caramel custard. Decorate each one with a spot of custard and sprinkle with almonds. Serve with cream.

MRS. SUTHERLAND, Koforidua.

Cassava Cakes.

Cassava tubers (about 1 lb.), dripping for frying. Peel cassava, cut it into half lengthwise and cut out the centre wood. Put into a saucepan and cover with water, then boil for about ½ an hour, or until the cassava becomes soft and floury. Beat in fufu beater till the cassava looks like potato. Make it into a round bar squeezing it and rolling it. Cut it into slices and fry them in frying pan with enough dripping to form a $1/_8$ -inch layer on the pan. Fry to a golden brown. The rounds should be inches in diameter and 4 inch thick,

MRS. BECKETT, Accra.

Chocolate Cream.

One pint milk, I oz. sugar, oz. gelatine, 1 oz. chocolate powder (or 1 oz. cocoa powder and a dessertspoon of sugar), a few drops of vanilla essence.

Mix the chocolate powder with a little cold milk to a smooth paste. Boil the rest of the milk and pour it into the mixture, stirring well. Return to the saucepan to cook, adding the sugar and the vanilla essence; stir till it begins to thicken. (A double saucepan is best). Remove from the fire, and stir well over cold water till it is cool. Dissolve the gelatine in about 3 tablespoons of warm water, and add to the mixture, stirring in thoroughly. Pour into a glass dish or small cups and leave till set. It can be decorated with whipped cream.

Coffee essence or orange juice may be used instead of chocolate but double the quantity of gelatine will be required.

MRS. WILKINSON, Dunkwa.

Chocolate Mousse.

Two dessertspoonfuls of cocoa or grated unsweetened chocolate, 4 dessertspoonfuls castor sugar, 2 ozs. butter, ½ teacupful water, 2 eggs.

Put the cocoa, butter, sugar and water into a saucepan and stir until it boils. Then take off the fire and let it cool. Separate the eggs, add the yolks to the chocolate mixture and stir for a few minutes over the fire. Do not let it boil. Take off and let it cool slightly. Beat up the whites to a stiff froth—fold lightly into the mixture and pour into a glass dish on top of custard. It should be made about half an hour before wanted and served cold.

MRS. PUCKRIDGE, Accra.

Chocolate Pudding.

Two tablespoons corn flour, 5 teaspoons cocoa, 1 pint milk, 3 tablespoons sugar, vanilla essence. Mix the corn flour and cocoa together with a little of the milk to a smooth paste, slowly adding the rest of the milk, and the sugar, put it into a saucepan, bring to the boil, stirring well. Let it boil for 8 minutes, stirring continually, add a few drops of vanilla and remove from fire. Rinse mould in cold water and immediately pour in the pudding. When set serve in glass dish with whipped cream.

MRS. LYNCH, Cape Coast.

Chocolate Soufflé.

6 ozs. slab chocolate
2 ozs. sugar
3 eggs
½ gill cream
½ oz. gelatine
1 gill milk
1 oz. almonds.

1. Melt 4 ozs. chocolate in the milk.
2. Melt the gelatine.
3. Separate yolks from whites, put yolks in basin with sugar and whisk over hot water till thick and creamy, add melted chocolate.

154

4. Whip cream, then whites and add each to yolks, folding them in, not stirring.

5. Strain melted gelatine and add to mixture.

6. Pour into soufflé dish or deep bowl and allow to stand in cold place.

7. Before serving sprinkle top thickly with grated chocolate and chopped browned almonds.

Orange Soufflé.

Same as above, substituting 1 gill of orange juice for milk. Rind of 2 oranges for chocolate.

MRS. BEACH JOHNSTONE, Accra.

Custard Baskets.

One orange per person. Custard according to number of persons. Cut a slice from the top of each orange large enough to insert dessertspoon. Scoop out pulp into bowl, removing skin and pith; make sufficient custard according to number of persons. Add to this the orange fruit and boil all together and when done return to orange skins. Cut a strip of orange skin and place to form handle. Cool and serve as cold as possible.

MRS. SILCOCK, Takoradi.

Baked Custard.

1 qt. milk
6 egg yolks
¾ cup sugar
4 tablespoons sugar
Whites of eggs.

Put two tablespoons of sugar in baking pan, stir constantly over hot stove until melted to a syrup of light brown colour. Roll this syrup around sides of pan, place this to one side, then take 1 qt. of milk and cup of sugar. Let this come to the boil, then pour this mixture gradually over the yolks of eggs. When thoroughly mixed together pour into the baking pan with the brown syrup. Bake in the oven, or cover and put coals on top of the lid and bake on top of stove. When baked set in dish of cold water until cool, turn out on platter. Beat whites of eggs with two tablespoons of sugar until stiff. Spread around custard.

MRS. SHIRER, Yendi.

Custard with Ratafias Baked.

Three-quarter pint milk, 3 yolks and 1 white of egg, 1 teaspoon sugar, ratafia biscuits. Beat the eggs with the sugar, heat, but do not boil the milk and pour onto the eggs, stirring well, strain into a greased pie-dish, cover the pudding with ratafia biscuits and place it in a shallow tin of cold water.

Bake in a slow oven. As the water gets too hot it must be changed, otherwise the pudding will be full of small holes and watery, serve cold, sufficient for 2 persons.

MRS. BANKS KEAST, Accra.

Danish Apple Pudding.

Stew enough apples to fill a medium-sized pie dish three-quarter full. Beat together 2 large eggs and 1 cup sugar, 2 tablespoonfuls butter, ¼ lb. ground almonds, and flavour with a little vanilla essence. Spread over stewed apples and bake slowly in a moderate oven. It is better cold.

LADY THOMAS.

Dough Nuts.

One pint flour, 1 teaspoon cream of tartar, ½ teaspoon baking soda, 1 oz. sugar, 2 eggs, milk, jam, fat for frying. Sift the flour, cream of tartar and soda into a basin, add sugar, mix into a light dough with egg and milk, roll out on floured board, cut out, put a little raspberry jam in centre and roll into balls, fry in deep fat for 5 minutes, take out and roll in castor sugar.

MRS. BROWNING, Cape Coast.

Eastern Pudding.

1 packet raspberry jelly
1 oz. corn flour
¾ pint water
½ pint milk
1 dessertspoon sugar
2 tablespoons grated coconut.

Dissolve the jelly in ¾ pint hot water. When cool line a mould with some of the jelly first decorating the bottom of the mould with a little coconut. Boil the milk and pour on to the corn flour previously blended with a little cold milk. Return to the pan, add sugar, simmer 5 minutes, cool slightly, stir in remainder of jelly and coconut, blend thoroughly; pour into the mould, serve with fruit salad or tinned raspberries.

ACHIMOTA.

Filling for Cakes or Sweets.

Two full tablespoonfuls of butter, beat to a cream, 2 tablespoons brown sugar (Barbados), beat to a cream with butter, 2 tablespoonfuls milk put in gradually, 2 tablespoons of boiling water added gradually, flavouring, vanilla or brandy, teaspoonful.

MISS WOOD, Accra.

Floats*

These are fried dumplings of very light dough: 4 ozs. flour, 1½ teaspoonfuls baking powder, ⅛ pint water or milk, salt, 1 level dessertspoonful of shortening, or less. Mix like pastry, and fry in deep fat (hot).

SISTER ANGELE, Cape Coast.

Floating Island.

One or 1½ pints custard, ½ lb. guava jelly, the white of I native egg. Whisk the white of egg till frothy, then add the guava jelly, a little at a time, beating thoroughly till the mixture is very stiff. Ice both ingredients, and before serving put the custard into a glass bowl and pile the island, in one or many small islets floating on the custard. Decorate with a few pieces of jelly or cherries.

MRS. BECKETT, Accra.

French Tart.

Make paste to cover outside of pudding basin. Bake upside-down. When cold take pastry off basin; put apricot jam in bottom, and fill with cold stewed prunes. Pour cream or custard over; serve hot or cold. Best cold.

MISS WOOD, Accra.

Fruit and Cream Sandwich.

1 sponge round
1 small tin strawberries, pears or peaches
¼ pint cream
Icing sugar
Apricot jam.

Split the sponge round and spread lower half with apricot jam. Drain the fruit thoroughly, cut into pieces and arrange closely to cover the jam. Sprinkle with icing sugar (this may be omitted). Whisk

* See also Bufflote.

158

cream stiffly and spread on top of fruit. Cover with top half of sponge round and dust icing sugar lightly over top.

MRS. CUTHBERT, Koforidua.

Fruit Cream.

One small tin apricots or peaches, 4 eggs whites, custard. Rub the fruit through a sieve, having strained off the juice. Beat up the egg whites till stiff and add them to the fruit puree. Heap on individual dishes and serve with custard made from the egg yolks, milk and sugar.

MRS. DRAKE, Tamale.

Fruit Jellies.

Cut up any kinds of fresh fruit, arrange in patterns and set in layers of a prepared jelly square.

MRS. OAKLEY, Accra.

Grape-fruit (Stuffed).

Scoop out the centre of the grape-fruit in the usual way, fill either with whipped cream mixed with nuts, shredded pineapple mixed with nuts and maraschino cherries, or cream cheese and shredded lettuce.

MRS. PASSELLS, Accra.

Guavas (Stewed).

Peel thinly 1 lb. ripe guavas, cut in halves or quarters and scoop out all the seeds. Barely cover the remainder of the fruit with water, to which the juice of a lime has been added; add ¼ lb. sugar and boil till the fruit is tender and syrup thickens slightly. Serve with milk, cream, or boiled custard.

ACHIMOTA

Honeycomb Mould.

One pint of milk, (Ideal diluted), 4 eggs, 2 lemons or 3 limes, 6 ozs. sugar, ½ oz. gelatine. Put milk, sugar, gelatine and the lemon rind into a saucepan and let it remain until flavoured. Now heat the milk slightly and strain into a basin. Beat the yolks of the eggs a little and put into the milk. Just bring to the boil, stirring all the time. Return to basin, beat the whites of the eggs to a stiff froth and stir in quickly, add the lemon juice. Pour into mould whilst hot and put in a cool place at once. Sufficient for 6 persons.

MRS. FIELDGATE, Koforidua.

Ice Cream (without cream).

1 tin Ideal milk
2 eggs
3 tablespoons sugar
1 small tin fruit or 2 oranges.

1. Separate yolk from whites of eggs.
2. Mix yolk with milk and beat thoroughly. Set aside till quite cold.
3. Beat whites stiffly and add to milk.
4. Squeeze and strain orange juice, or mash tinned fruit and juice thoroughly, and stir into mixture.
5. Put into refrigerator for about 6 hours.

MRS. BEECH JOHNSTONE, Accra.

Ice Cream Pudding.

1 tablespoonful butter or margarine
1 egg
1 pint milk
1 tablespoonful castor sugar
Vanilla flavouring
1 tablespoonful flour.

160

Blend butter and sugar and add egg, flour and flavouring. Mix well and add one pint boiling milk. Stir well and place in cool oven to set but must not boil. Allow to cool and place on ice.

MRS. CUTHBERT, Koforidua.

Iced Chocolate Shape.

6 oz. sugar
2 teaspoons vanilla
1½ oz. corn flour
1½ gills cream
3½ gills hot milk
2 squares chocolate, plain
Pinch of salt
Cold milk.

Add sugar and salt to the hot milk and stir it on to corn flour mixed with a little cold milk. Boil for 10 minutes stirring constantly. Add melted chocolate and leave to cool. Add vanilla and fold in stiffly whipped cream. Pour mixture into a mould and freeze. Decorate the shape with whipped cream and serve with wafers.

MRS. ELLIS, Kumasi.

Iced Cup Custards.

Beat till feathery 3 eggs (4 if small), add 1 quart milk (Bear brand), 1 cup full of granulated sugar, a pinch of salt and stir well for several minutes. Pour the mixture into 6 teacups, stand them in a tin or basin of hot water in a cool oven and bake gently till quite firm—remove from oven, carefully dry the outside of the cups and stand on ice till required. Iced tinned fruit or stewed fruit may be served if desired.

MRS. W. HILL.

Jellied Blancmange.

Set a blancmange first in a mould, then pour in a jelly square to set.

MRS. OAKLEY, Accra.

Jellied Coffee.

Make a pint of strong coffee, add ½ pint water, melt 1 oz. gelatine in a gill of water, stir it in and set in a mould. Serve with whipped or Devonshire cream, very cold.

MRS. NICHOLSON, Accra Ice Co.

Jelly Cream.

Take 1 jelly and prepare in the ordinary way. When nearly cold beat in 1 tin of Ideal milk and allow to set.

MRS. ROTHWELL, Koforidua.

Varieties with Jelly Squares.

Dissolve a jelly square in half the usual quantity of water (nearly boiling) add the rest of the water cold. Whisk till frothy and just setting.

MRS. OAKLEY, Accra.

Lemon Cream.

One breakfast-cupful sugar, 1 tablespoonful corn flour, 3 tablespoonfuls lemon juice (or more), 3 egg yolks. Stir well together. Put 1 breakfast-cupful water on fire. When boiling, add the mixture (sugar, corn flour, lemon juice, yolks), stir well until it becomes thick. Beat white of eggs and mix with the cream.

MRS. MARTIN, Agogo.

Lemon Cream.

Two lemons, 1 pint water, 2 ozs. corn flour, 4 ozs. sugar, 2 eggs. Pare the lemon thinly and boil the rind with the water for 5 minutes. Mix the corn flour smoothly with the strained juice of the lemons. Add the liquid from the rinds and boil for 3 minutes, stirring all the time. Add the sugar, and allow it to cool slightly. Mix in the well-beaten yolks and stir over a gentle heat till they thicken. Whip the whites stiffly and mix them in gently. Pour into a wet mould and when cold turn out.

SISTER ANGELE, Cape Coast.

Lemon Soufflé.

Beat 3 yolks of egg and 4 ozs. castor sugar till well frothed, then add the grated rind and juice of lemon. Stir in 5 sheets of gelatine (¼ oz.) which have been melted in a little water and lastly the stiffly beaten whites. Set in a mould.

MRS. OAKLEY, Accra.

Lemon Soufflé.

One lemon, 3 eggs, 3 ozs. castor sugar, ¼ oz. gelatine, 1 teacup water.

Beat yolks and sugar for five minutes. Dissolve gelatine in hot water and add it, with juice and grated rind of the lemon yolks and sugar. Beat whites very stiffly and mix them carefully in. Put in soufflé mould to set. Whipped cream may be added before serving.

MISS. LAMONT, Krobo Girls' School.

Lemon Sponge.

Rind and juice of 1 lime
1 pint water
4 ozs. sugar
1 tablespoon sherry
4 whites of eggs (African)
1 oz. leaf gelatine.

Wipe the lime with a damp cloth, peel rind thinly, and put in a saucepan with the gelatine broken in pieces and the water. Dissolve slowly, strain, cool, and add the sherry, beat up the whites of eggs with the lime juice, and add to mixture, whisk well in a basin surrounded with broken ice. Care must be taken it is not whisked too long, or it will become lumpy. It may be put either in a mould, or heaped on a glass-dish.

Decorate with angelica and serve with custard in glasses flavoured with sherry, sufficient for 6 persons.

MRS. BANKS KEAST, Accra.

Mrs. Pelly's Lime Sponge.

(From the recipe-book of a lady living in India about 1860). Whites of 3 eggs, 4 limes (or 1 large lemon), ½ lb. white sugar, ½ oz. gelatine dissolved in a cup of warm water. Dissolve gelatine ; add the lime-juice, sugar and whites of egg. Beat for half-an-hour; pour into a wet mould and leave to set. The sponge can be served covered with custard sauce made from the yolks of the eggs, and flavoured with lemon peel, if liked.

MRS. WILKINSON, Dunkwa.

Loganberry Sherbert.

1 small tin loganberries
4 ozs. loaf sugar
1 gill cream
1 gill water
1 egg white (2 native eggs)
A few drops carmine.

Drain the loganberries, reserving some as a garnish, and rub the rest through a sieve. Boil the sugar, water and loganberry syrup for five minutes; add the purée and cool. Freeze to a semi-solid consistency, and then beat until light in colour and frothy. Whip the egg white and the cream, and fold into the mixture with a little carmine. Pile in a glass dish and allow to freeze firmly.

MRS. DRAKE, Tamale.

Macaroni Custard.

¼ lb. macaroni
2 tablespoons of whipped cream
¾ pint custard
1 oz. sugar
Vanilla flavouring.
Boil the macaroni, place in a pie dish, add sugar and vanilla. Pour the hot custard over, and let it stand for 2 hours, serve with whipped cream and fruit.

MRS. HILDITCH, Tarkwa.

Mango Cream.

Sufficient mangoes to give ½ lb. purée, ½ oz. gelatine, 1 oz. castor sugar, 1 tin cream. Pass sufficient ripe mango through a sieve, to give ½ lb. purée; add the sugar to this. Dissolve the gelatine in a little water, and add to the puree. Mix well, and finally add a tin of whipped cream. Turn into a prepared mould (or individual moulds) and set.

MRS. E. McELROY, Accra.

Mango Fool.

Take 1 lb. pulp from mangoes that are not quite ripe and stew with ¼ lb. of sugar. Rub through a fine sieve. When cool add ½ pint of custard or evaporated milk and whisk for a few minutes.

ACHIMOTA.

Milk Jelly.

One pint milk, 4 sheets gelatine, ½ oz. sugar. Melt the gelatine in a little cold milk, boil the milk and sugar and pour over gelatine, slowly boil, strain, cool, and put on ice. Serve with custard in glasses flavoured with sherry. Sufficient for 3 persons.

MRS. KEAST, Accra.

Milk Jelly.

Make up a jelly square by melting it first in ¼ of the amount of water allowed, when quite cool add the remaining ¾ amount of liquid as cold milk instead of water.

MRS. OAKLEY, Accra.

Norwegian Cream.

Four eggs, ½ oz. powdered gelatine. Melt the gelatine in about 2 tablespoonfuls of hot water, allow to cool. Beat the yolks of eggs lightly with a fork, and add to them, beating well, a handful of castor sugar. In a large basin put the whites and beat to a very stiff froth, fold in the yolks lightly, but thoroughly—with any flavouring desired, lastly add the melted gelatine which must only be blood-heat.

Pour at once into a glass dish or soufflé mould—when set, put lumps of lemon jelly on top or whipped cream.

MRS. C. E. DE B. BIDEN.

Compote of Oranges and Grape-fruit.

8 ozs. sugar
3 oranges
1 gill water
1 grape-fruit.

Make a syrup by boiling sugar and water together. Divide oranges into sections, removing the pith, and cut grape-fruit into small sections taking care that no pith, or pips are allowed to remain. Drop the pieces of grape and orange into the syrup and stew very slowly until they are cooked, the time required varying from 10 to 15 minutes. When cool turn into a glass dish.

MRS. CUTHBERT, Koforidua.

Orange Baskets.

Three oranges, ½ pint jelly, cream, 2 ozs. of angelica and cherries. Cut oranges in half, squeeze out the juice into a basin, remove all pith and inside skin from the orange cases. Take half of a ½ pint jelly, dissolve in a quarter of a pint of hot water, add the orange juice through a strainer and a squeeze of lime juice and fill the orange cases. Place the orange cases in a cold place to set and, before serving, add a spoonful of whipped cream in the centre with crystallised cherries on the top. A handle for each basket should made with a narrow strip of angelica bent over and fixed into the jelly.

MRS. DONNATT, Winneba.

Orange Baskets.

Cut off about ¼ of the orange from the top leaving a piece of peel across about ½ an inch wide to form a handle. Scallop round the edge of orange, scrape out all the inside. It is best to use a sharp pair of scissors with which to form the baskets. Fill the oranges with orange jelly (when set) and decorate with whipped cream and baked ground nuts. To ensure the basket standing upright cut a small piece away from the bottom of the orange.

MRS. HEMANS, Takoradi.

Orange Folly.

1 cupful sugar
1 pint water
Pinch of salt
Pulps of 3 oranges
2 tablespoons corn flour
Juice of a lemon
Juice of 2 oranges.

Mix sugar with corn flour and add salt, slowly add water to the mixture. Put into a saucepan and bring to the boil and then boil until corn flour is cooked. Let it cool and add fruit juices and orange pulp, stir thoroughly and put into a mould to chill. When set decorate with tiny multi-coloured sweets.

MRS. COE, Wenchi.

Orange Fruit Soufflés.

Oranges as required, 1½ ozs. flour, 1½ ozs. sugar, 1½ ozs. butter, 3 eggs. Cut a circular slice off the top of each orange. Scoop out the pulp, but do not break the skins, rub sufficient pulp through a sieve to make half a pint.

Melt butter in a stewpan, add the flour and, when well blended, stir in orange pulp and boil until it thickens. Remove from the heat and cool it.

Add sugar and three egg yolks, one at a time. Whisk the whites very stiffly and stir into the mixture, fill orange cases with the preparation and set on a baking sheet in a moderate oven for 20 minutes. Serve very quickly.

MRS. ELLIS, Kumasi.

Orange Jelly.

One pint of orange juice, strained, 1 pint of boiling water, 2 ozs. of loaf sugar, 4 ozs. of gelatine, the juice of 2 lemons, the thinly cut rind of oranges. Put water, gelatine, sugar and orange rinds into a stewpan, bring to the boil, and let mixture stand by the side of the fire for about 10 minutes. Have the strained orange and lemon juice ready in a basin, add the contents of the stewpan pouring them through a piece of muslin or a strainer. When cool pour into mould. This filling is never cleared, as it spoils the flavour.

MRS. NORTH.

Orange Pudding.

Six oranges, ½ lb. sugar, 2 eggs, 1 tablespoonful cornflour, 1 pint milk. Peel and cut and slice oranges, removing skin and pips, sprinkle with sugar on layers. Make cornflour into a smooth paste with a little cold milk, and beaten yolks of eggs, stir well and pour in boiling milk, simmer until fairly thick, pour over oranges. Whip white of eggs stiffly, add 1 tablespoonful sugar, pile on top of pudding, place in cool oven to harden the meringue, serve hot or cold.

MRS. DOWLING, Winneba.

Orange Snow.

Dissolve ½ oz. gelatine in ½ pint hot water, add the juice of three oranges and the grated rind of one and heat until boiling. Allow to cool, then add the whites of three eggs and whip together until very stiff and frothy.

MRS. LYNCH, Cape Coast.

Orange Soufflé.

Three eggs, 3 tablespoons sugar, 3 oranges, sponge cakes, a little lemon juice. Separate yolks from whites, beat yolks with sugar and lemon juice and orange juice, also 1 tablespoon of grated orange rind. Cook on fire till it thickens. Beat in whites which have been stiffly beaten and pour over sponge cakes. Put on ice to set.

ACHIMOTA.

Orange Sponge.

Two or 3 oranges (according to size), ½ pint water, ½ lb. loaf sugar, 1 oz. gelatine, whites of 2 eggs. Boil the sugar and water together until dissolved, and add 1 oz. gelatine (previously dissolved in a little cold water). Add to this the rind of two oranges, finely grated, and the juice of two or three oranges, according to taste. Mix well, and allow to stand until almost cold, then add the stiffly whipped whites of two eggs, and put into a prepared mould to set.

MRS. McELROY, Accra.

Orole.

Half lb. flour, 2 tablespoons of sugar, a pinch of salt, 1 egg, ½ teaspoon baking powder, ½ teaspoon butter. Mix all ingredients well together and work in a smooth paste. Cut this in pieces and roll out separately, leave each spread out and dry for about half an hour. Fry in boiling oil. Can be served hot or cold.

SISTER ANTONIA, Keta.

Peach Foam.

Pulp peaches, beat in white of egg and castor sugar to a stiff foam. Any fruit pulp will be equally nice.

MRS. V. R. COE, Wenchi.

Peach Pie.

Pastry, 6 ozs. self raising flour, 4 ozs. margarine, 2 dessertspoonfuls castor sugar, yolk of egg and little water if necessary, pinch of salt. Filling—Large tin of sliced peaches, custard—can be made with custard powder, syrup of peaches and milk—or to taste. Stiffly whipped cream to decorate. Pastry—Sieve flour into baking basin, add a good pinch of salt, rub in margarine, add sugar with beaten egg, mix to a stiff dough (in this country when making pastry try to have cool hands and use iced margarine, butter or lard and always iced water).

Have ready a greased pie plate, roll out pastry thinly, put on to plate, putting a double layer on edge, joining with white of egg or water, decorate or mark with knife, prick pastry on bottom of plate and line with buttered paper and scatter rice on paper to prevent rising, fire in a hot oven for 20 minutes until a pale brown colour and allow to cool. Fill the centre of pastry with cold custard and decorate with slices of peaches and piped whipped cream alternately around the edge and also on top of custard. (I find when using tinned cream, turn into bowl, beat slightly, add a little sherry and a small teaspoonful Cox's powdered gelatine melted, with a little lukewarm water added and put on the ice will give a good stiff cream.)

MRS. WILKINS, Kumasi.

Pêche Melba.

Rub some raspberry jam through a hair sieve with not more than a tablespoonful of hot water. Colour with a little carmine. Make a vanilla ice cream mixture and half-fill some glass goblets. Colour some peaches slightly with carmine and place half a peach in each goblet, and cover with the raspberry puree.

MRS. KEAST, Accra.

Peter Pan Cream.

Three tablespoons semolina, 2 eggs (whites and yolks separated), 1 small tin milk, 2 large cups water, 2 ozs. castor sugar, juice and rind of an orange or lemon, Put the milk and water into a saucepan and bring it to the boil. Stir in the semolina, grated rind and the sugar and allow to boil gently for 15 minutes, stirring frequently. Add the beaten egg yolks; allow to cool and then beat in the orange or lemon juice a little at a time. Turn into a fireproof dish. Whip the egg whites, pile on top, sprinkle with sugar and lightly brown in the oven.

MRS. DRAKE, Tamale.

Pine-apple (To Serve).

Cut off the green tops and cut the pineapple in slices with a stainless knife. Remove the skin leaving no tough fibre behind. Place the slices in a dish (round or cut up), sprinkle generously with castor sugar and leave several hours.

A little sherry at the bottom of the dish gives a good flavour and a few maraschino cherries dotted about give an attractive colour.

The green top placed in a sauce of water will keep green a long time and makes a good table decoration.

MRS. PASSELLS, Accra.

Stuffed Pine-apple.

Cut off the top of the pineapple, scoop the inside and cut into small pieces, removing the core. Mix with soft fruit like pears, peaches, etc., sweeten with soft sugar and flavour with essence or liqueur, put the mixture back into the pineapple and serve very cold.

MRS. NICHOLSON, Accra.

Pine-apple Charlotte.

½ cup cream
1 cup crushed pineapple
½ cup marshmallows
Sponge gingers
1 cup castor sugar
½ cup cold water
1 tablespoonful powdered gelatine
1 tablespoonful lemon juice.

Beat cream until thick. Add marshmallows, cut in small pieces. Soak gelatine in cold water, then dissolve and add to pineapple. Add sugar and lemon juice. Let it stand in a pan of cold water till cold, stirring constantly. When it begins to thicken, fold in the beaten cream and marshmallows. Line a glass dish with sponge fingers and pour mixture in centre. Chill and serve. Enough for 4 persons.

MRS. LLOYD WILLIAMS, Tamale.

Pineapple and Orange Mould.

1 pineapple, 2 oranges and water to make one pint
10 lumps sugar
1 tablespoon corn flour
1 dessertspoon custard powder.

1. Squeeze the juice from the pineapple and add the juice of 2 oranges. Make up the quantity to 1 pint, either by adding water or more orange juice.
2. Take a small quantity of the juice and with this mix the cornflour and custard powder to a smooth paste.
3. Put the rest of the juice and sugar in a saucepan and bring to the boil.
4. Pour the juice on to the paste and stir all over the fire until the mixture boils and thickens.
5. Pour into a wet mould and stand in cold water to set.
This may be served with or without cream.

Variations—This same mould may be made with pineapple alone or orange alone—or the pineapple may be grated and the pulp used instead of only the juice. This makes the mould thick and not clear.

MRS. GIDDINGS, Wenchi.

Pine-apple Ice.

Mix an ice cream mixture according to the directions for rum ice pudding. Cut the top off a large pineapple and scoop out the inside. Fill with the mixture. Decorate the top with cut cherries. Surround the pineapple with ice-cubes which have had a cherry frozen in each, and place 9 slices of tinned pineapple among the ice-cubes. Sufficient for 8 persons.

MRS. KEAST, Accra.

Pine-apple Melange.

1 large pineapple stewed (or tin pineapple)
4 ozs. sweet almonds
1 tablespoonful rum (or sherry)
2 bananas
2 ozs. glace cherries
½ oz. gelatine
3 dessertspoons orange juice
Cream.

Drain the pineapple and put through a mincer, keeping back 3 pieces for decoration. Blanch and chop up all the almonds, cut up the cherries, peel the bananas and cut into small dice, dissolve the gelatine in a saucepan with ½ gill of the pineapple juice warmed, then strain into it the remainder of the juice, add the rum and orange juice. Stir in the minced pineapple, other fruits and almonds. Set in a wetted mould. Turn out when set and decorate with cream and pineapple.

MRS. SINCLAIR, Kumasi.

Pine-apple Mould.

Four ozs. corn flour, 1 pint milk, 1 large cupful of pineapple cut in dice, 1 pint pineapple syrup, whites of eggs, sugar to taste. Put the corn flour into a basin, mix with a little milk to a smooth paste, boil the remainder of the milk and pour over the mixture stirring all the time, return to fire and simmer for 8 minutes. Whip white of eggs to a stiff froth, mix with pineapple syrup and corn flour. Serve cold.

MRS. NICHOLSON, Accra.

Pine-apple Pudding.

Half of a pineapple, 2 cups milk (small), 1 oz. butter, ½ cup flour, ½ cup sugar, 2 eggs. Cut pineapple into chunks and put into ¼ pint water, cook until tender, leave to cool. Boil milk and butter together, mix flour with the juice of pineapple, add yolk of eggs and sugar. Pour this mixture into boiling milk and boil for 3 minutes. Pour over the pineapple chunks and leave to cool and decorate with the whites of eggs and sugar.

MRS. LOCKHART, Mfantsipim, Cape Coast.

Pine-apple Pudding.

One tin pineapple (or a fresh one can be used), 2 tablespoons corn flour, grated rind of 1 lime and juice, 1 cup of water, ½ cup sugar, 2 eggs. Mix the sugar and corn flour, and place in a double boiler. Stir in the juice of pineapple, lime and rind, and cook till smooth. Pour on to the well-beaten yolk of eggs, then fold in the beaten white of egg; and then the cubes of pineapples (1 cupful). Pour into a buttered dish and set in a slow oven for 20 minutes. When cool top with whipped cream, chopped almonds or any nuts.

MRS. MILLER LOGAN, Accra.

Pine-apple Salad (Sweet).

Slice a pineapple—Cut each slice across and remove core— Place in a dish, and sprinkle each slice with sugar or brandy an hour before serving.

MRS. C. E. DE B. BIDEN.

Pine-apple Sponge.

Half oz. gelatine, ½ pint syrup from the tin and water, rind and juice of lemon, some tinned pineapple, 2 whites of egg. Dissolve gelatine, water, fruit juice, rind and juice lemon and sugar, allow to get cool. Whip whites stiffly, add a little of the liquid at a time, beat well; continue till the liquid is all added, beat till stiff, add the pineapple cut up (reserving some for decoration), pile into a glass dish, decorate with pineapple and chopped pistachios.

MISS BELLAMY, Cape Coast.

Pine-apple Sponge.

Half tin pineapple (medium size), whites of 3 eggs, ½ oz. gelatine, juice of 1 lemon, 4 ozs. castor sugar, ½ pint liquid pineapple syrup and water. Drain the syrup from the pineapple and dissolve gelatine in the given quantity of liquid. Cut the pineapple into dice (small). Whisk the whites until very stiff, add sugar, dissolved gelatine and lemon juice, whisk until it becomes stiff then whisk in fruit. Pile up in a glass dish and sprinkle some fruit over; keep in cool place until used. Sponge may be moulded if liked. Custard sauce may be served with sponge.

N.B.—Other fruits may be treated similarly.

MRS. HENDRY, Accra.

Princess Pudding.

Stew 1 tin of apricots or any kind of fruit and sieve them. Make the yolks of 3 eggs and 1 teacupful of milk into custard, adding 1½ tablespoon of sugar (or make ½ pint of Bird's custard powder, not too thick and sweetened). Melt ½ oz. gelatine in 2 tablespoons hot water and strain into the custard (or make a thick custard of Bird's to set and omit gelatine), add the fruit juice and the whites of egg stiffly frothed (if an egg custard) and put to set in a mould.

MRS. OAKLEY, Accra.

Prune Jelly.

Half lb. prunes, 1 packet lemon jelly. Boil prunes in a pint of water, when tender, remove the prunes and boil up the syrup (making sure there is ¾ pint). Make the jelly with this syrup. Crush up the prunes, removing stones, and add to the jelly. Put in a wetted mould and leave to set.

MRS. STRADLING, Accra.

Prune Jelly Mould.

One-quarter lb. prunes, 1 packet jelly, 1 tablespoon sugar, a few almonds. Soak the prunes in 1 pint of water. Stew till tender with sugar added, strain the prunes and dissolve the packet of jelly in the juice. Cut the prunes in pieces and add the almond (blanched). Place all in a mould, and allow to set. Serve with cream or custard.

MRS. CRANSTON, Accra.

Pumpkin (As a Sweet).

1½ cups steamed and strained pumpkin
¾ cup brown sugar or ½ cup white sugar and 2 tablespoons golden syrup
1 teaspoon cinnamon
½ teaspoon ginger.
½ teaspoon salt
2 eggs
1½ cups milk.

Cook the pumpkin in a very small amount of water until it is soft. Drain thoroughly, and mash by forcing it through a colander or strainer. Mix ingredients in order given, and bake. It may be baked in an ordinary pudding dish, or in a pastry crust, or the bottom of a shallow dish may be greased, dusted thoroughly with rolled oats, and the mixture baked in it. In the two latter cases cut and serve as pie. Serve cold, with whipped cream on top.

MISS SPEARS.

Cooked Rice and Fruit.

1. Take the skin off some cold rice pudding, break it up and soften it, or make it more creamy by adding a little milk.

2. Put a little in individual glasses.

3. On this put a few tinned raspberries or strawberries and 1½ tablespoons of the fruit juice. Top up with boiled custard.

MRS. CAPON, Winneba.

Rice Meringue.

Three ozs. rice (about ½ a tumblerful), 2 tumblers milk (1 ideal tin mixed with water), 3 eggs, 5 lumps sugar (smashed), a little jam. Put rice in milk (cold), boil until soft, turn into basin, mix in the beaten yolks of eggs (in beating egg yolks alone add teaspoonful of water, it makes them beat better), and sugar, beat all together well and pile on glass dish. When cold spread jam on top and then the stiffly whisked whites of eggs.

N.B.—Be sure to put egg yolks in as soon as rice is taken from fire and is still very hot as that is the only cooking they get.

MISS WARRINGTON, Kumasi.

Rice Surprises.

3 oz. rice
1 oz. butter
1 teacupful water
Flavouring
1 pint milk
Some jam
2 oz. sugar.

Wash the rice in several waters and put it into a saucepan with a teacupful of fresh cold water. Let it boil quickly until the water is absorbed then add the milk and butter. Simmer slowly until the rice is thoroughly cooked and the mixture rather thick. Stir occasionally as it will be inclined to stick to the foot of the saucepan. When ready remove the saucepan from the fire and add the sugar and flavouring. Rinse out some dariole moulds or small cups with cold water, three-quarter fill them with rice and make a little hollow in the centre. Put a teaspoonful of jam into each, cover and fill up with more rice and set aside to cool. Turn out in glass dish and serve with custard sauce poured round.

MRS. HEMANS, Takoradi.

Rum Ice Pudding.

4 ozs. sugar
9 eggs (African)
9 half peaches
Cocktail cherries
Pistachio nuts
Hot chocolate sauce
3 small tins milk
3 dessertspoons rum.

Boil the sugar and milk diluted with 1½ tins of water. Beat together 9 yolks and 6 whites of eggs, and pour gradually into the milk. Stir until it thickens, add the rum. Freeze in the usual way. Rinse out the ice pudding mould (which should he made of pewter or copper) with iced water, and pack tightly with the frozen mixture.

178

Cover with a piece of wetted paper and put on the lid. Seal round the join of the lid and the mould, with butter. This hardens and makes the mould watertight. Place the mould in the wooden pail of the ice machine and pack it with ice and coarse salt. The pail should then be put in the Frigidaire or ice-chest for 2 hours.

To unmould, scrape off the butter and quickly rub off all the ice and salt. Dip the mould in cold water for a few seconds and dry. Take off the lid and invert on a dish. Draw the mould off slowly. Decorate the top and sides with a sprinkling of chopped pistachio nuts and surround with the half peaches and a cherry placed in each. Serve with hot chocolate sauce. Sufficient for 8 persons.

MRS. KEAST, Accra.

Russian Cream.

Four sheets gelatine, 1 tin (small) pears, 4 tablespoons sugar or 12 lumps, 4 eggs (coast), 1 teaspoon vanilla, 2 tins Ideal milk (small), 1 cup water or juice of fruit from tin.

Melt gelatine in cold milk and water for hour or more, add sugar and dissolve gradually by heating in double saucepan. When almost boiling add yolks of eggs (well beaten up previously) bring to boil until it thickens, remove from fire and add flavouring. Beat white of eggs and stir into mixture. Pour into mould or dish into which pears have been previously placed and leave to set (about 2 hours), on ice.

MRS. DONNATT, Winneba.

Russian Cream.

Two tins Ideal milk, 3 eggs, 12 pieces lump sugar, 1 tin cream, 6 sheets gelatine, glace cherries and almonds. Put the milk and equal quantity of water, the sugar, yolks of eggs and gelatine in the top of a double boiler. Stir until the mixture boils. Beat the white of eggs. Take from fire and add beaten whites of eggs and vanilla flavouring and stir. Turn into a mould and leave to set. When firmly set turn into a dish. Beat the cream with a little milk and sugar and put round the sweet, and decorate with cherries and almonds.

MRS. SUTHERLAND, Koforidua.

Savoy Creams.

(Enough for six persons.)

Two tablespoons of raspberry jam, 3 small bananas, pint of custard. Divide the jam between six custard or sundae glasses. Cover with custard till all are equally full, slice half a banana on top of each. Cover with whipped sweetened cream, flavoured with vanilla. Sprinkle with chocolate, or grated coconut, and serve ice-cold.

MRS. HILDITCH, Tarkwa.

Semolina Cream.

Three tablespoons sugar, 2 tablespoons semolina (farola preferred), 3 teacups water, pinch salt, juice of one lemon. Put two cupfuls of water, sugar, salt, and lemon juice on to boil. Mix semolina with the other cup of water, add to the other ingredients in the pan and boil a few minutes. Take off fire and beat for half an hour. Pour into a mould and turn out when cold.

MRS. HENDERSON, Accra.

Sponge Cakes in Jelly.

Pour prepared jelly over sponge cakes with or without jam, arrange in a glass dish. Decorate when set with whipped cream, etc.

MRS. OAKLEY, Accra.

Strawberry Cocktail.

One tin strawberries, custard according to number of persons. Make custard with the yolks of eggs only, three quarter fill a tumbler or whisky glass for each person. Put some strawberries in each. Whisk white of eggs to stiff froth, place a little on top of each and serve cold. Custard may be cooked or not according to taste.

MRS. SILCOCK, Takoradi.

Strawberry Cream.

One tin of strawberries or any other fruit, 1 tin of Ideal milk previously boiled in the tin, allow to cool and put on ice till required, 1 oz. gelatine, 3 ozs. sugar.

Dissolve ½ oz. gelatine and the sugar in the fruit juice. Sieve the fruit. Whip up the cold tinned milk with ½ oz gelatine melted in a little cold water until stiff (becomes like cream), fold in the juice and gelatine and add pulp, whisk well and set in a wetted mould.

MRS. OAKLEY, Accra.

Strawberry Cream.

One pint strawberry jelly, 1 tin Ideal milk (unsweetened). Melt the jelly with half usual quantity of water. Switch milk until thick, add jelly, and switch together the cream. Pour into a mould and turn out when set.

MRS. HENDERSON, Accra.

Strawberry Dream.

One large tin strawberries, 2 whites of eggs (or whites of 4 native eggs), sugar to taste (about two dessertspoonfuls), whipped cream.

Strain the juice from the strawberries, mash them and add sugar. Whip the whites of eggs to a stiff froth and fold into the mashed pulp. Fill individual glasses with the mixture, chill, and serve topped with whipped cream.

MRS. DRAKE, Tamale.

Strawberry Ice.

One tin strawberries, 1 tin Nestlé's cream, 1 tin Ideal milk, 1 dessertspoonful castor sugar. Crush the strawberries and beat to a pulp, then add the cream, milk and sugar. Beat well together. Place in tray of Frigidaire, cold control at No. 1. Turn to No. 2 for half an hour, this will remain hard in pan for days without chipping.

MRS. ALLARD, Sekondi.

Strawberry Sundae.

Half lb. strawberries (bottled or tinned), 1 packet jelly, ½ pint milk, cream and chopped nuts. Dissolve 1 packet jelly in ½ pint of hot water. Boil ½ pint milk. When both cool, stir the jelly into milk. Place a little fruit at bottom of custard glasses, cover with milk jelly and allow to set. Garnish each sundae with whipped cream, a few chopped nuts and strawberries. Raspberries may be used in the same way.

MRS. CRANSTON, Accra.

Sweets (Cold).

Cut the following fruit into slices: Oranges, pawpaw, bananas and pineapple. Place in separate layers in glass dish. Between each layer of fruit shake freely ground roasted coconut. Serve with ice-cold Bird's custard powder, Ideal milk or cream.

MRS. W. HILL, Accra.

182

Tapioca Cream.

One egg, 1 heaped tablespoonful tapioca (fine), 1 pint milk, 1 level teaspoonful custard powder, sugar to taste, flavouring. Boil milk and tapioca until latter is cooked. Mix custard powder with a little milk and add it to the paste, separate the white and yolk of egg, beat yolk with a little water and add with flavouring and sugar to taste. Boil a few minutes, take off fire and stir in the white of egg beaten to a stiff paste. Serve it iced.

MRS. STRADLING, Accra.

Tigernut Cream.

Four cupfuls tigernuts, I dessertspoonful of sugar, 4 tablespoonfuls of milk, water. Steep the nuts in cold water overnight. Wash thoroughly in cold water. Beat them to a paste in a mortar. Add the water and strain through a fine cloth. Put the liquid in a clean saucepan with the milk and sugar. Boil slowly until sufficiently cooked. Put in a bowl to cool.

SISTER ANGELE, Cape Coast.

Vanilla Ice Cream.

(Very good).
1 tin cream
1 coffee cup sugar
1½ tins Ideal milk
1½ sheets gelatine
1 teaspoon vanilla.

Soak gelatine in a little hot water, mix cream and milk together, add sugar and vanilla essence, and lastly gelatine, and put into freezing tray and turn controller to No. 2. It will be ready in 6 hours.

MISS BARCHI, Sekondi.

Victoria Pudding.

Three ozs. breadcrumbs, 3 ozs. castor sugar, 2 eggs (English, or 3 coast), 1 oz. butter, ¾ pint milk, grated rind and juice of one large lime (or 2 small). Beat well together, grease pie dish well with butter before pouring in the mixture, then bake slowly for about ½ hour, when cold turn into entrée dish, cover thickly with jam (apricot). Whipped cream on top is an improvement; only a moderate oven is required, pudding must not boil.

MRS. DONNATT, Winneba.

Walnut Blancmange.

1 pint milk
2½ dessertspoons corn flour
1 tablespoonful sugar
3 dessertspoons sherry
1½ ozs. shelled walnuts.

Mix corn flour to a smooth paste with a small quantity of milk, heat the remainder in a saucepan with the sugar and stir it on to the corn flour. Return the mixture to the pan and bring to boil, stirring all the time; add butter and boil gently for a few minutes, then take it off the heat and add the walnuts (chopped), gradually stir in the sherry. Turn mixture into a wet mould, and when set, decorate with shelled walnuts and serve.

MRS. ELLIS, Kumasi.

VEGETABLES AND SALADS

Apple and Cheese Salad.

Red apples, cream cheese, walnuts, or groundnuts, salad lettuce, salad cream. Wash, polish and core the apples but do not peel them, cut across into slices 1-inch thick, rub the cheese to a thick cream with a spoon, add chopped nuts and salad cream. Arrange apples on individual plates on the lettuce, with a layer of mixture between each slice. Serve very cold.

MRS. NICHOLSON, Accra.

American Tomatoes.

Four medium very firm tomatoes, 1 tablespoon chopped parsley, ½ gill of cream, small tablespoon chopped walnuts, small tablespoon chopped Brazil nuts, pepper, and salt and a few drops white vinegar, to garnish a little curled celery and small cress, rounds of buttered bread, decorated with parsley and rounds of cooked ham.

Cut round top from tomato and with handle of teaspoon scoop out soft mixture, leaving enough to keep good shape; leave upside down to drain, cut rounds of bread, size so that tomatoes can rest, butter on one side and coat with chopped parsley, place rounds of cooked ham on top of bread. Half whip the cream and add to it seasonings—salt and pepper, wash and scrape celery and chop finely, add chopped nuts and celery, and two teaspoonfuls of tomato pulp taken from centre, and lastly vinegar and mix all lightly with two teaspoons and then stuff tomatoes (apples can be treated in the same way), cut a few sticks of celery, leave in cold water, drain and you will find it curled—and with a fork arrange on top and then cress. Arrange on a bed of lettuce.

(Also good for brown bread sandwiches.)

MRS. WILKINS, Kumasi.

Asparagus Salad.

One tin of asparagus, 1 lettuce, 1 tomato, 1 hard boiled egg, salad dressing. Put the broken leaves of lettuce into a bowl, place the cut-up asparagus on top, pour over the dressing, decorate with slices of tomato and egg.

MRS. NICOLSON, Accra.

Banana Salad.

Cut bananas in half, lengthways, allowing one-half for each person. Place half banana on a lettuce leaf—on the banana spread mayonnaise (not too sweet) and sprinkle chopped-up groundnut on top. Serve alone or with cold chicken.

ACHIMOTA.

Banana and Tomato Salad.

Take 2 large tomatoes, skin and cut into 4 slices, arrange on individual plates or a bowl with small lettuce or cress. Peel and slice 3 small bananas on top, mix salad dressing and a little whipped cream together and place on top, then sprinkle. with chopped walnuts.

Salad: Two or 3 crisp lettuce leaves for each plate on which put orange quarters.

MRS. LOGAN, Accra.

Blackbeauty Garden Egg.

(Fried.) Peel the garden egg and slice it in ½-inch slices. Sprinkle each slice with salt, pile together on a plate and put a weight on top to express the juice. Let it stand 1½ hours. Dredge with flour, and fry slowly in butter.

(Baked.)

Pare an egg plant, cut in ¼-inch slices, cut crosswise, and soak in cold water to cover for 2 hours. Drain and cook in boiling salted water until soft. Drain and mash. Add breadcrumbs, 2 eggs well beaten, a few drops onion juice and small salt and pepper. Fill moulds or baking dish with mixture and cover top with crumbs. Bake in hot oven 15 minutes.

MISS SPEARS.

Cassava Cake.

Cassava, a little salt.
1. Peel, clean and grate the cassava.
2. Mix the grated cassava with a little cold water.
3. Put in a clean cloth and press well until all the water is out.
4. Sieve the grated cassava on a native strainer, add salt, put an enamel pan on the fire, heat it well, put a little of the sieved cassava into the pan and shape it. Roast golden brown then turn. When done put on a clean dish and serve with coconut milk.

SISTER ANTONIA, Keta.

Chicken and Grape-fruit Salad.

Grapefruit, cold chicken, lettuce, seasoning, plain cream or mayonnaise sauce. Wash and cut the grapefruit in half and remove a piece from each end so that the shells will stand firm on a plate. Scoop out all fruit and chop up finely, cut chicken into cubes. Fill grapefruit shells with a mixture of finely shredded lettuce, grapefruit, diced chicken, dressing and seasoning, serve very cold. An excellent luncheon dish.

MRS. SINCLAIR, Kumasi.

Coco—Amangkani-leaves (Spinach).

Take the youngest, not yet unrolled leaves and prepare in the same way as spinach.

MRS. MARTIN, Agogo.

189

Coco-yam Fritters.

The plebeian coco-yam has been subjected to much unmerited scorn by cooks. Here is one way of making it palatable to the European. Take 1 breakfastcup grated coco-yarn, 1 finely chopped onion, yolks of 2 eggs, ½ teaspoonful baking powder, pepper and salt to taste. Beat well together in a bowl to a smooth paste. Drop from a spoon into a frying pan of smoking hot fat, fry to a golden brown. Do not use the whites of the eggs ; the thinner the fritters are the better.

MRS. MOOR, Koforidua.

Coco-yam Leaves.

The young leaves of the coco-yam can also be used as a vegetable. They should be cooked like spinach.

MRS. GIDDINGS, Wenchi.

Corn (As a Vegetable).

If you shrink from gnawing at the plebeian cob, cook the corn on the cob as usual, then cut it off, heat it with a small amount of milk, and add butter, salt and pepper to taste.

Corn Chowder.

2 slices bacon
1 small onion
3 potatoes
3 cobs corn (cooked)
About 4 cups milk
Salt, pepper.

Fry bacon, add sliced onion to the fat and cook until light brown. Strain fat into saucepan, add sliced potatoes and 2 cups hot water, and cook until potatoes are soft. Then add milk and corn which has been cut from the cob. Heat all together and season with salt and pepper. Serve with cheese, biscuit or toast as a luncheon dish.

MISS SPEARS.

Corn Toast.

¼ tablespoon finely chopped onion
2 cups creamy milk
1 cup corn (cooked)
1 ½ tablespoons butter
Small salt, pepper.

Cook onion with butter 2 minutes, stirring constantly. Add corn, milk, and seasoning. Bring to boiling point and simmer 5 minutes. Pour over toast and serve at once. This recipe is sufficient for 6 slices of bread.

MISS SPEARS.

Cucumber Jelly to eat with Cold Salmon.

One and a half cups peeled grated cucumber, 1 saltspoonful salt, ¼ oz. gelatine, ¼ cup lemon juice, 1 teaspoon chopped onion and lettuce. Mix cucumber, lemon juice, onion and salt, turn into a saucepan, stir in gelatine dissolved in a little cold water, stir constantly and cook for 10 minutes, turn into a mould. Just before serving place some freshly minced cucumber and salad dressing in the centre of the mould and serve on lettuce. This must be served very cold.

MRS. NICHOLSON, Accra Ice Co

Curried Vegetables.

One tin peas, 1 tin asparagus, 1 tin mixed vegetables or any mixture of vegetables liked, cabbage, cauliflower, 1 oz. curry powder, 1 oz. butter, 1 gill cream, pepper and salt, onions. Cook all the vegetables first. Then make a sauce with the curry and cream and, when cooked, add the cooked vegetables. Place all in a casserole and keep hot in the oven.

MISS SUTHERLAND, Aburi.

191

Dry Vegetable Curry.

(For two persons.)

Two carrots, 1 apple, 1 banana, 1 plantain, 1 large or 3 small onions, 2 tomatoes, 4 okras, 1 tablespoonful of sultana raisins, 1 dessertspoonful curry powder. Dice the vegetables and fry till golden brown. Mix curry powder with sufficient stock or water to cover the vegetables and simmer gently for 2 to 2½ hours until all the liquid has been absorbed. Serve with boiled rice accompanied by chutney, ground nuts and coconut.

MRS. SHAW, Accra.

Dry Velvet Beans.

Soak overnight, or at least 10 hours, in cold water, and boil until soft (about 2 hours). Jackets will then be split and some will drain off with the water, cook should remove the rest. Add 1 cup milk and 2 tablespoons butter and reheat.

MISS SPEARS.

I—Escalloped Corn.

2 cups corn
1 cup breadcrumbs
¼ cup butter
¼ cup flour
½ teaspoon salt
1½ cups milk.

Heat the milk. Mix butter and flour together and add milk, stirring constantly. Then add corn, salt and sugar. Let it come to the boiling point and turn into a baking dish. Cover the top with breadcrumbs moistened slightly with milk, and bake 15 or 20 minutes.

II—Escalloped Corn.

2 cups corn
2 eggs

192

2 tablespoons melted butter
2 cups scalded milk
1 green pepper
Salt, pepper.

Discard seeds from pepper and chop the shell. Mix ingredients in order given and bake until firm.

MISS SPEARS.

French Bean Salad,

Cold cooked French beans, 2 tablespoons of chopped onion, 2 tablespoons salad oil, 1 tablespoon vinegar, salt and pepper. Cover onion with oil and stand for two hours, add salt, pepper and vinegar, then pour all over the beans.

MRS FRASER, Achimota.

French Dressing.

One teaspoon salt, 1 teaspoon sugar. Mix all together. One-quarter teaspoon pepper, add 3 tablespoons vinegar, ¾ cup olive oil. Beat all thoroughly with a fork.

MISS SPEARS.

Green Pawpaw (Stuffed).

Half lb. minced beef, mutton or chicken, 1 minced carrot, 1 minced onion, small minced parsley. Little stock or water, pepper and salt. Peel and cut in half one green pawpaw, scoop out pithy centre and seeds, mix minced meat and vegetable and stock together, place in the pawpaw. Cut off the end so that each half will stand upright and roast for 4 hours in a moderate oven. Serve on a dish covered with thick gravy.

MRS. SHAW, Accra.

Green Pawpaw (Stuffed).

Green pawpaw
Minced groundnut
Salt and pepper
Tomato
Egg
Onion.

Take a green pawpaw—this may be either cut into 2 halves or the centre scooped out, leaving the pawpaw whole—and boil until tender.

For the Stuffing—Take about 4-6 tablespoons of ground nuts roasted and minced. Add a tomato skinned, and chopped, a little onion—previously boiled and chopped—salt and pepper, and any other seasoning desired. Bind this mixture together with the egg and either fill the whole pawpaw or the 2 halves and bake in the oven until brown. Serve with brown sauce.

Variation.—The mixture used for stuffing might also be made into small cakes and fried and served as nut rissoles.

MRS. GIDDINGS, Wenchi.

Goodwood Salad.

Two dozen prawns, 1 tin asparagus tips, 1 hard boiled egg, lettuce, 2 cups chopped boiled potatoes, mayonnaise, 1 teaspoon chopped onion and parsley. Wash prawns, mix with potato, onion and parsley, and mayonnaise, lay on the lettuce, sieve the yolk of egg over the mixture, plant asparagus tips evenly round the edge, cut the white of egg into dice, make a ring of it round the dish.

MRS. NICHOLSON, Accra.

Italian Salad.

For those who like something unusual, here is a good salad to be served with a hot roast joint or fowl, without any accompanying potatoes or other vegetable; but gravy should be served with the meat.

One large lettuce, or failing this the heart of a small cabbage, uncooked; three medium-sized potatoes, previously boiled; three apples, raw; three tomatoes, two oranges, a few chopped nuts. Tear the lettuce into fairly small pieces, or if cabbage is being used, after careful washing shred it very finely. Shred the apples, peel and slice the tomatoes, slice the potatoes thinly; peel and cut up the oranges, mix all together, and pour over all enough of the following dressing to moisten the salad without making it too wet. Enough for four people.

Dressing—1 tablespoonful dry mustard, 2 tablespoonful granulated sugar, pinch of salt, 1 teaspoonful Worcester sauce, ½ pint milk, ¼ pint vinegar and 3 eggs.

Dissolve sugar and mustard with vinegar and Worcester sauce, stir in drop by drop, very carefully to mixture of beaten eggs and milk. Stir over fire until it thickens. This will keep for several weeks in a well stoppered bottle.

ACHIMOTA

Jellied Salad.

Any cooked vegetables such as carrots, peas, beans can be used for this, the vegetables can be set in individual moulds of aspic or calves-foot jelly served with salad dressing on young lettuce leaves.

MRS. NICHOLSON, Accra.

Macaroni Salad.

Cold macaroni, tomatoes, salad dressing, salt, pepper, and eggs. Season the macaroni with salt and pepper, mix with some sliced tomato and add a little salad dressing. Toss lightly together with a fork and serve on crisp lettuce leaves, garnish with quarters of hard boiled eggs, sprinkle with minced parsley, if possible, or with a little minced-up onion.

MRS. DIXON, Salaga.

Maize (Boiled).

Choose young, tender ears of corn, plunge into salted boiling water for 15 minutes. Serve in a napkin, as the corn hardens if allowed to get dry. Eat with butter.

ACHIMOTA.

Native Spinach.

Spinach, onions, eggs, lard, pepper (white) and salt. Remove stems and wash the leaves thoroughly. Put leaves in boiling water and boil until soft. Strain and add a pinch of salt. Then fry in a frying pan with a little lard, white pepper and onions. Serve in a hot dish and trim with hard boiled eggs, cut in halves or rings.

SISTER ANTONIA, Keta.

Onions (Stuffed).

Sheep's kidneys
Butter
Spanish onions
Pepper and salt.

Boil some Spanish onions in salted water for about an hour till tender, cut the small tops nearly off, and scoop out the hearts. Skin the kidneys, cut in two and put a portion in each onion. Replace the tops. Melt an ounce of butter in a baking dish, and stand the onions in it, sprinkle with pepper and salt, and pour a little salted butter over each and bake, basting frequently till kidneys are cooked through.

MRS. HILDITCH, Tarkwa.

Onions stuffed with Tomato.

Parboil as many large onions as desired. Then pierce a small hole through the heart of each (but not quite through the bottom), fill the cavities with tomato sauce or ketchup to which has been added a little salt and pepper. Then roll each onion in egg and breadcrumbs, put into a baking tin or a shallow fireproof dish, with a

196

little butter to cover the bottom of the dish. Over all sprinkle a little finely-grated cheese; bake until a golden brown. The stuffing may be varied; a little well-minced half-cooked kidney is good, or cold meat minced.

MRS. DIXON, Salaga.

Orange Salads.

1. Cut peeled oranges in pieces. Serve on water cress (or lettuce) and serve with French dressing (oil and vinegar, salt and pepper).

2. Equal parts of oranges, pineapple and banana, cut in pieces. Serve with French dressing.

3. Equal parts of pineapple, celery and nuts cut in pieces. Serve with mayonnaise dressing.

MRS. FRASER, Achimota.

Palm Cabbage.

The young cabbage which comes out of the centre of a palm tree when it is cut down for palm wine, makes an excellent vegetable boiled.

MRS. GIDDINGS, Wenchi.

Pawpaw.

Pawpaw as a vegetable may be improved if it is served:

(a) Boiled as usual, then mashed, and butter, salt and pepper added. (b) Creamed with onion. Boil as usual, and at the same time boil one or two onions. Make a cream sauce by adding a small amount of flour to hot milk and butter, and when it is well cooked pour over the pawpaw and onions. Bachelors: if the cream sauce is lumpy, tell the cook to mix the flour into a smooth, thin paste by adding a little water to it gradually, before putting it into the milk.

MISS SPEARS.

Pawpaw (Stuffed).

1 green pawpaw
1 cup breadcrumbs
1 cup groundnut paste
3 tomatoes skinned and chopped
½ teaspoonful salt and pepper to taste
6 onions chopped.

1. Peel and remove seeds from pawpaw, keep whole, boil in salt water until soft, but unbroken.
2. Prepare groundnut paste.
3. Skin tomatoes and cook with chopped onion in salt water.
4. Prepare breadcrumbs.
5. Mix nuts, tomato, onion, salt, and pepper into stiff paste, eggs can be used to bind.
6. Stuff inside pawpaw. Steam in a basin or steamer to reheat.
7. Serve with rich brown gravy or tomato sauce. Pawpaw may also be stuffed with minced meat, thyme stuffing or cheese mixture.

MISS SPEARS.

Pea Timbale.

Beat 4 eggs and add 2 cupfuls of pulped peas, 3 tablespoonfuls thick cream, a few drops of onion juice, 2 tablespoonfuls melted butter and salt, and pepper to taste. The whole mixture to be turned into a well-buttered ring mould; the mould set in hot water and steamed for 30 minutes or until firm. The centre filled with creamed mushrooms.

MRS. BARTON, Kumasi.

Peach and Nut Salad.

Fill halves of chilled canned peaches with blanched and chopped nuts or almonds. Arrange on a bed of lettuce leaves, decorate with boiled beets. Serve with French dressing or mayonnaise.

MRS. FRASER, Achimota.

Peppers (Stuffed).

I.—Remove seeds. Cook Book says "boil for small time on top of stove before stuffing"; but cook says, "no do so". Suit yourself. Stuff with equal parts of finely chopped left-over meat and breadcrumbs. Season with onion juice, salt and pepper, and bake about 20 minutes.

II.—Prepare as above. Stuff with rice well moistened with tomato (about one cup of tomato pulp and juice to one cup of rice). Sprinkle tops with breadcrumbs and bake.

III.—Prepare as above. Cut corn from cob and slowly cook in a very small amount of milk. Season with butter, salt and pepper. Stuff pepper with this mixture and bake.

MISS SPEARS.

Pine-apple Salad.

Lay whole slices of pineapple on lettuce leaves on the required number of individual salad plates. Fill the centre of each round of pineapple with finely diced cucumber which has been moistened with mayonnaise sauce. Place two narrow strips of red pepper over the top for garnish.

MRS. MILES.

Piquant Salad.

Arrange a bed of lettuce on a salad dish. Cut 4 tomatoes into thick slices and arrange in a ring on the lettuce. Cover tomato with 1 teaspoonful of grated cheese or cream and place 1 teaspoonful of mayonnaise on each. Pile sliced cucumber in the centre and dress with mayonnaise. Or in place of the tomatoes and grated cheese, take three hard boiled eggs, cut them in halves, and carefully scoop out the yellow. In a separate basin beat up a little butter till creamy, add the hard boiled egg yolks and 2 spoonfuls of grated cheese. Replace this creamy mixture into the hollowed out egg whites and serve with the salad as above.

As a variety, anchovy sauce, or pounded sardine may be used in place of the cheese.

MRS. DRAKE, Tamale.

Potato Salad (Stripped).

6 cold potatoes
1 lettuce
1 onion
Salad dressing
2 beetroots.

Cut the potatoes into slices, spread a layer in the bottom of a salad bowl, chop the beetroot into small pieces, and spread a layer over potatoes. Cover with another layer of potatoes. Chop up part of lettuce and then spread a layer of finely chopped onion on top. Add seasoning and dressing over all.

MRS. HILDITCH, Tarkwa.

Prune Salad.

20 large prunes
½ cup mayonnaise dressing
1 cream cheese
½ teaspoon salt
2 tablespoons peanut butter
Shredded lettuce.

Wash prunes and let stand in cold water all night. Heat up, cool and dry on a towel. Mix the cheese, peanut butter and salt, and if too stiff to form into balls, add cold milk, and stuff into prunes. Press together, or leave open showing filling. Serve on lettuce with the dressing.

MRS. FRASER, Achimota.

Pumpkin (As a Vegetable).

Some people prefer it if it is boiled as usual, then mashed and salt, butter and pepper added.

MISS SPEARS.

Raisin and Apple Salad.

1 cup seeded raisins
1 cup mayonnaise
½ cup lemon juice
2 cups apples (chopped)
2 cups shredded lettuce
Red jelly.

Wash and dry raisins, add with lemon juice to the chopped apples. Serve on the lettuce, cover with mayonnaise and garnish with red jelly.

MRS. FRASER, Achimota.

Roasted Yams and Cassava.

Vegetables usually have a better flavour roasted than boiled. The potato roasted in its jacket is well known, but yams and cassava are not often seen on the table. These should be placed over an open fire and turned continually until every part of the surface is charred. They should then be taken from the fire, well scraped with a knife and put back to char again. Repeat until the vegetable is soft to the touch and shows a clear brown, crisp skin. Serve in place of jacket potatoes.

Spinach with Cheese.

One cup cooked spinach, 2 eggs, ½ cup milk, 2 tablespoonfuls butter or margarine, ¼ lb. cheese. Make a cheese sauce by cooking together the yolks of the eggs, the milk, butter and cheese. Take the cupful of cooked spinach which must be very finely chopped, mix half of the cheese sauce with it, and fold in the white of the eggs, after beating them stiffly. Fill individual moulds or cups with this mixture, place in a pan of hot water and bake until firm. When serving pour the remainder of the sauce round the spinach moulds which have been turned out on to a dish. Garnish with slices of hard boiled egg or fingers of fried bread. Enough for two people.

ACHIMOTA.

Spinach with Cheese.

The following makes a nutritious dish for lunch:—Make a cheese sauce by cooking together 2 egg yolks, ½ cup milk, 2 tablespoons butter and ¼ lb. cheese. Take 1 cup of cooked spinach (it should be chopped very fine or mashed) mix half of cheese sauce with it, and fold in stiffly beaten egg whites. Fill individual moulds or cups with this mixture, place in a pan of hot water, and bake until firm. Turn out on a platter, pour the balance of the cheese sauce around the timbales, and garnish with slices of hard boiled egg. This recipe should serve two people.

MISS SPEARS.

Surprise Lentils.

½ lb. of lentils
1 small onion
2 ozs. of streaky bacon
4 eggs
Seasoning.

Wash the lentils, chop the onion very finely and add it and the seasoning to the lentils. Put into a greased pie dish or casserole, cover with plenty of water, put the lid or greased paper on and bake gently in a moderate oven for an hour, stir occasionally. When the lentils are tender and the mixture thick and soft place the bacon rashers on top and bake in the oven. Break the four eggs on top, season and bake gently until set, if preferred the eggs may be fried separately and then put on top of the bacon.

MRS. BUTLER, Accra.

Sweet Potatoes.

Baked or boiled and sprinkled with grated coconut are quite appetising.

MRS. CUTHBERT, Koforidua.

Sweet Potato Rechauffé.

One lb. cold potatoes, 2 tablespoons minced onions, 2 tablespoons flour, 1 oz. margarine, a little milk. Press into a mould, turn out and bake in moderate oven until brown.

MISS SPEARS.

Sword Beans.

Sword beans may be made palatable for some of us if they are served with French dressing poured over. They may be either hot or cold.

MISS SPEARS.

Sword Bean Tomato Salad.

Peel tomatoes, chill and slice thin. Arrange lettuce on small individual plates, put 3 or 4 slices of tomato on each plate, top with a small mound of sword beans, and garnish with slices of boiled egg. Serve with your favourite salad dressing.

MISS SPEARS.

Tomatoes.

As a hot vegetable they may be stewed and seasoned with a little salt, butter, pepper, and sugar to taste. Or they may be cut up, mixed with about an equal quantity of breadcrumbs (perhaps a little less), seasoned and baked for a short time.

MISS SPEARS.

Tomato, Cherry and Nut Salad.

Scoop out the centres of the tomatoes, refill with canned cherries stuffed with nuts and cover with mayonnaise or French dressing. Serve on lettuce leaves.

MRS. FRASER, Achimota.

Tomato Salads.

Peel medium-sized tomatoes. Take out seeds and some pulp. Sprinkle inside with salt, invert and let stand half an hour. Fill tomatoes with:

1. Pineapple cut in small cubes and chopped nuts.
2. Cucumber cut in small cubes.
3. Finely cut celery and apple.
4. Finely shredded white cabbage.
5. Cold boiled vegetables and chopped chicken.
6. Cold hard boiled egg whites—yolks powdered. Serve with a teaspoon of mayonnaise dressing on each tomato.

MRS. FRASER, Achimota.

Tomato and Green Pepper Salad.

Peel tomatoes by immersing for half a minute in very hot water to loosen jackets; peel and allow them to thoroughly cool, chill in icebox if possible. Cut top off from each tomato, and scoop out pulp from centres. Remove seeds from one green pepper, and chop the shell. Mix the finely chopped green pepper with the tomato pulp and season with a little salt, pepper, and enough mayonnaise to hold the ingredients together. Fill the tomato shells with this mixture. Serve on lettuce leaves, garnish with strips of green pepper and dots of mayonnaise.

MISS SPEARS.

SAVOURIES.

Anchovy Toast.

For every person take the yolk of one egg and a teaspoon of anchovy sauce, mix on a plate over hot water until it is like a custard, stir in a little butter, and soak the buttered toasts in this preparation on both sides. Push into the oven for a minute, and serve very hot. Decorate with grated egg and anchovies.

MRS. LYNCH, Cape Coast.

Apples and Bacon.

Select medium-sized cooking apples, core and cut in slices, do not peel. Fry in bacon drippings over a fire until well cooked but not broken. Remove to hot plate, sprinkle with little sugar and nutmeg; serve with fried bacon and garnish with sliced lemon and parsley. Can also be served on circles of bread dipped in beaten egg and fried in the bacon drippings. Makes a more substantial dish and is very good.

MRS. FRASER, Achimota.

Apple and Bacon Savoury.

One apple, 8 slices thin bacon 3 inches long. Peel and cut the apple into eight slices. Roll each piece in a rasher of bacon and put on skewers. Fry till brown and crisp and serve at once on toast. Stoned prunes, sardines or soft herring roes can be substituted for the filling given above.

MRS. SHAW, Accra.

205

Apple Sauce.

Green pawpaw
Butter
Lime juice
Sugar.

Boil green pawpaw until quite tender and then beat up with a little lime or lemon juice, sugar and butter. Served with roast duck, pork chops, etc., this is hardly distinguishable from real apple sauce.

MRS. GIDDINGS, Wenchi.

Asparagus Cheese.

1 tin asparagus
2 tablespoons grated cheese
2 ozs. butter
1 tablespoonful of breadcrumbs.
1 egg.

Beat up the egg, dip the tips of asparagus into it, sprinkle the grated cheese over them, dip again into the egg and crumbs. Fry in melted butter and serve quickly.

MRS. HILDITCH, Tarkwa.

Asparagus Fingers.

Squares of bread and butter. Put asparagus from corner to corner, fold over points and toast.

MISS WOOD, Accra.

Bacon and Cheese.

Thin slices of bacon, grated Cheddar cheese, strips of hot buttered toast. Roll up each slice of bacon leaving a small space in middle. Fill with grated cheese, fry, and serve on strips of buttered toast.

MRS. CUTHBERT, Koforidua.

Bird's Nests.

Four eggs, 2 ozs. suet, 2 ozs. breadcrumbs, 1 tablespoon chopped ham, 1 tablespoon chopped parsley. Grated rind of half lemon, 1 egg, salt and pepper. Boil egg hard, chop suet finely and mix breadcrumbs, ham, parsley, lemon rind, salt and pepper. Mix and bind together with beaten egg. Roll in flour then cover with stuffing, brush over with some of the egg and toss in crumbs, fry in smoking fat to a golden brown, divide with a sharp knife. This is quite good with salad.

MRS. BROWNING, Cape Coast.

Bird's Nest Sausages.

Half lb. vermicelli, sausages, parsley and eggs. Cook vermicelli in frying-basket in boiling fat. Have some hard boiled eggs, one for every sausage, remove shells. Skin sausages and press round egg. Egg and breadcrumbs. Fry, arrange in dish with vermicelli here and there and garnish with parsley.

MRS. THOMAS, Cape Coast.

Bombay Toast.

One oz. anchovies, 1 oz. butter, 2 eggs, 4 rounds toast, cayenne to taste. Take anchovies and butter and rub through a sieve. Melt in a saucepan and when it melts add the beaten yolks of 2 eggs, stir till it thickens. Serve hot on buttered toast.

MRS. PUCKRIDGE, Accra.

Cheese Creams.

Take 2 slices of bread about inch thick and make sandwiches with butter and cheese, the cheese being about ¼ inch thick. Turn off the crusts, and cut into convenient sizes, fry on both sides in boiling fat and serve very hot.

MISS BARCHI, Sekondi.

Cheese Croquettes.

Two and a half ozs. fine breadcrumbs, salt and cayenne pepper, 1 egg, deep hot fat, 5 or 6 ozs. grated cheese. Mix the dry ingredients well together and moisten them with the egg. Form the mixture into small balls and dip each one into beaten egg. Coat it with fine breadcrumbs, and fry the croquettes in boiling fat and serve hot.

MRS. ELLIS, Kumasi.

Cheese Croustades (Hot).

Grate some Kraft or Cheshire cheese. Pound it with some undiluted Ideal milk until it is thick and smooth. Cut some stale bread into squares and butter them. Spread the mixture on thickly, dip in some butter and fry in deep fat.

MRS. KEAST, Accra.

Cheese Fritters.

2 tablespoons cheese (grated)
2 eggs
1 oz. flour
1 oz. butter (melted)
Salt, pepper.

Mix cheese, flour and butter with seasoning, add the egg yolks beaten and lastly the whites stiffly whisked. Sometimes a little milk is necessary if too stiff. Drop bits of mixture into smoking fat and fry till a golden brown.

MRS. OAKLEY, Accra.

Cheese Potatoes.

Six potatoes, 1 piece butter the size of an egg, 2 tablespoons grated cheese. Boil potatoes with salt till tender. Cut potatoes lengthwise. Brush with melted butter, sprinkle with cheese. Put in greased tin and bake in a hot oven till brown.

MRS. SWAN, Tamale.

Cheese Pudding.

2 ozs. breadcrumbs
2 ozs. grated cheese
½ teaspoonful dry mustard
½ pint milk
1 egg
½ oz. margarine
Seasoning.

Bring margarine and milk to boiling point, and pour over dry ingredients. Leave soaking for half an hour. Add beaten egg and pour all into greased pie dish. Bake in a moderate oven till firm and brown.

MRS. CUTHBERT, Koforidua.

Cheese Pudding.

Two and a half ozs. grated cheese, 2 eggs, pinch of salt, ¼ pint boiling milk. Put grated cheese in a bowl and pour on boiling milk and let it stand until cool. Beat up eggs, add with a pinch of salt, and place in buttered pie dish and bake in a moderate oven.

MRS. CRANSTON, Accra.

Cheese Pudding.

Six ozs. white breadcrumbs, ¼ lb. grated cheese, 1 tin milk and 2 teacups water, 3 eggs, salt, pepper and made mustard, 1 oz. butter. Put the crumbs and cheese into a greased pie dish. Beat the eggs, add milk and water and seasoning, and pour over the crumbs. Add the butter. Cook in a moderate oven for 1 hour. Stir twice during the first half hour cooking.

MRS. DRAKE, Tamale.

Cheese Puffs.

Two ozs. grated cheese, white of an egg, pepper and salt. Beat up the white of egg stiffly and mix with the cheese and seasoning; drop a teaspoonful of the mixture in boiling fat and fry brown.

ACHIMOTA.

Cheese Savoury.

Four ozs. of grated cheese (Cheddar or Parmesan), 1 pint of milk, 1 oz. of butter, 2 ozs. of cornflour, nutmeg seasoning. Break down the corn flour with a little of the milk, heat the remainder of the milk and add to it the corn flour, stir until thickened, add butter, cheese and seasoning. Turn out on to a wet dish, spread evenly, when cold cut into shapes egg and breadcrumb and fry in deep fat.

MRS. BUTLER, Accra.

Cheese Soufflé.

Two and a half ozs. butter, 1 tablespoonful flour, 1 pint milk, 4 eggs, 3 tablespoonfuls cheese (grated). Melt butter and roast flour in it a short time. Add milk and beat all to a thick cream. Cool it down and add yolks, cheese, salt and froth of eggs. Pour all in a well-buttered dish (fireproof) and bake it (30-45 minutes). Serve cheese soufflé with any salad.

MISS COUTZ, Agogo.

Cheese Straws.

Two oz. butter, 2 oz. flour, 2 oz. cheese, pinch of baking powder. Cream the butter and add the flour, cheese and baking powder, salt to taste, mix thoroughly and bind with a little milk. Roll out, cut into strips and make into bundles, bake until crisp in a hot oven.

MRS. ROTHWELL, Koforidua.

Cheese Straws or Biscuits.

2 ozs. flour
1 oz. butter or margarine
1 oz. grated cheese
1 yolk of egg.
½ teaspoon dry mustard
Seasoning
Red pepper

1. Rub fat into flour and add all dry ingredients.
2. Mix to a firm paste with yolk and a little water.
3. Roll out one-eighth-inch thick and cut in strips 2½ inches or circles, and rings made by using two cutters of different sizes.
4. Bake in a warm oven till straw colour.
5. Dish in bundles with straws passed through rings.
N.B.—The biscuits make an excellent basis for all kinds of hot small chop.

MRS. BEACH JOHNSTONE, Accra.

Cheese Straws.

Two ozs. butter, 2 ozs. grated cheese, 2 ozs. flour, little salt and cayenne, yolk of 1 egg. Mix cheese and flour, rub in butter, egg last of all. Knead into a paste and roll out in a thick piece. Cut into straws. Bake on a grated tin in a slow oven 5—10 minutes. Allow to cool before removing from tin.

MRS. STEELE, Tamale.

Cheesy Tarts.

Two tablespoons flour, 1 tablespoon butter, salt (a pinch of), water (a few drops), egg yolks, beaten. Mix and roll the paste very thin and line some patty-pans with it. Fill up with the following: 2 tablespoons grated cheese, 2 well-beaten yolks of eggs, small salt and pepper, a few drops of lemon juice, lastly 2 spoons of cream, mix well.

MRS. DIXON, Salaga.

Chicken Forcemeat.

Livers of chicken
1 chopped onion
3 rashers of fat bacon
2 ozs. dripping
1 egg
2 ozs. breadcrumbs
1 dessertspoon milk.

Mince or chop the liver and bacon, very fine. Mix them with dripping, salt, pepper, and chopped onion, and breadcrumbs, then the milk, and lastly, the beaten egg, then fry in dripping.

MRS. HILDITCH, Tarkwa.

Colombus Canapé.

Place a teaspoon of chopped olives in the centre of rounds of toast, surround with a circle of chopped hard boiled egg white then a circle of hard yolk sieved. Place a border of chopped olives round this and season with French dressing.

MRS. OAKLEY, Accra.

Pickled Cucumber.

Peel the cucumber and slice a layer thinly sprinkled with salt and then another layer and so on until the cucumber is finished, put a small plate or saucer turned the wrong way up at the bottom of the dish for drainage, leave this for 12 hours, then place the cucumber into a pickle jar and cover with vinegar (2 chillies if required). To be eaten the next day and the vinegar can be used again. This prevents the cucumber from being indigestible.

MRS. MILNE, Winneba.

Cucumber Cheese.

1 cucumber
White sauce
3 spring onions
1 oz. cheese (grated)
Salt
Pepper.

Peel the cucumber, and cutting off one end scoop out the inside. Peel the onions and put them into a stewpan with the cucumber to boil. In another stewpan make sufficient white sauce to fill the cucumber, to this add the cheese and the boiled onions. The onions should be cut up or mashed so that the sauce is smooth. The cucumber should be boiled for 15 minutes, then taken out and drained, but not allowed to go cold. When the cucumber is ready, thoroughly mix a raw native egg with the cheese sauce and stuff the cucumber. Put into a dish and bake for a few minutes (5-10), serve sprinkled with bread-crumbs. Enough for two persons. Tomatoes stuffed with the same sauce and baked are delicious.

MRS. BECKETT, Accra.

Alpine Eggs.

4 eggs
6 ozs. cheese
2 ozs. butter.
A little finely chopped parsley
Pepper and salt.

Butter a baking dish and line with greater part of cheese cut in thin slices, break in the eggs, keeping the yolks whole. Grate the rest of the cheese and mix with parsley, season the eggs liberally, and sprinkle over them the grated cheese and parsley, add butter broken in small pieces. Bake 10 minutes in quick oven.

MRS. SAMPLES, Takoradi.

Baked Eggs.

Two eggs, 3 ozs. cheese, 1 oz. butter, a little chopped pepper and salt. Butter baking dish, thickly line with 3 parts of the cheese cut in thin slices, break eggs over, keeping yolks whole, grate remains of cheese, mix with chopped parsley, season, and sprinkle over eggs, add remains of butter, bake in quick oven 10 minutes, serve very hot.

MRS. DOWLING, Cape Coast.

Egg Cutlets.

One oz. butter, 1 oz. flour, ½ pint milk, 3 eggs, 1 tablespoonful lean ham, 1 teaspoonful chopped parsley, salt and pepper. Hard boil 2 eggs. When cold remove shells and chop them up. Melt butter in pan, add flour and stir well and then add the milk and cook this sauce for about seven minutes, then add the raw yolk of egg and cook slightly, then add the ham, eggs, and parsley to the sauce. Mix all well together and put on a plate to cool. When cold form into cutlets, using flour, egg and breadcrumbs. Fry a light brown.

MRS. EMMETT, Accra.

Egg and Caper Canapé.

Half oz. butter, 1 egg, 1 teaspoonful of capers, chopped small, rounds of buttered toast. Beat the egg, season with pepper. Melt butter in a small saucepan, stir in the egg, when slightly thickened add the capers and a teaspoonful of vinegar. Serve piled up on hot buttered toast.

MISS WOOD, Accra.

Sherried Eggs.

Boil 4 eggs for 10 minutes, while still warm shell and remove yolks. Blend yolks with ½ oz. butter, salt and pepper, into a smooth paste and add a good teaspoonful of sherry, return to whites, which should be filled with the mixture. Prepare white sauce and add to it 1

214

heaped dessertspoonful cheese. Pour sauce over eggs and shake a little grated cheese on top.

MRS. DIXON, Salaga.

Eggs (Two ways of serving).

1. Take as many hard boiled eggs as required, halve them and remove the yolks. Cut the yolks up finely and mix with chopped anchovies in the proportion of 1 anchovy to 2 hard boiled eggs. Add a little butter to bind smoothly, pepper, salt and a few drops of lime juice. Fill up the white with the mixture and serve standing on rounds of buttered toast. (Cut off rounded ends to enable them to stand.)

2. Instead of anchovies, mix yolks with good cream cheese, after piling the mixture in the cases, place half a slice of tomato, or a dash of tomato sauce on top of each.

MRS. PASSELLS, Accra.

Eggs in Mayonnaise.

4 or 6 hard boiled eggs
¼ pint mayonnaise sauce
Lettuce
Tomatoes
¼ oz. gelatine.

Divide the hard boiled eggs in half, and cut a small piece from the bottom of each so that they will stand upright. Dissolve the gelatine in the least possible amount of water and add to the mayonnaise. Coat each egg with this mixture, and when cold place each piece on a slice of tomato, on a bed of lettuce.

MRS. DRAKE, Tamale.

Florentine Eggs.

Put mounds of cooked spinach in a casserole, break an egg over each one and cover with Béchamel sauce, sprinkle with grated cheese and small pat of butter and cook in oven, watching that eggs do not get hard.

ACHIMOTA.

Foie Gras in Aspic (Cold).

Make some aspic jelly and put a little in some small moulds. Let this partly set and three-quarter fill with foie gras which has been mixed with cream. Fill up with partly set aspic jelly and put on ice. Serve on a bed of mustard and cress and dress the top of each with chopped truffles. Surround the dish with thin slices of lime.

MRS. KEAST, Accra.

Golden Eggs.

4 hard boiled eggs
4 tablespoonfuls breadcrumbs
1 teaspoon chopped parsley
Brown sauce
1 oz. butter
1 uncooked egg.

Mix together the breadcrumbs and parsley. Add the melted butter. Beat up the raw egg and add a little to the mixture. Cover each boiled egg with the mixture; dip them in the remainder of the beaten egg and sprinkle with breadcrumbs. Fry in the butter until a nice golden brown. Cut across, place on a dish and serve quickly with a little brown sauce poured round them.

SISTER ANTONIA, Keta.

Eggs au Gratin.

Butter fireproof ramekin-dishes and put a tablespoonful of white sauce into each, put in two or three slices of hard cooked eggs, spreading white sauce and grated cheese between the layers of egg, season each layer with salt and pepper, coat the top with white sauce, sprinkle grated cheese over the top and add a few tiny pieces of butter. Bake in a hot oven for 10 minutes. Serve with a slice of hard cooked egg on top.

MRS. FRASER, Achimota.

Eggs with Creamed Potatoes.

Cold boiled potatoes
Butter
Eggs
Milk
Grated cheese
Pepper and salt.

Put potatoes through masher or sieve, melt a little butter in a saucepan, add potatoes and stir in milk, mix well until it becomes creamy; season with pepper and salt. Butter a fireproof baking dish, cover with a layer of creamed potatoes and make as many depressions in the surface of potatoes as there are eggs. Break the eggs one at a time and pour one into each depression. Cover with a layer of grated cheese and bake in a moderate oven until eggs are set.

MRS. BRUCE CRABB, Accra.

Parmesan Eggs.

Boil the eggs hard. When cold remove the yolks and mix with grated Parmesan cheese and a little butter. Refill the eggs with the mixture and serve cold.

MRS. ROTHWELL, Koforidua.

217

Scotch Eggs.

Two hard boiled eggs, 4 small cooked sausages, 1 egg beaten, breadcrumbs—light brown—fat or oil for deep fat frying. Remove shells from hard boiled eggs, coat with flour. Remove skin from sausages, press all round eggs until evenly coated. Brush over with beaten egg, coat with crumbs, fry till golden brown in boiling fat, drain well on paper. Cut small rounds of bread and fry—drain. Cut the eggs through the centre, neatly trim ends to make them stand, arrange bread down centre of dish, place egg on each and pour tomato sauce around.

MRS. STRADLING, Accra.

Tripe Eggs.

4 or 6 eggs (hard boiled)
1 small tin milk
½ pint water
2 or 3 large onions
Small lump butter
2 tablespoons flour
Pepper, salt
3 cloves.

Cut up the onions and simmer them in the milk and water till tender, together with cloves. Melt the butter in a saucepan, stir in the flour, add the stewed onions together with all their liquid, and stir gently over a fire until sauce has thickened; add seasoning to taste. Roughly break up the hard boiled eggs and add them to the thick onion sauce. Serve hot.

MRS. DRAKE, Tamale.

Boil an egg 4 minutes, cool and mix with some chopped mint and pulp of two tomatoes, season and spread on bread rounds.

MRS. DEVEREUX, Accra.

218

Gherkin Toast.

Five rounds of toast, 8 gherkins, 2 ozs. parmesan cheese, cayenne and salt to taste. Sprinkle the grated cheese on the toast. Chop the gherkins very finely and cover half the toast with them and cover the other half with the yolk of the hard-boiled eggs chopped up. Season with salt and cayenne.

MRS. PUCKRIDGE, Accra.

Gnocchi (Semolina Cheese).

Four ozs, semolina, 1 pint milk and water, 1 tablespoonful butter or margarine, 2 tablespoonfuls grated cheese, 2 yolks of eggs. Sprinkle semolina into milk, simmer in double pan till quite thick and well cooked. Add butter and yolks of eggs well beaten, allow to simmer for 5 minutes. Season to taste, and pour into buttered dish. When set, sprinkle half of the cheese on top; cover all with white sauce, sprinkle on the rest of cheese, add a few small pieces of butter. Brown in oven.

MISS S. F. LAMONT, Krobo Girls' School.

Ham Sandwiches.

When making ham sandwiches, add the made mustard to the butter, and beat well before spreading on the bread. Chop the ham in small pieces.

Ham Toast with Mushrooms.

Chop finely 1 teacupful of cooked ham, using a fair proportion of fat. Put it into a saucepan with a piece of butter the size of a small egg and season with mustard and cayenne. Add two eggs well beaten and a little salt if the ham is very mild. Stir over the fire until thick. Serve on rounds of toast or fried bread and garnish with grilled toasted mushrooms.

MRS. MILES, Accra.

219

Baked Kidneys.

(A Delicious Breakfast Dish.)

Three sheep kidneys, 4 potatoes, 2 ozs. butter, 1 small onion, breadcrumbs (brown), salt and pepper. Skin the kidneys and slice finely, removing cores. Peel and wash the potatoes and cut into large dice, very finely chop the onion, melt butter in pan, put in the onion and fry a little, add the kidney and cook quickly for 1 minute then stir in the potatoes. Mix well, and turn all into a greased fireproof dish, sprinkle with breadcrumbs and cook 40 minutes in a slow oven. Serve in same dish piping hot. Enough for two people.

MRS. STRADLING, Accra.

Kipper or Haddock Savoury.

Half of a small Finnan haddock or kipper, 1 hard-boiled egg, a little chopped parsley, walnut of butter, dessertspoonful flour, teacup of milk, pepper and salt. Simmer the haddock in the cupful of milk till soft then bone and shred adding the chopped parsley and hard-boiled egg, pepper and salt. Melt the butter, add flour and milk the haddock was cooked in, till a thick sauce is made. Stir in fish, egg and parsley and when thoroughly heated put on hot toast or in small ramekins and brown slightly in a quick oven.

MRS. SHAW, Accra.

Lobster Canapés.

2½ oz. lobster
1 oz. butter
2 level tablespoons chopped cress
1 small level teaspoon curry powder
2 small level teaspoons flour
2 teaspoons chopped onions
Pimento
Fried bread.

Melt butter in pan, add onion and the cress and cook for a few minutes without browning, mix flour with the curry and add to onion and cress. When it is well blended stir in the flaked lobster and make it hot, spread fried bread or buttered toast, about 1½ -inch wide and 3-inch long, with the mixture. Decorate the top with a piece of pimento.

MRS. ELLIS, Kumasi.

Lobster Canapés.

Fry 1 dessertspoonful chopped onion in one tablespoonful butter until it is a golden brown. Add one tablespoonful of chopped parsley, 1 dessertspoonful flour, a good pinch of curry powder, a teacupful of Ideal milk. Stir until smooth and add a cupful of lobster meat, either tinned or fresh, season to taste and heat thoroughly, heap the mixture on rounds of bread which have been fried brown in hot butter. Sprinkle with red pepper and set in a hot oven until brown. Serve hot, garnished with parsley and cut lemon.

MRS. MILES, Accra.

Macaroni Cheese (Hot).

Boil some macaroni, or preferably milkaroni, until tender. Make a thick white sauce and add some grated cheese, and made mustard. Mix well and stir over fire until the cheese is melted. Add the macaroni and pour mixture into a greased pie dish. Sprinkle with breadcrumbs which have been mixed with a little grated cheese, and put small pats of butter on the top. Brown in the oven.

MRS. KEAST, Accra.

French Omelet.

5 eggs
1 saltspoonful salt
2 oz. butter
5 shakes of pepper pot
1 teaspoon chopped parsley
1 tablespoon tepid water
½ teaspoon chopped onion.

Clean pan with tissue paper and a little butter. Put 1 oz. butter in pan and heat until smoke rises. Beat eggs slightly with a fork and not more than 8 beats; add the parsley, onion, pepper, salt and water. Lastly stir in 1 oz. butter. Pour mixture into pan and break quickly with a fork. After it has set, tilt pan, and let liquid run under omelet. Let it cook a little longer, then slip palette knife under and fold over. If liked, add champignons which have been cut in half and mixed with a thick brown sauce. Put this mixture on to half the omelet before folding over. For cheese omelet, sprinkle the top (after it has been folded over) thickly with grated parmesan.

MRS. KEAST, Accra.

Puffy Omelet.

Four eggs, ½ teaspoonful salt, ½ teaspoonful pepper, 2 teaspoonful baking powder, 1 tablespoonful corn flour, ½ cup milk, or half milk and half water. Separate eggs, mix salt, pepper, baking powder, corn flour and milk with yolks of eggs. Beat whites until light though not done, and mix in well with yolks. Put into greased hot frying pan and cook slowly until well puffed up, dry out in oven, fold over in half and serve immediately on hot platter. If desired serve with tomato sauce added before omelet folded.

MRS. SINCLAIR, Kumasi.

Onions au Gratin.

Six medium-sized onions, ½ pint white sauce, grated cheese, breadcrumbs, pepper and salt. Boil onions until tender, drain, arrange

222

in pie-dish, or casserole, pour over the white sauce to which half the grated cheese had been added, sprinkle with the balance of cheese also breadcrumbs and bake until brown.

MRS. STRADLING, Accra.

Onion Pie.

Sixpence soup bone, 2 large onions, ¼ lb. cheese, 2 slices bread. Boil the soup bone for about two hours, then strain, add sliced onions and season with pepper and salt, allow to simmer for half an hour, put into a pie-dish and cover with the toasted bread, grate cheese to thickly cover the whole, sprinkle with milk and put pie-dish into oven for about twenty minutes, serve hot.

MRS. SUTHERLAND, Koforidua.

Onion Ramekins.

Two large onions, 1 oz. dripping or margarine, 1 oz. flour, 2 tablespoons breadcrumbs, 1 tablespoon chopped parsley (if possible), whites of 2 eggs, salt, etc. Peel the onions and parboil, drain them and chop them, melt the fat, stir in the flour, add the onions, chopped parsley, salt and pepper, and a little piece of butter, cook mixture for about 5 minutes, then stir the beaten whites of the eggs lightly in. Turn the mixture into well-greased ramekin dishes and bake in a moderate oven for about half an hour.

MRS. DIXON, Salaga.

Onions (Stuffed).

Three large onions, ½ teaspoonful lemon juice, 3 tablespoons breadcrumbs, ½ oz. dripping, 3 tablespoons of cold meat (minced), pepper and salt, 3 teaspoonfuls grated cheese. Peel the onions, put in boiling water with a little salt, cook for an hour or longer if the onions are large. Take out the centres and stuff with the above ingredients mixed together and the centre of the onion minced, sprinkle with grated cheese. Put in a hot oven for 20 minutes and baste with the dripping. Serve very hot.

MRS. EMMETT, Accra.

Orange.

Orange slices may be used instead of apple sauce, as an accompaniment for roast pork. Cut the oranges into thin slices, soak for half an hour in lime juice, a little sugar, salt and pepper and place around the joint or pork chops. Garnish with parsley.

MRS. HILL, Accra.

Pawpaw with Cheese.

Take a green pawpaw, peel, remove the seeds and cut into good-sized pieces. Place in a large pie dish; add an onion cut in halves, a few cloves and pepper and salt. Pour half a pint of milk over, cover with greased paper and bake in a moderate oven till tender. When cooked, drain off the liquor. Melt 1 oz. of margarine in a saucepan, add 1 tablespoonful of flour, then the liquor and stir and simmer for 10 minutes. Add 4 ozs. grated cheese and pour all over the marrow in the pie dish. Sprinkle with grated cheese and brown in the oven. Serve in the dish in which cooked.

MRS. NICHOLAS, Kumasi.

Potato Soufflé.

Six large potatoes, ¾ cup tinned milk, yolks of 2 eggs, salt and pepper. Scrub and roast potatoes and cut off tops, scoop out the insides and mash in a bowl till smooth. Add milk, yolks of eggs, pepper and salt. Beat all together thoroughly and put back in the skins. Bake for 20 minutes.

MRS. SWAN, Tamale.

Prune Savoury.

Soak prunes overnight, stew the prunes and remove stones as carefully as possibly, roll one prune in one slice of bacon and tie with thread. Fry, and serve on fried bread or toast.

MRS. HEMANS, Takoradi.

224

Stuffed Prunes.

Six cooked prunes, a little chutney, 6 fingers of fried bread and bacon. Take out the stones and stuff the prunes with a little chutney. Then cut the bacon into pieces large enough and wrap round the prune. Roll and tie and cook quickly and then place one roll of bacon on each finger of fried bread and serve as hot as possible. Sufficient for six persons.

MRS. FIELDGATE, The Residency, Koforidua.

Stuffed Prunes.

Six olives, 6 prunes, 6 capers, 6 fillets of anchovies, bacon and squares of hot-buttered toast. Stone the olives, put a fillet of anchovy and a caper into each and pack all into the stoned prunes. Wrap a piece of bacon round each prepared prune, tie in place with sewing cotton and bake for 10 minutes in a quick oven. Remove the cotton and dish up on squares of hot-buttered toast which have had a few drops of anchovy essence sprinkled on them. Serve immediately.

MRS. EGG, Accra.

Pumpkin Breakfast Omelet.

Stew pumpkin till tender. Mash and season with salt, pepper, butter, a little sage. Fry like an omelet and serve with bacon.

ACHIMOTA.

Pumpkin Omelet.

Stew pumpkin until tender, mash and season with salt, pepper, butter and a little sage and a bit of sugar, if necessary, fry like an omelet in bacon fat, serve with bacon.

MRS. FRASER, Achimota.

A custard mixture of 1 egg to 1 cup of milk, well seasoned and mixed with chopped cooked beans, or any left-over vegetables and baked slowly as an ordinary custard makes an unusual meat substitute.

SAVOURIES

Ramekins of Eggs.

Two eggs, 1 tablespoon chopped mushrooms, 1 tablespoon chicken or ham, 1 teaspoon milk, 4 oz. butter, salt, pepper, browned crumbs. Beat eggs, seasoning and milk together, heat the butter in a pan, pour in the egg mixture and stir over a low heat till soft and creamy. Fill paper or china cases with alternate layers of egg mixture and chopped mushroom or ham. Heat up with brown crumbs on the top.

MRS. OAKLEY, Accra.

Rice Cases.

To each cup of cooked rice, 1 egg is added. Cover the outside of patty moulds with the mixture, leave for a short time, carefully remove invert and place on a baking sheet and bake in oven till delicate brown. Any left-overs of meat, chicken, fish or fruit, chopped fine and mixed with a white sauce can be added (in case of fruit mix with custard sauce).

MRS. FRASER, Achimota.

Rice and Egg Cutlets.

Four ozs. cooked rice, 3 hard boiled eggs, 1 oz. butter or margarine, 1 oz. flour, 1 gill of milk (or milk and water), salt, pepper, breadcrumbs, frying fat. Melt the butter in a pan, add the flour and blend well, gradually add the milk. Stir till the mixture thickens and boils, add the rice and simmer for 8 minutes. Chop the eggs and add. Season well and turn on to a plate to cool. When cold shape into cutlets. Brush over with milk and coat with breadcrumbs. Fry in deep hot fat. Drain on soft paper and dish leaning up against each other in a circle. Garnish with fried parsley. This can be made overnight and fried in the morning.

MRS. NORTHCOTE, Accra.

Rice and Tomatoes.

1 cup rice (cooked)
1 cup grated cheese
2 cups tinned tomatoes
2 tablespoons dripping
½ cup cut onion
1 teaspoon salt.

Put dripping and onion in frying pan, fry onion until cooked but not brown, add boiled rice, tomatoes and salt. Cook all for 10 minutes. Put in dish, cover with cheese and cook in oven till cheese is melted and brown. Serve hot.

MRS. FRASER, Achimota.

Risotto.

Take 6 ozs. rice and fry it in a frying pan with plenty of butter until quite brown. Then put it into a saucepan with 1 tin tomatoes and a few chopped onions and mix well over a slow fire. Serve on a flat dish and sprinkle with parmesan cheese.

LADY THOMAS.

Risotto Creole.

One cup rice, 1 cup tomato pulp, 3 cups water, ½ cup grated cheese, 2 tablespoons butter, 2 tablespoons chopped onion, 2 teaspoons salt, pepper. Cook the rice in plenty of water. Boil 5 minutes and drain and rinse. Melt butter in saucepan, add onion and rice, cook till the butter is absorbed. Add tomato pulp, salt, pepper and water. Cook till the rice is tender then stir in the cheese. Serve very hot.

MRS. FRASER, Achimota.

Salmon Toast.

1 small tin salmon
1 oz. butter
1 oz. flour
½ cup milk and water
½ tablespoonful ketchup
Salt and pepper
4 pieces hot buttered toast
Prawns to decorate.

Melt the butter in a saucepan. Stir in the flour; add the milk and water gradually and stir till it boils. Put in the whole tin of salmon, add the ketchup, mix well and let it boil for 3 or 4 minutes; season to taste and heap it on to the hot buttered toast. Decorate with prawns if available, or green peas. In place of the hot buttered toast, flaky pastry cases may be used.

MRS. DRAKE, Tamale.

Sardine and Bacon Rolls.

Roll thin rashers of bacon around sardines. Place on baking sheet and bake in a moderate oven.

MRS. LYNCH, Cape Coast.

Sardine Eggs.

Boil 4 eggs for 10 minutes and put them into cold water. Scrape 4 sardines gently and mash up thoroughly. Shell the eggs and cut them in half lengthways. Take out the yolks and add them to the sardines, with 1 oz. butter, a little white pepper and salt, and a dessertspoonful of parsley. Pound all together, then fill the whites with the mixture and put the two halves together and serve in a nest of small salad sprinkled with oil and vinegar.

MRS. W. EMMETT, Accra.

Chipped Sardines.

Take one tin of sardines, and tail them. Pour the sardine oil into frying pan. Cut some fingers of bread and fry in the oil until lightly brown. Remove from frying pan, place a piece of butter in the frying pan, fry the sardines, place them on fingers of toast. Garnish with parsley and serve with chips.

MRS. HOWE, Nkawkaw.

Cream Sardines.

Melt four tablespoonfuls of butter, add 1 cup stale breadcrumbs and 1 cup of milk. Cook until slightly thickened then add 2 hard-boiled eggs cut up, and 12 sardines, skinned and boned, season with salt and cayenne pepper. Serve hot on toast.

MISS WOOD, Accra.

Sardine Snacks.

Heat required number of medium-sized sardines in a little tomato ketchup to which has been added a good squeeze of lime juice. Butter strips of toast, each large enough to hold two sardines. When the fish are thoroughly heated remove from the sauce, coat them with brown breadcrumbs and lay them .on the toast. Pour a little of the sauce over each portion and garnish with cut lime.

MRS. MILES, Accra.

Small Chop.

Two eggs, 1 teaspoonful of curry powder, 2 teaspoonfuls of butter. Hard boil the eggs, separate the whites from the yolks. Mix the yolks, curry powder and butter, pepper, salt and beat well. Spread on buttered toast, placing a small strip of the white on the top. Picnic sandwiches are nice done this way, substituting thinly cut bread and butter for toast.

MRS. HOWE, Nkawkaw.

Savoury Balls.

Half lb. liver, 1 cupful breadcrumbs, 1 teaspoonful sage, 6 small onions. Mince the uncooked liver and onions, scald the sage, strain off the water and add to the mixture. Season well and add the breadcrumbs. Form into balls and flour well. Bake in well-greased tin for 20 minutes.

MRS. HOWE, Nkawkaw.

Savoury Biscuits (Cold).

Butter some Fortt's Bath Olivers or Carr's celery cheese biscuits. Grate some cheese and pound well until smooth with some undiluted Ideal milk. The mixture must be thick, spread generously on the biscuits. Mix some yolks of hard boiled eggs with a little butter and fold in the chopped whites. Put this on the top of the cheese. Dress with mustard and cress or lettuce. Prepare not more than 2 hours beforehand, or the biscuits will become soft.

MRS. KEAST, Accra.

Sherried Eggs.

Boil eggs (per person) for 10 minutes; shell, and remove yolks. Blend yolks with oz. of butter and seasoning into a smooth paste and add a good teaspoonful of sherry. Return to whites until each half is full. Prepare a white sauce and add to it one heaped dessertspoonful of grated parmesan cheese. Pour sauce over eggs and shake a little of the grated cheese over the top. Place in hot oven for 5 minutes, then it is ready to send to table.

MRS. DE CARTERET, Kumasi.

Tomato Toasts.

Two tomatoes, 1 egg, ½ oz. butter, pepper, salt, 1 tablespoonful of grated cheese, rounds of hot-buttered toast and gherkins. Sieve the tomatoes and put the purée into a saucepan with the egg, butter and seasoning, mix together and stir over the fire until thick—without boiling; add the grated cheese and pile on rounds of hot-buttered toast. Garnish each with a little finely chopped gherkin and serve hot.

MRS. EGG, Accra.

Savoury Tomatoes.

Half lb. tomatoes, ¼ lb. macaroni, 2 ozs. Cheddar cheese and a little butter; season with pepper and salt to taste. Stew the tomatoes well and boil the macaroni till soft. Stir the ingredients well together and serve. Sprinkle chopped parsley over all.

MRS. THOMAS, Cape Coast.

Savoury Tomatoes.

Six tomatoes, 2 tablespoonfuls minced cucumber (not essential), 3 tablespoonfuls tinned salmon (flaked), 1 lettuce, ½ pint of mayonnaise, salt and pepper. Dip tomatoes in boiling water then peel carefully. Cut a small slice from each top and remove the centres. Mix the pulp together with the salmon, cucumber (if any), seasoning and mayonnaise to taste and then pile into tomatoes. Stand in a cold place if possible and when chilled put a teaspoonful of mayonnaise on the top of each tomato and serve on a bed of lettuce. The appearance of the tomatoes would be improved if a little parsley was sprinkled over the mayonnaise on the top of each tomato.

MRS. FIELDGATE, Koforidua.

Tomatoes au Gratin.

Six tomatoes, 3 ounces of grated cheese, 4 ounces of breadcrumbs, 1 ounce of margarine or butter, salt and pepper to taste. Mix the cheese, crumbs and seasoning together and put a thin layer at the bottom of a greased pie dish. Cover with sliced tomato and fill the dish with alternate layers, crumbs forming the last layer. Divide the margarine or butter into small pieces, and dot over the top. Bake in a moderate oven for about 20 minutes.

MRS. BUSH, Sekondi.

Tomato Cheese.

One oz. of butter in stewpan, 1 tablespoon tomato sauce, stir well, add 2 tablespoons grated cheese, a few drops lemon juice and a little cayenne, stir and beat thoroughly. Serve on buttered toast.

MRS. BROWNING, Cape Coast.

Tomato Cheese.

2 tablespoonful breadcrumbs
2 tablespoonful grated cheese
2 good-sized tomatoes.

Cook the tomatoes until tender, then rub through a sieve. Stir in the crumbs and cheese, a pinch of salt and a little pepper and butter. Spread on buttered toast and serve hot.

MRS. SAMPLES, Takoradi.

Tomato Egg Rice.

Boiled rice, tomato pulp, eggs, pepper and salt, breadcrumbs and butter. Butter a shallow dish or individual dishes and put in

1. A layer of rice.

2. A layer of tomato pulp.

3. Eggs broken as for poaching, pepper and salt.

4. Cover with breadcrumbs (fresh) and dot liberally with butter.

Bake in a quick oven for about ten minutes.

ACHIMOTA.

Tomato Pan-cake.

Four ozs. wholemeal flour, 2 new laid eggs, 1 gill milk, 1 tablespoonful olive oil, 2 large onions, 3 tomatoes, 2 teaspoonfuls mixed herbs. Break eggs into the flour and beat well for 5 minutes. Add the milk and lastly the oil. Let the mixture stand for 1 hour. Then put a little fat into a pan, make very hot and pour in the mixture. Add minced onions and tomatoes and herbs, fold over and serve hot.

MISS. EVELYN BELLAMY, Cape Coast.

Tomato Welsh Rarebit.

Cut a half pound of cheese into small pieces, put in a saucepan, and cook, stirring until it melts. Add half a tin of tomato soup, season with salt and pepper, and mustard, and serve on toast.

MRS. PASSELLS, Accra.

232

CAKES

Almond Biscuits.

Quarter lb. butter, 6 ozs. sugar, 1 egg (2 Gold Coast eggs), ½ lb. flour. Cream butter and sugar, add egg and 2 drops almond essence, then flour mixed with 1 teaspoonful of baking powder. Take piece of mixture in the hand, roll in a round ball, then roll out the shape of a finger and flatten. Put an almond in the middle of biscuit and brush over with beaten egg. Cook about ten minutes.

ACHIMOTA.

Australian Jack.

Put into a pan and melt 1 oz. butter, 1 tablespoon syrup, 1 tablespoon sugar. Mix together 1 tablespoon grated cocoanut, 4 handfuls Quaker oats. Add dry ingredients to ingredients in pan. Turn into greased sandwich tin and bake in moderate oven till golden brown—about fifteen minutes.

MRS. SWAN, Tamale.

Banana Cake.

Four bananas, 3 eggs, ½ lb. of flour, 4 ozs. butter or margarine, 6 ozs. castor sugar. Peel the bananas and mash them to a smooth pulp. Sieve the flour, add a pinch of salt. Beat the butter and sugar to a cream, add the yolks of the eggs one by one, beating each in well. Beat in the banana pulp, then stir in the flour gradually. Whip the whites of the eggs to a stiff meringue and stir lightly to the mixture. Put in a well-greased tin, lined with greased paper, and bake in a moderate oven for about one hour. Turn on to a sieve to cool.

If liked, the cake may be iced with white glace icing, and decorated with cherries and angelica.

MRS. BARTLETT, Accra.

Banana Cake.

Three ripe bananas, 2 cups flour, 1 cup castor sugar, ½ cup butter, 4 eggs beaten, 4 tablespoonfuls milk (sour), 1 teaspoonful baking soda, pinch salt, 2 teaspoonfuls baking powder, 1 teaspoonful vanilla. Cream butter and sugar, add bananas and eggs, milk with soda dissolved in it. Then add the flour, etc., and beat well. Bake in a moderate oven. Open oven door and allow cake to cool there before taking out.

MISS SUTHERLAND, Aburi.

Brandy Wafers.

Put into a saucepan 4 ozs. butter, 4 ozs. sugar, 4 ozs. golden syrup, warm slightly and mix with 4 ozs. flour, ½ teaspoon ground ginger. Stir all together and drop a small quantity on to a well-buttered baking sheet, cook till brown. When nearly cold curl round handle of wooden spoon.

MRS. FRASER, Achimota.

Brown Cake without Eggs.

¾ lb. flour
¼ lb. margarine
6 ozs. moist sugar
3 ozs. mixed peel
½ lb. raisins
1 tablespoonful golden syrup
1 teaspoonful bicarbonate soda
1 teacupful milk.

Rub the butter in the flour. Add sugar and fruit. Melt treacle in little warm milk and lastly the soda. Mix all well together, it must be rather moist. Bake in a moderate oven.

MRS. EMMETT, Accra.

Brown Scone.

Two cups wholemeal flour, ½ cup flour (white), ½ teaspoon bicarbonate soda, 1 teaspoon cream of tartar, 1 teaspoon margarine, 1 teaspoon sugar, a little milk. Mix all dry ingredients together and moisten, knead and roll out and cook in a moderate oven.

MRS. LOCKHART, Mfantsipim, Cape Coast.

Method of Cake Making.

1. Beat the butter to a cream.

2. Add the sugar sieved one teaspoonful at a time, and beat well. Beat until the mixture is perfectly white.

3. Beat the eggs well, and add to the mixture one dessertspoonful at a time. Beat all lightly.

4. Add the flour which has been sieved and dried in the sun. The flour must be added in small quantities and gently beaten in.

5. Add any fruit last.

The success of the cake depends on the good beating before the flour is added.

Use self-raising flour, but if unobtainable, add 1 teaspoonful of baking powder to 4 ozs. flour. It should be sieved with the flour.

MRS. KEAST, Accra.

Preparation of Tin.

It is unnecessary to line cake tins with paper unless a plum cake is required. Clarify a little butter by melting it in a small saucepan and take off the scum. It should be clear before using. Brush the tin over with this, mix equal quantities of flour and castor sugar (about a teaspoon of each) and shake into tin so that it is well coated. Turn tin upside down and tap it, so that the surface has an even coating. After the cake is baked, the outside will not be greasy if the tin is treated thus.

MRS. KEAST, Accra.

Cake Mixture.

Ten ozs. flour, 4 ozs. butter, 4 ozs. sugar, 4 eggs, 3 teaspoons baking powder, 3 ozs. currants, 3 ozs. raisins, flavouring of vanilla and lemon essence. A little milk if necessary. Sift dry ingredients. Cream the butter and add the well-beaten eggs. Beat well. Add the baking powder, then the fruit and flavourings. Bake in a moderate oven.

SISTER ANTONIA, Keta.

Chantilly Puffs.

Two ozs. butter, 4 ozs. flour, ½ pint water, grated lemon rind, 3 eggs. Put the water, lemon rind and butter into a pan, when boiling, beat in the flour. Stir over a gentle heat until the mixture leaves sides of pan quite clean. Remove from fire and beat in three eggs one at a time. Place this paste on a baking tin in round balls. Bake for half an hour then cool on a rack, split, and fill with sweetened whipped cream.

MRS. LYNCH, Cape Coast.

Cherry Cake or Sultana.

Half lb. flour, 5 ozs. butter, 5 eggs (African), 5 ozs. sugar, a little milk, cherries, some halved and mixed in, some to decorate top, or sultanas about 4 oz., 2 teaspoons baking powder, add last. Cream the butter and sugar, and the beaten eggs, then flour gradually beaten in and a little milk; add fruit and baking powder. Mixture should be just thin enough to pour into cake-tin, if too thin fruit sinks to bottom. Pour into greased tin, or line tin with greased paper. Bake in moderate oven about one hour. May be put into small tins.

MRS. BEVERIDGE, Accra.

Chocolate Butter Icing.

Two ozs. butter, 3 ozs. Cadbury's chocolate powder, few drops of vanilla essence. Beat well together.

MRS. KEAST, Accra.

236

Chocolate Cake.

3 oz. sugar
3 African eggs
2 oz. flour
1 teaspoon baking powder
½ bar milk chocolate.

Beat sugar and eggs until thick. Add flour and baking powder and grated chocolate. Put into a cake tin and bake 10 minutes. Split when cool and spread with chocolate filling.

MRS. LOCKHART, Mfantsipim, Cape Coast.

Chocolate Filling.

One tablespoon butter, 3 tablespoons icing sugar, ½ bar milk chocolate. Beat all together smooth and use for filling. Note—This sponge mixture can be used equally for a plain jam roll or coffee cake, coffee being used in mixture and filling instead of the chocolate.

MRS. LOCKHART, Mfantsipim, Cape Coast.

Chocolate Cake.

4 eggs
4 ozs. self-raising flour
4 ozs. sugar
2 ozs. Cadbury's chocolate powder
4 ozs. butter
½ teaspoon vanilla essence.

Mix as in the method given and bake in a sandwich cake tin. If a valour-perfection stove is used bake 25 minutes on the lower shelf and 10 minutes on the top shelf. When cold cut in half and spread with chocolate butter icing. Cover the top also with the icing, and put round a border of halved shelled walnuts. Spread the centre with some of the nuts, peeled and chopped finely and coloured with Marshalls' vegetable green.

MRS. KEAST, Accra.

Chocolate Cake.

Four ozs. butter, 4 ozs. castor sugar, 4 ozs. chocolate powder, 2 eggs, 4 ozs. flour, 1 teaspoon baking powder. Beat butter with sugar, when white and thick add eggs unbeaten. Beat together, then add chocolate powder previously dissolved in a little water. Lastly, add flour and baking powder; bake one hour.

LADY THOMAS.

Chocolate Fruit Cake.

Six tablespoons flour, 1 tablespoon Bourneville cocoa, 4 tablespoons butter, 4 tablespoons castor sugar, 3 tablespoons currants, 3 tablespoons sultanas, 1 teaspoon baking powder, 4 eggs, milk to mix. Wash and dry the fruit, line a tin with two layers of greased paper and sieve flour, cocoa and baking powder together. Beat the butter and sugar to a cream and add the eggs one by one, beating in each thoroughly. Stir in the flour, etc., and the fruit alternately with some milk until of a thick creamy consistency. Place in the lined tin and bake in a moderate oven for about 45 minutes.

MRS. FREELAWN, Asokore.

Chocolate Swiss Roll.

3 eggs
3 ozs. self-raising flour
3ozs. castor sugar
1½ ozs. Cadbury's chocolate powder
3 ozs. butter.

Mix as in the method given, adding the chocolate powder to the flour, and bake according to the recipe for Jam Swiss Roll. When cold, unroll gently, and spread with melted chocolate, and roll again. Spread some of the chocolate on the top and sides of the roll and mark it with a fork to represent more or less a log of wood. Cover with chopped pistachio nuts.

To Melt the Chocolate.

Grate a slab of plain chocolate, and with 1 teaspoonful of water only, put into a basin which place in a pan of boiling water. Keep the water boiling and stir occasionally. It takes a very long time to melt.

MRS. KEAST, Accra.

Cinnamon Biscuits.

One cup sugar, ½ cup butter, 2 eggs, ½ teaspoon soda bicarbonate, 1 teaspoon cream of tartar, 1 teaspoon powdered cinnamon, 1½ cups flour, or enough to make a soft dough. Take a teaspoonful of the dough; make into balls; roll in granulated sugar; flatten a little and place on greased tin. Bake in quick oven.

MRS. BEVERIDGE, Accra.

Coconut Biscuits.

Ten ozs. of sifted sugar, 3 eggs, 6 ozs. grated coconut. Whisk the eggs until they are very light. Then add the sugar and the grated coconut. Roll the paste into balls, about a tablespoonful in each. Place on papered tins and put in a moderately hot oven till they are a light brown.

SISTER ANGELE, Cape Coast.

Coconut Cakes.

One tablespoon butter, 2 tablespoons sugar, 2 eggs, 1 cup grated coconut, 2 cups flour, 2 teaspoons baking powder. Cream the butter and sugar, add the eggs well beaten, add the coconut and the flour which has been mixed and sifted with the baking powder. Chill the dough, roll out thinly, cut with a small round cutter, and bake in a hot oven until nicely browned.

SISTER ANTONIA, Keta.

Coconut Cakes.

One cup grated coconut, 1 cup granulated sugar, 1 white of egg, 1 cup flour, or less. Mix coconut and sugar; add well-beaten white of egg and flour. Place in little heaps on greased tin (or lined with greased paper). Bake in hot oven.

MRS. BEVERIDGE, Accra.

Coconut Cones.

Whip up white of 1 egg and add 4 ozs. castor sugar mixed with 3 ozs. dried desiccated coconut. Form into cones and place on wafer paper, bake in slow oven until pale golden brown and crisp.

MRS. COE, Wenchi.

Coconut Macaroons.

One and a quarter cups desiccated coconut, 1 egg white, $\frac{1}{3}$ cup condensed milk, teaspoon vanilla. Mix coconut, condensed milk and vanilla thoroughly, beat egg white until stiff, combine mixtures, shape into cakes, bake in moderate oven 15 minutes.

MRS. FRASER, Achimota.

Comox Chocolate Cake.

One-quarter cup butter or margarine, 1 cup sugar, 2 eggs (separate yolks and whites), 1½ cups flour, ½ cup milk, 3 teaspoons baking powder, 2 tablespoons cocoa powder, grated rind of an orange. Cream butter, adding gradually half the sugar, and the cocoa made into a smooth paste with a little of the milk. Beat yolks of egg till thick and lemon-coloured, and add gradually the remaining sugar. Combine mixtures, and add milk alternately with flour sifted with baking powder, add grated rind, and lastly whites of egg beaten stiff. Bake 40 to 50 minutes in a moderate oven. If liked the cake can be iced with orange icing made with the juice of the orange.

MRS. WILKINSON Dunkwa.

Corn Cake.

(Ewe Kakla).

Corn dough, sugar, plantains and a pinch of salt.

(1) Pound the plantains, mix with the dough.

(2) Add sugar and salt, roll into small balls, put on leaves and bake for half an hour in a moderate oven.

SISTER ANTONIA, Keta.

Corn Cakes.

One cup of corn-grains, 1 tablespoonful flour, 1 egg, 1 tablespoonful milk. Corn must be cooked well beforehand, grind corn, mix milk, flour and eggs, add corn, bake little lumps swimming in hot lard, scatter sugar over the corn cakes, serve them with fruit salad or without sugar to any roasted meat.

MISS. GOETZ, Agogo.

Cornmeal Scones.

Make the same as other scones, using half cornmeal and half flour.

MISS SPEARS.

Cream Scones.

Half lb. or 1 breakfastcup flour, 1 teaspoon cream of tartar, ½ teaspoon bicarbonate soda, 1 dessertspoon sugar, ¼ teaspoon salt, 1 tablespoon margarine, a little milk, rub dry ingredients together, moisten and roll out to ½ inch thickness, cut into squares, bake slowly on a griddle, turning as required until cooked.

MRS. LOCKHART, Mfantsipim, Cape Coast.

Currant Cakes (To improve).

To improve currant cakes, after they are cold, pour a little rum or brandy over the top.

SISTER ANTONIA, Keta.

Cream Sponge Cake.

Yolks 5 eggs
1 cup sugar
Flour
1½ teaspoons baking powder
3 tablespoons cold water
¼ teaspoon salt
1½ tablespoons cornflour
Whites 5 eggs
1 tablespoon lemon juice.

Beat yolks of eggs and water until thick and lemon-coloured, add sugar gradually, and beat two minutes. Put corn flour in a cup and fill up with flour. Mix and sift corn flour and flour with baking powder and salt, and add to first mixture. When thoroughly mixed add whites of eggs beaten until stiff, and flavouring. Bake 30 minutes in a moderate oven.

MRS. SHIRER, Yendi.

Currant Buffers.

Half lb. flour, 2 eggs, 4 spoons milk, half a cup water, a teaspoon baking powder, some currants, a little salt. Mix all ingredients well and let the batter stand for 2 or 3 hours, Fry in small quantities in a little butter, lard or oil. When brown, turn on other side for a minute and serve hot.

MRS. KEAST, Accra.

Cumberland Cake or Pastry.

Prepare some dough for pastry, spread a layer of pastry on an old plate (which has been well buttered), then fill the hollow with well-cleaned currants, and a little candied peel, when quite level sprinkle over with castor sugar, and put three or four small pieces of butter on the top. Cover the whole plate with a thin layer of pastry and bake it in the oven. After it is cooked, sprinkle sugar over, it can be eaten hot or cold. Tinned gooseberries (without the juice), also sliced apples, well sugared, and no butter are very nice for a change.

MRS. BUTLER, Accra.

Easter Cakes.

6 ozs. flour
1 egg (2 native eggs)
3 ozs. butter
1 oz. currants
3 ozs. sugar
1 teaspoon cinnamon essence.

Sieve the flour; put the butter and sugar into a basin and work together until they are pale in colour and creamy. Beat in the egg and fold in the dry ingredients, and add cinnamon essence. Mix to a fairly soft dough, but stiff enough to roll out. Flour a board, roll out the mixture to about thickness, cut into rounds, bake in a moderately hot oven until they are brown and crisp.

MRS. DRAKE, Tamale.

Date Cake (For the filling).

½ lb. dates
½ cupful flour
½ cupful brown sugar
1 cupful rolled or Quaker oats
½ lb. cup sugar
½ cup butter
Pinch of salt
½ teaspoonful baking powder
Water.

Wash dates, cover with water and boil till soft with sugar. Rub butter into flour, add the rolled oats and powder. Place half of mixture in greased tin, place dates on top, then put the remainder of rolled oats mixture on top Bake in moderate oven for one and a half hours.

MISS SUTHERLAND, Aburi.

Dropped Scones or Tea Pan-cakes.

Half lb. flour, 2 ozs. butter, 2 ozs. sugar, 2 eggs, 2½ cups milk (1 part tinned, 3 water), ½ teaspoon soda bicarbonate, 1 teaspoon cream of tartar. Beat butter and sugar to a cream; add beaten eggs; then add milk and flour alternately, and add soda and cream of tartar. This batter should be fairly thick, just thin enough to spread into rounds when dropped on hot griddle or iron-plate which must be greased with butter or dripping. Turn with knife when air-bubbles begin to come through, and brown the other side.

MRS. BEVERIDGE, Accra.

Ginger Bread.

Sift together ¼ lb. flour, ½ teaspoonful carbonate of soda, 1 teaspoonful ginger, 1 teaspoon mixed spices. Melt in a saucepan 2 ozs. butter, ½ lb. syrup, 2 ozs. brown sugar, without allowing the mixture to boil. Pour this with 2 beaten eggs and 1 teacupful of milk into the flour, stir until smooth, beat a few minutes, then bake in a moderate oven.

MRS. LOGAN, Accra.

Ginger Bread.

Three-quarter lb. plain flour, ¼ lb. lard or butter, ¼ lb. sugar, 1 teaspoon carbonate of soda, 1 dessertspoonful ground ginger, 2 eggs, pinch of salt and milk. Dissolve fat and sugar with half syrup (two heaped tablespoons), mix well, bake 1 hour.

MRS. BROWNING, Cape Coast.

Ginger Bread.

One tablespoon butter, 2 tablespoons sugar, 4 tablespoons flour, 1 egg, ½ teaspoon carbonate of soda, 1 teaspoon mixed spices, 1 teaspoon ginger, 2 tablespoons treacle, milk to mix. Beat butter and sugar to a cream, add egg and beat again. Add treacle, then dry ingredients, and finally milk to make a soft mixture. Drop into a greased and floured tin and bake in a moderate oven for about one hour.

SISTER ANGELE, Cape Coast.

Ginger-bread Cake.

1 lb. flour, 6 ozs. butter, ½ lb. brown sugar, ½ lb. (or more) golden syrup, ½ oz. ground ginger, 1 teaspoonful carbonate of soda, 1, 2 or 3 eggs. A little chopped candied peel. Mix flour, soda, and butter. Add sugar, peel, and ginger, stir in the beaten eggs and mix with warmed syrup.

ACHIMOTA.

Ginger Biscuit.

Half lb. flour, ¼ lb. fresh butter, ¼ lb. castor sugar, ½ oz. ground ginger, 1 egg and a little milk. Rub the butter and ginger into the flour on the board. Make a hole, break in the egg, and wet into a paste, using a little milk if necessary. Roll out thinly and cut with a plain round cutter. Put on a greased baking tin and bake in a fairly cool oven for about five minutes.

MRS. HENDERSON, Accra.

Ginger Cake.

The weight of 3 eggs in butter, sugar, and flour. Replace the flour with the corn flour as in the orange cake, and add teaspoon of ground ginger to it. Finally add 3 ozs. ginger cut up in pieces and a little of the ginger syrup. Bake in a sandwich cake tin.

MRS. KEAST, Accra.

Ginger Nuts.

½ lb. flour
2 ozs. brown sugar
¼ lb. golden syrup
1 tablespoon brown ginger
2 ozs. butter
¼ tablespoon carbonate of soda.

Mix all dry ingredients. Melt butter in the treacle in the oven. Add, while hot, to the dry ingredients, mix with a knife. Take a piece the size of a walnut in the hand, form into a round ball, place on a greased tin. Bake quickly in a moderate oven for 10 minutes.

MRS. STEELE, Tamale.

Groundnut Biscuits.

Groundnuts, brown sugar. Crush the groundnuts. Melt sugar in frying pan. Stir in the groundnuts and when well browned, turn out and roll out very thin with a glass rolling pin or bottle.

MRS. STEELE, Tamale.

Groundnut Cakes.

Four ozs. flour, 4 ozs. sugar, 4 ozs. butter, 2 eggs, ½ teaspoonful baking powder, 1½ ozs. chopped groundnuts.

1. Cream the butter and sugar.
2. Beat in the eggs one at a time.
3. Sift the flour and baking powder, add 1 oz. chopped nuts.
4. Add all this to the butter, eggs, and sugar.
5. Fold in very lightly.
6. Put into small greased tins and sprinkle ½ oz. groundnuts on the top.
7. Bake in a quick oven 10 to 15 minutes.

N.B.—A few drops of almond essence improves the flavour, but is not necessary.

ACHIMOTA.

Groundnut Macaroons.

Two large or 3 small egg whites, 5 ozs. groundnuts, 6 ozs. white sugar. Blanch nuts and pound in a mortar or put three times through a mincing machine. Beat eggs, sugar and nuts to a smooth paste with a wooden spoon for 30 minutes. Place in small lumps on greased paper and place 2 nuts split on top of each and bake in a cool oven.

LADY THOMAS.

Jam Sandwich.

Two eggs, 1 teaspoon baking powder, 2 tablespoons sugar, 2½ tablespoons flour, 1 dessertspoon warm water, pinch of salt, jam, vanilla or lemon flavouring. Mix the flour, baking powder and salt together. Whisk the whites of eggs to a stiff froth, then add the yolks one at a time beating well. Beat in the sugar till dissolved. Add the flour and baking powder, etc., with the warm water and flavouring. Mix all lightly with a wooden spoon. Poor into greased sandwich tins and bake in a hot oven for five to seven minutes. Cool on tray and spread with jam.

MRS. LYNCH, Cape Coast.

Lime Cake.

One and half breakfast cupfuls of flour, 2 tablespoonfuls of butter, 3 tablespoonfuls of sugar, 2 teaspoonfuls of baking powder, 2 eggs, juice of one lime. Cream the sugar and butter, add well beaten eggs and lime juice adding the flour and baking powder last. Sprinkle a few groundnuts on the top and bake in a moderate oven.

MRS. HOWE, Nkawkaw.

Unsweetened Lunch Biscuits.

One lb. of dry sifted flour, ½ oz. of butter or margarine, ½ pint of milk, a pinch of salt, 1 teaspoonful of baking powder. Dissolve the fat in the milk and make it lukewarm, pour it by degrees on to the flour, sieve with the salt and baking powder, beating meanwhile. Beat very thoroughly, turn on to a board and knead until smooth, roll it out very thin, cut into rounds with a cutter, prick with a fork, and bake lightly on a floured tin in a moderate oven 15 to 20 minutes. Keep in a tin and if necessary crisp up in the oven for a minute or two before serving.

MRS. BUTLER, Accra.

Lunch Cake.

Half lb. flour, 4 ozs. raisins, 4 ozs. butter, 4 ozs. currants, 4 ozs. sugar, I oz. candied peel, ½ teaspoon mixed spices, ½ teaspoon baking powder, two eggs (small) and a little milk. Bake in a moderate oven an hour a half to two hours.

MRS. NORTHCOTE, Accra.

Meringues.

Whip 1 white of egg to a stiff froth, add 3 ozs. castor sugar and bake slowly for 45 minutes, must not be brown, but white.

MRS. COE, Wenchi.

Mocha Cake.

3 eggs
3 oz. sugar
3½ ozs. flour (sifted)
1 tablespoon coffee.

1. Whisk eggs and sugar and coffee essence until thick.
2. Fold in flour.
3. Pour into tin.
4. Bake one hour.
5. When cold add cream made by heating together butter and sifted sugar, flavoured with coffee essence or strong coffee.

MRS. KEEVIL, Sekondi.

Nut Bread.

Four teacups self-raising flour, 1 teacup sugar, 1 teacup sultanas, 1 teacup chopped walnuts, 2 eggs and a good pinch of salt, 1 dessertspoonful of golden syrup in 2 teacups of warm milk. Mix and pour into tin and let it rise for 20 minutes. Bake in oven not too hot, about 1½ to 2 hours.

MRS. EMMETT, Accra,

Nut Bread.

One egg, ¾ cupful sugar, 2 cupfuls flour, ½ cupful chopped walnuts, ¾ cupful milk, 2 teaspoons baking powder, pinch salt. Beat egg and sugar together. Sift flour, baking powder and salt together and add to egg and sugar alternating with the milk. Mix in chopped walnuts and bake in a greased and floured tin for about one hour in a moderate oven.

MRS. HENDERSON, Accra.

Oat Cakes.

One lb. coarse oatmeal, pinch salt, 1 teaspoon dripping, pinch soda bicarbonate, ¼ cup water. Mix salt and oatmeal, put soda and fat into a cup, add little hot water enough to melt fat. Mix all together with rest of the water into soft paste. Make into a round cut in four, rub top and bottom with oatmeal. Fire on hot griddle and toast when ready.

MRS. BIDEN.

Orange Cake.

Six ozs. flour, 3 ozs. butter, 3 ozs. sugar, 3 eggs, 2 teaspoons baking powder, juice and rind of half an orange. Cream butter and sugar, add eggs, flour and baking powder and orange, bake in fairly hot oven. For icing this cake: 3 or 4 tablespoons icing sugar, 2 teaspoons orange juice, mix together and spread on cake when half cold.

MRS. BROWNING, Cape Coast.

Orange Cake.

The weight of 3 eggs in butter, sugar, and self-raising flour. Take out 1 dessertspoon of flour and replace with 1 dessertspoon of cornflour which will help to make the cake light. Add to the sugar 1 teaspoon of grated orange rind. Mix as in the method given, and put into sandwich cake tin, spreading the mixture well to the sides of the tin, otherwise it will rise in the middle. When cold turn upside down and pour over orange icing. Cut crystallised cherries each into four pieces and put a border of these round the cake.

MRS. KEAST, Accra.

Orange Icing.

Half lb. icing sugar and about 3 tablespoons of strained orange juice. Sieve the sugar and put in enamelled saucepan. Add the liquid and stir with a wooden spoon over the fire until it is warm. The icing must not be made hot or it will become lumpy. Colour faintly with carmine. Put the cake on a wire cake cooler, and stand on a soup plate. Pour over the cake and prick any bubbles with a pin. Let it stand for 2 minutes, then lift cake gently with palette knife on to a plate. The icing will crack if left longer.

MRS. KEAST, Accra.

Orange Icing.

Ten ozs. icing sugar, ½ gill orange juice. Sieve the icing sugar, mix well together with the juice until smooth. Place in a saucepan and make slightly warm, stir well all the time. Place sandwich on a cake rack. Pour the icing over. Leave until set.

NOTE.—If the sandwich has risen much cut a piece off the top and turn it upside down to ice it.

MRS. EMMETT, Accra.

Orange Cake.

4 ozs. flour
4 ozs. castor sugar
2 ozs. butter
Rind and juice of half orange
1 teaspoonful baking powder
2 eggs.

Beat butter and sugar to a cream, then add flour, beat well, then put in the eggs whole, beat all together, then the rind and juice of half orange, lastly, baking powder. Use paper baking cases and use 1 dessertspoonful of the mixture in each and bake in quick oven.

MRS. SAMPLES, Takoradi.

Orange Cake (No Butter).

Four ozs. flour, 2 teaspoonfuls of baking powder, juice of 2 oranges, grated rind of I orange, 6 ozs. sugar, the yolks of 4 eggs and the whites of 2 eggs. Cream sugar and eggs together for 10 minutes. Add the juice of the oranges and then the grated rind. Stir in the flour lightly, then add baking powder, pour into a well-greased tin and cover with greased paper. Bake for hour in a brisk oven.

Do not open the door until the cake is cooked.

MRS. FIELDGATE, The Residency, Koforidua.

Orange Filling.

Half cup sugar, 3 tablespoons corn flour, ¼ teaspoon salt, ¼ tablespoon flour, 1 tablespoon melted butter, 1 egg, ¾ cup water, 1 tablespoon lemon juice, juice and rind of 1 orange. Mix dry ingredients. Add water and melted butter and cook 15 minutes after mixture thickens. Beat eggs slightly—add to cooked mixture, add grated rind of orange with orange and lemon juice, when cold spread between layers of cake. Put plain white icing on top.

MRS. KEAST, Accra.

Orange Layer Cake.

One cup sugar, ½ cup water, 1 egg yolk, 2 whole eggs, juice and rind of 1 orange, 1½ cups flour, 3 teaspoons baking powder, ½ teaspoon salt. Separate eggs, beat yolks slightly, add sugar and 1 tablespoon water taken from water in receipt. Beat 1 minute with Dover egg-beater. Sift together, flour, salt and baking powder. Add grated rind of orange, add orange juice to rest of water and add to sugar and eggs alternately with dry ingredients. Cut and fold in beaten whites of eggs, cook in moderate oven.

MRS. FRASER, Achimota.

Iced Orange Sponge.

Three eggs, their weight in—butter, sugar and flour—1 teaspoonful of baking powder, rind of an orange (grated), juice of half orange (strained). Grease a jam sandwich tin and line with paper. Cream the fat and sugar together. Sieve the flour and baking powder. Add the grated orange rind to the flour. Beat the eggs separately into the creamed fat and sugar, beat well for a few minutes. Lightly fold in the flour, etc., and the juice of half the orange. Put into prepared tin. Bake in a hot oven for 10 to 15 minutes. Place on a sieve to cool. Then ice with orange icing.

MRS. EMMETT, Accra.

Palm-Oil Corn Cake.

(Ewe, Bongo).
Corn dough, Sugar, palm oil.
1. Take a little of the dough add water and mix into a thin paste. Add this paste to the remaining dough, mix well, add sugar and palm oil.
2. Divide the mixture, roll into balls. Put each on a clean leaf and bake for half an hour in a moderate oven.

SISTER ANTONIA, Keta.

Palm Wine Bread.

One and three-quarter lbs. flour, 1 teaspoon salt, 1 gill palm wine, ½ pint and ½ gill water, 1 tablespoon sugar.
1. Sieve the flour and salt into a basin.
2. Mix the palm wine, water and sugar, and add them to the flour.
3. Mix to a dough and knead on a clean floured table until smooth and elastic.
4. Put into a lightly floured basin, cover with a wet cloth and leave overnight.
5. Next morning mould into shapes required.
6. Prove in a warm place for 20 minutes.

7. Bake in a very hot oven to begin with, then lower the temperature.

N.B.—This quantity will make one big loaf (½ quartern) taking 1 hours to bake, or two smaller loaves taking ¾ hour to bake.

ACHIMOTA.

Pastry.

(Short Crust Pastry for pies, tarts).

Six tablespoons flour, 3 pieces butter the size of eggs, (dripping may be used), ½ teaspoon baking powder, 2 teaspoons sugar, pinch of salt, cold water. Put all dry ingredients into a bowl. With tips of fingers rub butter into flour till dry and like breadcrumbs. Add a little cold water and stir with fork till the dough will just stick. Turn on to floured board and roll out to size and thickness required. Bake in quick oven for 10 minutes, then cook slowly till crisp and brown.

MRS. SWAN, Tamale.

Peanut Crisps.

Cream together ½ cup of butter, and 1 cup sugar. Add 2 well beaten eggs, ground nutmeg to taste, 1 cup chopped peanuts, and sufficient flour mixed with 1 teaspoonful of baking powder to form a stiff batter. Beat the mixture well, and drop teaspoonfuls on a buttered baking tin, allowing plenty of room between as the biscuits spread in cooking. Bake 15 minutes in a quick oven.

MRS. NICHOLAS, Kumasi.

Plain Cake.

Two teacups of flour, ¼ lb. butter, 1½ cups of white sifted sugar, 3 eggs, ½ cup of milk, 2 teaspoons baking powder. Beat butter and sugar to cream, add beaten yolks of eggs then while well beaten, mix all together, then add milk, lastly the flour into which the baking powder has been added, pour into a greased tin and bake for 1 hours.

MRS. BROWNING, Cape Coast.

Potato Scones.

One teacup mashed potatoes, 1 teaspoon butter, 1 tablespoon milk, ¼ teaspoon salt, 1 teacup flour. Put potatoes, salt, milk, butter and half of the flour into a bowl—mash together till smooth. Turn out on board and knead in remainder of flour. Roll out thin, cut into four, and prick with fork. Bake on hot pan on both sides till brown.

MRS. SWAN, Tamale.

Quaker Oats Biscuits.

Half lb. Quaker oats, ¼ lb. butter or margarine, ¼ lb. Demerara sugar. Mix Quaker oats and sugar together, keep the butter all in one piece as far as possible, and work in the oats and sugar, press out to about half inch thick, and bake for about 20 to 30 minutes in a moderate oven.

If the mixture will bind enough, it can be cut into strips or rounds before baking; but if it is crumbly it is best to bake it in a shallow tin, mark it out into strips on taking it out from the oven, and leave in the tin till cold.

MRS. WILKINSON, Dunkwa.

Quaker Oats Biscuits.

Two ozs. sugar, 4 ozs. margarine, 2 ozs. flour, 6 ozs. Quaker oats, pinch of salt, flavouring. Beat sugar and margarine to a cream, add flavouring, mix well. Add flour and salt, then add Quaker oats; knead lightly till mixture sticks well. Turn on to floured board, roll out thinly, cut into fingers, bake in hot oven. Can be made with part Quaker Oats and part groundnuts.

MISS S. F. LAMONT, Krobo Girls' School.

Queen Buns.

The weight of 3 eggs in flour and sugar, the weight of 2 in butter, 1 teaspoonful lime juice, ½ teaspoonful baking powder. Beat together the eggs and the butter, add the sugar and continue beating, then the lime juice. Stir in gradually the flour in which the baking powder has been carefully mixed. Drop into small tins and bake in a quick oven.

ACHIMOTA.

Queen Cakes.

Six ozs. butter, 6 ozs. sugar, 8 ozs. flour, 3 ozs. currants, 4 English eggs, 2 teaspoonfuls baking powder, a little flavouring. Beat the butter to a cream, then add the sifted sugar and mix well. Well beat the eggs and pour on to the sugar and butter, mix again, lastly add the flour (well sifted), baking powder, currants and a little flavouring, if liked. Bake at once. This quantity makes about 40 small cakes.

MRS. BOOTH, Accra.

Raisin or Nut Bread.

Three cups of self-raising flour, ½ cup sugar, 1 cup of seeded raisins or almonds and walnuts, pinch of salt, 1 egg (2 Gold Coast eggs), 1 cup milk, 2 tablespoons butter. Soak raisins in boiling water, drain and dry in cloth; rub butter into flour, add raisins. Beat egg and sugar together and add milk—stir this into dry ingredients. Grease 3 Cerebos salt tins, pour the mixture in until tins are about half full. Bake 30 to 40 minutes.

ACHIMOTA.

Raspberry Sponge.

Three eggs and their weight in flour, butter and castor sugar, ½ teaspoonful Borwick's baking powder, raspberry jam. Sieve the flour. Cream butter and sugar, add by degrees flour and eggs. Beat well, mix baking powder with last flour, bake in a baking tray lined with greaseproof buttered paper. Spread evenly; bake 10 minutes in hot oven. Turn out on sugar paper and spread with jam. Cut the cake in two and fold together.

MRS. SAMPLES, Takoradi.

Rich Fruit Cake.

One lb. butter, 1 lb sugar, 1 lb. raisins, 1 lb. currants, 2 ozs. candied peel, 2 ozs. cherries, 1 lb. flour, 12 eggs. Beat butter and sugar together, add the eggs, well beaten, then mix in the fruit and the flour. Bake for 4 hours in a moderate oven.

MRS. ROTHWELL, Koforidua.

Sandwich Cake.

Four ozs. butter, 4 ozs. sugar, 4 ozs. flour, 4 eggs. Beat the butter and sugar together, then add the eggs, well beaten, separately; then add the flour. Bake in a moderate oven for 20 minutes.

MRS. ROTHWELL, Koforidua.

Standard Recipe for Sandwich Cake.

¼ lb. butter
¼ lb. sugar
3 ozs. flour
2 eggs
1 oz. corn flour
Pinch of baking powder.

Cream butter and sugar together, add eggs gradually beating well, then the flours and baking powder, a little at a time. Bake from 20 to 30 minutes. This makes two cakes 5 inches in diameter.

Fill with butter icing (2 spoons butter, 4 oz. sugar and vanilla) or coffee butter icing, or put chopped ginger in the cake mixture, or ginger syrup in the filling.

Orange—Add 1 orange rind finely grated to the cake mixture, when cool, fill with orange-flavoured butter icing and ice over the top with orange glace icing (½ lb. icing sugar, 1 orange juice), boiling water to mix and orange colouring.

MRS. OAKLEY, Accra.

256

Afternoon Tea Scones.

Four ozs. flour, 1 oz. butter, 1 tablespoon castor sugar, ½ teaspoon cream tartar, ¼ teaspoon carbonate soda, 1 egg, milk or water. Rub butter lightly into the flour, add the remaining dry ingredients. Beat and stir in the egg, adding milk or water to make the dough, roll out thin, cut into small rounds and bake about fifteen minutes in quick oven.

MRS. BROWNING, Cape Coast.

Scones.

One lb. flour, 3 ozs. butter, 4 teaspoons baking powder, pinch of salt and milk. Bake on griddle.

MRS. BROWNING, Cape Coast.

Scones (Plain).

½ lb. flour
½ oz. baking powder
1 oz. butter
½ gill sour cream or milk (Turn the milk by adding lime juice)
Pinch salt.

Rub in the butter, add salt and baking powder, mix to a stiff dough with sour milk, knead till smooth, roll out to ½-inch thick, cut into scones with small round cutter, bake on a greased tin in a hot oven for about fifteen minutes.

MRS. OAKLEY, Accra.

Shortbread.

One-quarter lb. castor sugar, ½ lb. butter, 1 lb. flour.
Put sugar and butter into a basin and cream very thoroughly with the hand, gradually work the flour into butter and sugar. Divide into cakes, pinch round edges with forefinger and prick on top with a fork. Paper a tin and put cakes on it, and bake in a moderate oven till a pale brown.

MRS. HENDERSON, Accra.

Shortbread.

One lb. flour, 1 lb. sifted sugar, ½ lb. butter. Knead into flour, roll out thinly, cut in pieces and bake quickly.

MRS. BROWNING, Cape Coast.

Shortbread Snippets.

Three-quarter lb. flour (plain), 6 ozs. butter, 4 ozs. castor sugar. Cream the butter with a wooden spoon till soft and white. Add a little sugar and a little flour alternately until all is used up. Knead the dough till quite smooth and evenly mixed (if it is much too dry add a very little water). Turn on to a floured board and roll out to about inch in thickness. Cut the dough into small squares, about inch. Place them on a greased tin and leave for 20 minutes before baking. Bake in a moderately hot oven for about 20 minutes. White the snippets are still hot roll them in castor sugar. These are a tea-time favourite, easily made in this climate, and keep well in a tin.

MRS. DRAKE, Tamale.

Scotch "Dreip" Scones.

(For breakfast.)

Eight ozs. flour, 1 teaspoon cream of tartar, ½ teaspoon bicarbonate of soda, 1 egg or 2 native eggs, milk, salt and pepper. Make a batter: Sieve flour into dish, break eggs into baking bowl, gradually add flour and milk, beating well with wooden spoon until air bubbles form and of a dropping consistency, add seasoning and lastly, cream of tartar and baking soda (do not beat after raising agency has been added), leave, if possible in a cool place for half to 1 hour.

Fry in smoking fat (use pan after frying bacon, it adds to flavour of scones)—a spoonful of batter dropped from point of spoon will form a scone, fry to a golden brown colour on both sides. Serve on hot plate immediately.

MRS. WILKINS, Kumasi.

Scotch Tea Scones.

Half lb. flour (2 teacups), 1 oz. butter, 1 teaspoon castor or granulated sugar, ½ teaspoon soda bicarbonate, 1 teaspoon cream of tartar, 1½ (about) teacupfuls milk (1 part tinned to 3 water). Mix flour, soda bicarbonate, cream of tartar and sugar; rub in butter; pour in the milk and mix lightly into a soft dough. Turn on to a well-floured board; roll out very lightly till about inch thick; cut into rounds with floured cutter or tumbler, place on floured tray, and bake in fairly quick oven.

MRS. BEVERIDGE, Accra.

Shrewsbury Biscuits.

¼ lb. butter
¼ lb. castor sugar
½ lb. flour
1 egg.
Grated rind of ½ orange, and a little juice, a pinch of salt.

Cream the butter and sugar, then add the beaten egg and half the flour. When well mixed, add the orange and rest of flour and salt. Roll the mixture very thin and cut into small biscuits. Bake in moderate oven until a pale fawn colour. The addition of currants makes a pleasant change.

MRS. ALLARD, Sekondi.

Quick Sour-milk Scones.

Half lb. flour, ¼ lb. dripping, butter or margarine, 3 ozs. sugar, 1 egg or a little sour milk. Mix, roll flat and cut into rounds; bake in a hot oven for a very few minutes. N.B.—This recipe is very useful for using up milk that has begun to turn sour

ACHIMOTA.

Sponge Cake.

Four egg yolks and 2 whites, 6 ozs. castor sugar boiled for 10 minutes in pint water, dessertspoonful marmalade and ¼ lb. flour. Beat the eggs, add boiled sugar, beat again for 15 minutes, add marmalade (jelly part only), stir in flour lightly. Bake for an hour or more in a slow oven.

LADY THOMAS.

Sponge Cake.

3 eggs
½ teaspoon grated lime
3 ozs. sugar.

Beat the eggs and sugar together until very stiff for 40 minutes. Add the flour gradually and fold in gently. On no account must it be beaten or the cake will be heavy. Put in a deep cake tin. Do not open oven door for ½ hour and when the cake begins to shrink from the sides of the tin it is ready.

MRS. KEAST, Accra.

Small Sponge Cakes.

(Should be eaten same day as cooked).
3 eggs
3 ozs. flour
4 ozs. castor sugar
Salad oil.

1. Oil some patty-pans and sift with castor sugar.
2. Separate yolks from whites.
3. Put yolks in a basin with castor sugar and whisk over hot water till thick and creamy—about ten minutes.
4. Whip whites stiffly.
5. Add flour and then whites to yolks, turning the mixture over the flour and stirring as little as possible.
6. Half-fill prepared tins and sprinkle a little castor sugar on the mixture.
7. Bake in a fairly quick oven about ten minutes.

MRS. BEACH JOHNSTONE, Accra.

Sponge Sandwich.

One cup of sifted flour, 1 teaspoonful baking powder, 1 cup of sifted sugar, 4 English eggs. Beat the eggs and the sugar together for 20 minutes. Lightly mix in the flour and baking powder. Bake in a cool oven about ½ hour. This quantity makes two good-sized sandwich cakes.

MRS. BOOTH, Accra.

Sugar Cracknels (Tea Cakes.)

Eight ozs. flour, 4 ozs. butter, 4 ozs. sugar, 2 yolks and 1 egg. Beat butter and sugar to cream. Sift flour and add it in turns with yolks and egg. Form rolls as thick as finger and 7-inch long. Form cracknels or rings. Brush them over with whites of eggs. Scatter coarse sugar over them. Bake on baking board light brown. (15 to 20 minutes.)

MISS GOETZ, Agogo.

Sweet Potato Cakes.

Make the same as potato cakes.

MISS SPEARS.

Swiss Roll.

The weight of 3 eggs in self-raising flour, butter and sugar. Prepare the tin as above. It is advisable to bring out a special Swiss roll tin which is very thick, and is less than 4 inch in depth. Mix the cake as in the method given, and bake in a very hot oven for 6 minutes.

Have ready a cloth (a tea-towel can be kept for the purpose) which has been wrung out in hot water, and turn the tin upside down on to this. Remove tin, and spread cake quickly with some warm jam. Trim the four sides with a sharp knife, and roll up with the help of the towel. It must be done quickly else the cake will break. Cool on a wire cake-stand, and when quite cold sieve a little icing sugar along the top of the roll.

MRS. KEAST, Accra.

Vinegar Cake.

(No egg required.)

One-quarter lb. flour, 2 ozs. butter, 2 ozs. sugar, 2 ozs raisins, 2 oz. candied peel, ½ teaspoonful baking powder, ½ teaspoonful carbonate soda, 1 teaspoonful spice, 1 teaspoonful malt vinegar, a little milk, pinch salt. Mix all together and bake in hot oven in buttered and floured tin.

MRS. C. E. DE B. BIDEN,

Walnut Bread.

Two breakfastcupfuls flour, ½ breakfastcupful sugar, ½ cupful chopped walnuts, 1 teaspoonful salt, 1 teaspoonful carbonate of soda, 2 teaspoonfuls cream of tartar. Mix all dry ingredients together, make into a soft dough with the milk. Bake in a slow oven for about an hour in a greased Quaker oats tin.

MISS SUTHERLAND, Aburi.

Wholemeal Sultana Scones.

Twelve tablespoons wholemeal flour, 2 tablespoons Demerara sugar, 3 tablespoons butter, 3 tablespoons sultanas, ½ teaspoon salt, 1 teaspoon bicarbonate soda, 1 teaspoon cream of tartar. Mix the salt well with the flour. Rub the butter into the flour, add sugar, sultanas, bicarbonate soda and cream of tartar. Mix to a stiff paste with cold milk, roll on to a floured board, divide in two portions and mark each into six sections. Brush with milk and bake on a greased tin for 15 to 20minutes.

MRS. FREELAWN, Asokore.

263

THE PRIZE RECIPE.

Take a little Time
Add a little thought
Procure a few details
Stir the imagination
Allow to simmer gently
Study the need for economy
Weigh the facts carefully
Buy a new 8 h.p. Ford Car
Add very little petrol
License for Two Pounds
Run 40 to 45 miles per gallon
Then taste the joys and thrills of
THE NEW 8 H.P. FORD CAR!

CONFECTIONERY

Banana Jam.

Twelve large bananas, 6 sweet oranges, 4 lemons, sugar. Peel and cut the bananas into thin round slices. Add ¾ lb. preserving sugar to each lb. of sliced bananas. Boil slowly for ¾ hour. Squeeze oranges and lemons in a glass squeezer. Use all the pulp that is pressed out excluding the pips.

N.B.—Large coarse bananas which are not too ripe should be used.

SISTER ANGELE, Cape Coast.

Cangika.

Fresh corn, 2 or 3 grated coconuts, sugar. Grate coconuts, mix with warm water, strain, and keep for use later, grate corn and mix with coconut, put in sugar and put on fire, boil until quite liquid, serve cold.

SISTER ANGELE, Cape Coast.

Chocolate Caramels.

One-quarter lb. chocolate, ¼ lb. butter, ¾ lb. castor sugar, 1 cup milk, vanilla essence. Boil milk for 10 minutes with the sugar, add grated chocolate, boil for 10 minutes longer and beat in creamed butter, add essence to taste, pour in buttered tin and cut in shapes.

MRS. BROWNING, Cape Coast.

Chocolate Fudge.

2 cups granulated sugar
1 cup milk
1 tablespoon butter
¼ cake unsweetened chocolate.

Put in sugar and milk, and when this becomes hot put in the chocolate, broken up into fine pieces. Stir constantly. Put in butter when it begins to boil. Stir until it forms soft ball in cold water. Then remove and beat until quite cool and pour into buttered tins.

MRS. SHIRER, Yendi.

Coconut Squares.

One coconut, 1 lb. granulated sugar, 1 teaspoon of butter 1 teaspoon milk, vanilla essence.

Grate one coconut (dry) add all ingredients together and put into saucepan, let it boil (stirring now and again) until the coconut begins to leave the sides of the saucepan and very little juice is left. Then drop on a wet board in flat cakes when it hardens—then turn them over and cut into squares. Don't put these sweets into a bottle or tin as they go rancid quickly.

MRS. EGG, Accra.

Coconut Toffee.

One coconut, ½ packet sugar, 1 lime. Cut the coconut very fine. Put in a shallow dish, and add 2 tablespoonfuls of cold water and the sugar. Bring to the boil and add the lime. Allow it to cook until brown, but keep stirring all the time. When a golden brown, turn out and divide immediately into pieces and let it cool. Serve when cold.

SISTER ANGELE, Cape Coast.

Fudge.

Twelve ozs. sugar, 2 ozs. butter or margarine, 1 small tin Ideal milk (6 ozs.), 1 tablespoon golden syrup. Put all into a saucepan, bring slowly to the boil and allow to boil half an hour, stirring occasionally. When it forms a soft ball on dropping it into cold water it is cooked. Take off fire and add three drops vanilla essence. Beat until creamy then turn into a greased tin and allow to set. Cut into squares before quite cold.

MRS. KEEVIL, Sekondi.

Grape-fruit Jam.

One grape-fruit, 1 lb. sugar (lump sugar), 1½ pints water. Cut the grape-fruit into quarters, and peel the skin off, now peel the rind

266

off leaving only the white part of the skin, this put to soak for 20 hours in water. After soaking take and rinse slightly in new water and cut into pieces of about half-inch square, put into a stewpan with 1½ pints of water and half the sugar, when it has boiled a little add the remainder of the sugar and cook slowly till it is reduced to half the volume, put into a 1-lb. jar. The whole should be quite firm jelly when cool. Cook slowly from the first.

MRS. BECKETT, Accra.

Grape-fruit Marmalade.[1]

Wash 1 large grape-fruit, 1 orange and 1 lemon, slice as thinly as possible, discarding all seeds, cover with 3 quarts cold water and let stand till next day, bring to the boil slowly and boil for 5 minutes, remove from the fire, add 5 lbs. sugar stirring till sugar is dissolved. Allow to stand in the pan till next day, boil slowly, stirring occasionally to prevent burning until marmalade is thick and rich. Makes 12 glasses.

MRS. HILL.

Grape-fruit Marmalade.

Two grape-fruit, 4 oranges, sugar and 1 leaf of gelatine. Slice the grape-fruit thinly, removing the inner pith and pips. Weigh it and to each 1 lb. add 3 pints of filtered water and the juice only of the oranges. Let the whole remain covered in an enamel vessel for 24 hours, then turn the whole preparation into an enamel saucepan and boil until tender. Let it remain another 24 hours. Weigh again and add to each lb. of pulp 1 lb. of sugar and bring it gently to boiling point; skim and cook for about an hour, then add the gelatine and boil for half an hour until it thickens and sets, when tested in a cold saucer. Orange Marmalade can be made in the same way, only taking 4 oranges and the juice of 2 limes.

MRS. MILNE, Winneba.

---

[1] This appears to be a sweet dessert rather than a preserve. DS

Ginger Pawpaw Jam.

Four ozs. ginger, ½ lb. prepared pawpaw, (green pawpaw) 1½ lbs. lump sugar. Scrape all the skin from the ginger and boil for 2 hours, remove the ginger and put the prepared pawpaw and half a lb. of sugar into the ginger juice. If the liquid is not enough to cover the pawpaw some hot water should be added. The pawpaw must be peeled, and the seeds, etc., scraped from the inside. Cut it into pieces of about quarter-inch square. When the pawpaw has boiled till tender add the remainder of the sugar and cook slowly till the syrup thickens, or until the syrup is just sufficient to cover the fruit.

MRS. BECKETT, Accra.

Goa or Guava Jelly.

Wash nearly ripe goas, cut them up roughly and remove the tops. Cover them with water and boil, let it drip through a jelly-bag all night. Add 1 lb. of sugar to each pint of juice. Take from fire when it is just beginning to jelly on the spoon.

MRS. MARTIN, Agogo.

Groundnut Biscuits.

Two egg whites, 8-10 ozs. castor sugar, minced groundnut. Beat up the eggs and sugar until quite stiff. Stir in very slowly enough minced groundnut to make a fairly stiff mixture. Drop the mixture on to greased paper in little heaps and bake in a fairly slow oven until the biscuits are set and light brown in colour. If less groundnut is added the biscuits will be more meringue-like.

Groundnut Filling for Biscuits or Cakes.

Take equal quantities of groundnut (minced) and castor sugar and mix with beaten white of egg. Add a few drops of almond essence and this may be used as a substitute, for almond paste.

MRS. GIDDINGS, Wenchi.

Groundnut Toffee.

Groundnuts, 2d. worth, sugar ¼ packet, 1 lemon. Roast the groundnuts and clean them. Put the sugar into a pot and fry until brown. Pour in the groundnuts and stir until cooked. Divide at once into pieces, tie them in white clean paper and leave to cool.

SISTER ANGELE, Cape Coast.

Guava Jam.

Ripe guavas, sugar and limes. Top and tail the guavas, cut them in halves and scoop out the centre with a teaspoon, to each 1 lb. of fruit add 1 lb. of sugar and ½ lb. of grated lime rind and boil for 4 hours, skimming all the time.

MRS. MILNE, Winneba.

Guava Jelly.

Wipe and cut the guavas in half, just cover with water, boil to an absolute pulp, then strain it all night, next morning measure liquid, put in saucepan and heat it, then add ¾ lb. sugar to each pint liquid, let it come to the boil and then add 4 tablespoons lemon juice to each pint, boil ½ hour to a pint or till it stiffens on a cold plate.

LADY THOMAS.

Guava Jelly.

Four lbs. of ripe guavas, 6 pints of cold filtered water, 1 dessertspoonful of whisky, sugar and 1 gelatine leaf. Do not cut the guavas, just break them in halves into an enamel saucepan and add the water, and allow this to remain overnight 12 hours, then boil until tender (about an hour) and stand this aside until the same evening, make a bag of mosquito netting and strain all night (squeeze very gently or the jelly becomes thick).

To every pint of juice add 1½ lbs. of sugar and boil for 1 hour skimming meanwhile. Add the gelatine about ten minutes before it is done. See that the jelly is kept boiling otherwise it will not set.

MRS. MILNE, Winneba.

Guava Jelly.

Some half-ripe guavas, fairly sour ones are best, sugar (granulated or lump sugar should be used). Wash the guavas thoroughly and cut off the top and the stern ends, cut them into quarters, put into a stewpan and cover with cold water, bring to the boil and boil till the fruits are tender, they should then be strained and squeezed through a cloth until nearly all the juice is extracted from the fruit. Strain twice to ensure having no grits. Measure the juice and put into a saucepan, allowing ½ lb. of sugar to every pint of juice, dissolve the sugar before putting it on the fire, bring to the boil quickly and keep boiling as quickly as possible until, when a drop of the jelly is tried in cold water in a saucer it does not dissolve early, and no film is left on the surface of the water.

If a film-like layer of jelly is left floating on the surface of the water when the other part of the drop has sunk, the jelly is not boiled enough. Perfect jelly should be light red and translucent. If it is dark and cloudy, but not " thick" and sticky it has been boiled too slowly, if dark, thick and sticky, it has been over-boiled—made too concentrated.

MRS. BECKETT, Accra.

Guava Jelly.

1. Wash the guavas thoroughly.

2. Cut each fruit into four.

3. Put fruit into saucepan with enough water to cover the bottom of the pan and stew very slowly until all juice has run from fruit.

4. Wring out a cloth in hot water and hang over a basin. Pour the fruit and juice into the cloth and allow to drip overnight. Do not stir or squeeze or jelly will be cloudy.

5. Measure juice carefully and allow ¾ lb. lump sugar to every pint of juice.

6. Put sugar and juice in saucepan and allow to heat; slowly, not boil, till all sugar is melted.

7. Boil quickly, removing scum as it rises, till jelly sets when a little is removed and cooled.

8. Pour into clean warm jam jars and screw up top immediately.

MRS. BEACH JOHNSTONE, Accra.

270

Guava Jelly.

Take guavas, better not too ripe, wash thoroughly, ends may be cut off, but do not peel. Place in enamel or aluminium saucepan; add sufficient filtered water just to cover them; boil till quite soft. Pour into jelly-bag and allow to strain for some hours. To each pint of the juice add 1 lb. sugar; allowing juice of ½ lemon to about 30 guavas, After sugar and lemon juice are added, boil quickly for about 15 minutes, or more, till it becomes a deep red and thickens when dropped on a cool plate. Pour out into jam jars. Cover when cold.

MRS. BEVERIDGE, Accra.

Helensborough Toffee.

One tin condensed milk (sweetened), 1 lb. sugar, a little Ideal milk, 1 dessertspoonful butter. Put sugar, butter and a little Ideal milk in pan and stir till warm. Then add the condensed milk. Boil till hard and flavour with vanilla essence. Before it gets too cold, cut into squares.

MRS. CRANSTON, Accra.

Orange Marmalade.

Six lbs. preserving sugar, 6 Seville oranges, 1 lemon, 6 pints water. Wipe oranges and lemon, and divide into 6 or 8 parts. Remove pips and tie them in a piece of muslin. Then soak in a half pint of boiling water. Cut oranges and lemon into thin shreds, and put into 5½ pints of cold water. Boil until foam appears on top then take from fire and put aside for 24 hours. Place on fire again, add water from the pips and sugar. Cook until a little of the jam will jelly on a cold plate. Then put in dry jars, cover and store in a dry place.

Jams and Marmalade.

Should be covered down hot, making a paste with flour and cold water if no tin cover to the bottle, then with 3 layers of grease-proof paper, each layer covered with paste made from the above, which will harden when cold and the jars must be perfectly dry.

MRS. MILNE, Winneba.

271

Lemon Curd.

Half lb. sugar, 4 ozs. butter, 3 English eggs, 1 good-size lemon or 3 limes. Place butter and sugar into brass or aluminium pan to simmer. Well beat the eggs, add to the mixture, lastly add well-strained lime juice. Let all simmer very slowly 15 minutes. Try a little on cold plate to see if the mixture is setting.

MRS. BOOTH, Accra.

Lemon Curd.

Two eggs, 1 lemon or 2 limes, 1 heaped tablespoonful of butter, 4 lumps of sugar. Beat the eggs well in a breakfast cup. Add the grated rind of the lemon or limes and three-quarters of the juice, butter and sugar. Put some cold water in a saucepan on the stove and stand the cup inside. Bring the water to the boil, being careful not to allow any water to get inside the cup. Stir the contents of the cup until it melts and begins to thicken, then take the cup out of the saucepan and allow the contents to cool; it is then ready for use.

MRS. FIELDGATE, Koforidua.

Lime Cream.

One lb. loaf sugar, 4 ozs. butter, the yolks of 6 eggs, the juice of 6 or 8 limes, a little finely shredded candied peel or grated coconut. Put the sugar, butter, shredded peel or coconut and lime juice into a stewpan and stir until the sugar is dissolved. Beat the yolks of eggs, add them to the contents in pan and stir and cook very slowly until the mixture thickens, if it does not get as thick as desired, add one teaspoonful of corn flour mixed to a smooth paste with a little water and stir. This is very nice for tart fillings or served with steamed sponge puddings.

MRS. HORSEY, Obuasi, Ashanti.

Lime Curd.

Six ozs. sugar, 3 ozs. butter, rind and juice of 2 large limes, 3 eggs.

1. Put butter, sugar, and grated lime rind into a pan.
2. Beat up the eggs in a basin.
3. Add the lime juice to the eggs.

272

4. Strain into the pan.

5. Heat gently until the sugar dissolves.

6. Bring to the boil, stirring all the time.

7. Boil for 2 or 3 minutes.

8. Put into a warm jar and tie down.

N.B.—This quantity fills a 1-lb. jar. It will keep several weeks if allowed to boil thoroughly.

ACHIMOTA.

Lime Toffee (Sweet Dish).

(Ewe Anyata).

One-quarter lb. packet of sugar, breakfastcupful fresh water, teaspoonful of the juice of lime, ground ginger to taste.

1. Turn sugar from packet into an aluminium saucepan.

2. Pour the water over it and boil for about ten minutes.

3. Add lime and ginger and cook to a tigernut brown

4. Wet a small round calabash and pour the brown sugar into it.

5. Let it stand in a cool place while the sugar gets cool and tough.

6. Take it out from the calabash and start to draw with both hands.

7. When you draw to about a yard long put the two ends in your hands together. After this you will get another end below. Take this and draw again.

8. Draw till the sugar gets a white colour, cut into pieces and serve.

SISTER ANTONIA, Keta.

Mango Jam.

1 lb. mango pulp
¾ lb. sugar
3 limes, juice only
¼ gill water.

1. Boil fruit and water till soft, add lime juice.

2. Rub through sieve, weigh, boil up and add sugar.

3. When thick, dish in hot, dry jars.

MISS SPEARS.

273

Marmalade.

Four bitter oranges, 1 sweet orange, 1 lemon, 4 lbs. sugar, 2 quarts water. Cut up the fruit, boil the water, add the fruit and boil for 1 hours, add the sugar and boil for 1 hour. If bitter oranges unobtainable, 6 sweet oranges and 2 limes, do just as well.

MRS. C. E DE B. BIDEN.

Milk Caramels.

Three-quarter lb. butter, 1 lb. moist sugar, 1 tin Swiss milk, ½ lb. golden syrup. Put butter in saucepan to melt, add sugar, milk and well-mixed syrup, boil gently over slow fire stirring well, turn a little in cold water, it is done when it sets like caramel, not toffee.

MRS. BROWNING, Cape Coast.

Orange Conserve.

Six oranges, 1 lemon, 2 lbs. sugar, ¼ pint hot water. Remove peel from the oranges in large pieces. Cover it with boiling water and boil until tender. Drain and scrape off the white piths. Mince the orange rind and scrape and grate the lemon rind. Cut the pulp into small pieces and throw away all the pips. Bring the hot water and sugar to the boil, add the fruit pulp and grated rind, and cook until it has the consistency of thick syrup when dropped on a cold dish.

SISTER ANGELE, Cape Coast.

Pawpaw Jam.

1 large pawpaw
2 cups sugar
1 cup water
1 handful root ginger.

1. Prepare pawpaw, cut into small dice.
2. Boil water and sugar, add pawpaw.
3. Wash ginger, put into muslin, add to jam.
4. Boil until mashed and thick.
5. Dish in hot, dry jars.

Note.—This is a cheap jam suitable for school use, it is popular with our girls, it will not keep long.

MISS SPEARS.

Pawpaw Jam.

Cut up ripe pawpaw in inch cubes. Add an equal amount of sugar, and either 2 or 3 pieces of preserved ginger or a little ginger root from market, cook over a slow fire until it is jammy.

MISS SPEARS.

Pine-apple Jam.

1¼ lb. pineapple (one pineapple)
2 limes
¼ pint water
1¼ lb. sugar.

1. Peel and chop pineapple, discarding tough inner core.
2. Cut thinly the rind off lime and squeeze out juice, put peel into muslin bag and boil with other ingredients.
3. Make syrup of sugar and water, add fruit and lime.
4. Boil about one hour till pineapple is soft and juice clear.
5. Dish in hot, dry jars.

MISS SPEARS.

Pine-apple Jam.

One pineapple (about one lb. when peeled, etc.), 2 lbs. sugar. Peel the pineapple and cut away all eyes carefully, chop, or slice thinly, or cut into small pieces as preferred, do not use the centre core, put the pulp into a saucepan with enough water to cover and 1 lb. of lump sugar, bring very slowly to the boil and keep covered till the pineapple is tender, add the other lb. of sugar, and when dissolved uncover, and cook slowly till syrup is thick. Bottle hot.

MRS. BECKETT, Accra.

Pine-apple Jam.

Any number of pine-apples and ¾ lb. sugar to every lb. of pine-apple. Mash and pound the pine-apples very well so as to obtain a pulp. Mix with sugar and put on the fire to cook. When the substance becomes clear, it may be taken from the fire and allowed to cool. Place in clean dry pots and keep in a dry place.

SISTER ANGELE, Cape Coast.

Pumpkin and Pine-apple Jam.

One pumpkin, 1 pine-apple, sugar, ¼ lb. green ginger. Peel and cut the pumpkin into small dice. Peel and core the pine-apple and put through a mincer, pound the ginger, weigh all and to each 1 lb. of fruit add ¾ lb. sugar and boil gently for about 1 to 1½ hours. Skim while boiling.

MRS. MILNE, Winneba.

Shrewsbury Biscuits.

Half lb. flour, ¼ lb. butter, ¼ lb. castor sugar. Mix together and wet it with one egg, roll out as thin as paper and bake.

MRS. BROWNING, Cape Coast.

Tablet.

Two lbs. granulated sugar, ¼ lb. butter, 1 teacup milk, 1 tin Nestlé's Swiss milk, 1 teaspoon vanilla essence. Put sugar, butter, and milk into a pan and bring to the boil. Boil 10 minutes stirring all the time, add Swiss milk and boil for half an hour. Add vanilla essence, stir for a few minutes quickly, and pour into buttered tins.

MRS. HENDERSON, Accra.

Tangerine Marmalade.

One dozen tangerine oranges, 3 small lemons or limes, sugar and water. Cut up oranges and lemons very finely removing pips. Put the fruit in a bowl after weighing and to every lb. of fruit add 2 pints water. Leave till next day Boil hard for half an hour and leave till next day. Weigh the marmalade and to each lb. allow 1½ lbs. sugar. Boil all together for of an hour, pour into jars and cover at once.

This marmalade should be a beautiful bright colour nearly transparent.

MRS. NORTHCOTE, Accra.

Tangerine Marmalade.

Twelve Tangerine oranges, sugar (1 lb. to 1 lb. fruit) and 1 pint of water, 1 lemon. Wipe and dry 12 Tangerine oranges, put them in a pan and barely cover with water. Let them cook until the rind is quite soft and easily pierced. Drain off the water, peel the oranges, remove the pips and soak them in cold water for 12 hours. Pound the pulp up, cut the peel in very thin shreds. Allow 1 lb. sugar for every lb. of fruit and each pint of juice. Put the sugar, the water from the pips and the strained juice of 1 lemon to boil to a thick syrup, then add the pulp and the rind and boil from 30 to 35 minutes.

MISS EVELYN BELLAMY, Cape Coast,

Tomato Jam.

One lb. ripe tomatoes, 1 lb. sugar, pint water.
1. Wipe the tomatoes, put into a basin, then cover with boiling water.
2. Skin tomatoes, cut into quarters and remove hard pieces at the end, and some of the seeds.
3. Boil the skins and seeds in the water for hour and strain.
4. Put sugar, strained liquid and tomato into pan and boil till it will set.
5. Dish in hot, dry jars.

MISS SPEARS.

Tomato Jam.

Tomatoes, sugar, cinnamon or ginger flavouring. Put the ripe tomatoes into a basin and pour over them boiling water and leave for five minutes, then peel and weigh and to each lb. of pulp add 1 lb. of sugar and flavouring and boil for 1½ hours. This makes a delicious jam for tarts.

MRS. MILNE, Winneba.

Treacle Toffee.

Half lb. butter, ½ lb. treacle (teacupful), 1 lb. brown sugar. Put treacle and butter on to melt, add sugar. Stir all the time and boil rapidly for 15 minutes. Take off fire and pour quickly into buttered tins. When cooling, mark into squares.

MRS. HENDERSON, Accra.

BEVERAGES.

Claret Cup.

(Eight to ten persons.)

One bottle claret, 1 dessertspoon sugar, rind of 1 lime, 3 slices orange, 3 slices lime, 1 slice cucumber peel, 1 teaspoonful angostura bitters, ¾ gin and bitters glass brandy, 1 gin and bitters glass Benedictine, ½ gin and bitters kirsch, 1 wine-glass sherry, 1 sprig mint. Mix in jug and allow to steep for 5 hours. Remove slices of orange, lime and peels. Add 10 cubes of ice and dilute before serving, with 30 per cent to 50 per cent, according to taste, of cold soda water.

MRS. MOOR, Koforidua.

Cocoa Syrup.

Boil together 2 cups sugar, ¼ cup cocoa and 1 cup boiling water for 5 minutes, add 1 teaspoon vanilla when cold. Store in a preserve jar. When using add required quantity of milk.

ACHIMOTA.

Concentrated Lemonade.

Rind and juice of 6 small lemons or limes, ½ oz. citric or tartaric acid, 2 lbs. sugar (put less if too sweet), 1½ pints boiling water. Put rind (peeled very thinly) and juice into a jug with the sugar and acid. Pour over 1½ pints of boiling water and leave for 24 hours, stirring occasionally. Strain, bottle and cork tightly, one tablespoon in a glass of water or soda water makes a refreshing drink. It will keep fresh about a fortnight.

MISS BARCHI, Sekondi.

Egg Orangeade.

1 egg
2 oranges
Sugar
1 lemon
Filtered water or soda water.

Pour a well beaten egg into a tumbler, add orange and lemon juice and sugar, water to fill glass.

MRS. COE, Wenchi.

Fruit Punch.

Half cup lime juice, 1 cup orange juice, grated rind of ½ orange, 1 quart water, ¾ cup sugar. Cook sugar and water for 3 minutes. Cool, mix with grated rind and juice, add any variation, e.g.

1. One cup grated pineapple, 1 pint soda water.
2. Quarter cup finely chopped preserved ginger, 1 bottle ginger ale, 1 quart tea, ½ cup maraschino cherries finely chopped.

MRS. FRASER, Achimota.

Fruit Punches.

Basic Recipe:—½ cup lemon juice, 1 cup orange juice, 1 tablespoon grated lemon rind, grated rind of ½ orange, 1 quart water, ¾ cup sugar. Cook sugar and water for 3 minutes, cool: mix with orange and lemon juice and grated rind—to this add any of the following variations:—

No. 1.— 1 quart ginger ale, cup preserved ginger cut fine.

No. 2.—1 quart tea, cup maraschino cherries cut fine.

No. 3.—1 glass currant jelly dissolved in 1 cup hot water, cook and add ¼ cup mint finely minced.

No. 4.—1 cup grated pineapple, 1 pint soda water, more sugar if necessary.

No. 5.—2 cups water-melon pulp, ½ cup raisins cut fine, ½ cup sugar.

No. 6.—3 tablespoons grated cucumber rind, 1 pint loganberry juice, ¼ cup sugar.

MRS. FRASER, Achimota.

Ginger and Lemon Drink.

Two lbs. castor sugar, 1 oz. tartaric acid, 1 bottle essence ginger, 1 bottle essence lemon, 1 quart boiling water. Pour boiling water on the sugar. When cool, add essences and acid and stir well. Bottle and use as required.

MRS. LOCKHART, Mfantsipim, Cape Coast.

Ginger Wine.

Three drachms of essence of cayenne, 3 drachms of essence of ginger, ¾ oz. tartaric acid, 3 lbs. loaf sugar, 1 dessertspoonful of essence of lemon, 1d. worth of burnt sugar. Mix all together. Then pour 5 quarts of boiling water over mixture. Serve when quite cold.

SISTER ANGELE, Cape Coast.

Lemon Squash.

One oz. tartaric acid, 2 oranges (limes or lemons), 2 lbs. sugar, 1 pint boiling water. Put all into a jug, add boiling water and stir until dissolved, when cold, bottle.

MRS. HILL, Accra.

Lemonade.

Six lemons, 3 pints boiling water, 6 ozs. loaf sugar. Wipe the lemons well. Take off the rind and put in a jug with sugar. Squeeze the juice in and pour boiling water over. Stir with a wooden spoon. Cover the jug with a cover or a clean cloth and allow the lemonade to get cold.

SISTER ANGELE, Cape Coast.

Orange Beverage.

Six oranges, 1 tablespoonful pearl barley, 1 pint of water. Place the barley in a teacup and cover with boiling water for 1 minute, then drain that water away, place steeped barley in a saucepan and add 1 pint of cold water, simmer gently for hour. Squeeze juice of oranges and place in jug, add barley water. This will be found to be a most refreshing drink—iced, it is much improved.

MRS. PANK, Cape Coast.

Orange Syrup.

Eight oranges, 4 lb. sugar, 2½ pints water, 1 oz. citric acid. Scrape off peels of oranges with lump sugar, or peel oranges and cut peels into small pieces. Put all in basin and add rest of sugar and water. Dissolve citric acid in one glass of water and add it. Leave the mixture until next day. Stir it up now and again. Strain the syrup and fill it in bottles, cork them up well. The syrup can be prepared in the same way with 4 oranges and 4 lemons.

MISS COUTZ, Agogo.

Orange Vermouth.

Juice of 4 oranges into a glass and add wine-glass of vermouth.

MRS. COE, Wenchi.

Pine-apple Lemonade.

Take ½ cup of grated pine-apple (or the juice) and the juice of 1 lime. Add 2 tablespoonfuls of sugar and ½ cup boiling water to dissolve the sugar. When cool, add 1 cup of ice-cold water and serve.

MRS. McELROY, Accra.

Rum Cocktail.

One glass lime juice, 2 glasses sugar, 3 glasses rum, glasses water or 2 glasses water and 2 lumps ice. Shake well—put on ice— and shake well again before serving.

MRS. NORTHCOTE, Accra.

Sour-sop Drink.

Sour-sop (about 2 lbs.), sugar, 1 pint water, $\frac{1}{3}$ pint evaporated milk. Peel and skin the sour-sop, removing any grits. Divide the fruit in half by pulling it apart with two forks. Take the centre core out, then remove all the seeds, pulling at them with two forks is best. Do not use a steel knife. When all the seeds are out put the pulp into a jug and add the water. Stir or swizzle till the juice is "washed" from the pulp. Then strain and squeeze the pulp. Add the milk to the juice and sweeten to taste. Iced, it is a cool refreshing drink.

MRS. BECKETT, Accra.

Tea Punch.

(Hot Weather Drink).

Make sweetened lime juice to taste with boiling water and pour this over the usual quantity of tea leaves, instead of plain boiling water. Allow the liquid to stand until cold and then strain off and serve in tall glasses with slices of lime on top and chips of ice (if available).

MRS. McELROY, Accra.

Tennis Cocktail.

One bottle of Crown Bird ginger beer, 1 bottle of Crown Bird soda water. Several drops of angostura bitters, gin. Get a large jug, shake the angostura bitters in first, then pour some gin, add ginger beer, and then soda water.

MRS. HILDITCH, Tarkwa.

White Wine Cup.

One bottle white wine, 1 bottle soda water, 2 liqueur-glasses brandy, 1 liqueur-glass curaçao, 1 large or several small lumps ice. Stir up well and add pieces of fruit (pineapple, orange, etc.) and a few slices cucumber. Put on ice till required.

MRS. NORTHCOTE, Accra.

MISCELLANEOUS

Ablemamu.

(Ablemamu is a flour made by the natives from maize corn. The corn is first fried and then pounded into a fine flour. Cook can get it very cheaply from market. A very good baking powder bread can be made from it.)

One cup white flour, 1 cup ablemamu, ¼ cup sugar, 1 teaspoon salt, 5 teaspoons baking powder. Sift all together and add a tablespoon melted lard or butter, ½ cup milk. Mix and bake about 20 minutes in a hot oven.

Note:—In all these recipes "cup" means about teacupful or about half of a pint; except the last recipe, "ablemamu bread," there "cup" means a coffee cup or pint.

MISS SPEARS, Methodist Girls' High School.

Acras.

(A Native Chop.)

Three ozs. salt fish (Bombay duck before it has been baked), 6 small onions, 2 tomatoes about 3 ozs. altogether, 3 ozs. flour, 1 teaspoonful baking powder, pepper, milk to mix. Boil the fish for a while (10 minutes), take it out of the water and take away any skin and bones. Put into a fufu beater, and beat until the fish is all fine threads. To this, add the chopped tomato and onion and pepper, mix well and add the flour and baking powder. When thoroughly mixed, add sufficient milk to make a paste-like substance. Form into balls and fry in hot fat, in a chip saucepan in 4 inches of fat.

MRS. BECKETT, Accra.

Asparagus Tips Sandwiches (Rolled).

Cut bread into slices, remove the crust—butter and then put a thin layer of mayonnaise cream on each slice. Cut asparagus tip in half lengthwise, put same on bread then roll. Stick with orange sticks and place them in a damp napkin; keep for an hour or two before serving when sticks can be removed.

MRS. EGG, Accra.

Apple Rings (Baked)

4 apples
½ cup water
Small piece stick cinnamon
1 tablespoonful lemon juice
1 teaspoonful cloves
½ cup castor sugar.

Wipe and core the apples. Cut into thick slices. Place in a buttered baking dish. Boil sugar, water and spices together for 5 minutes. Add lemon juice and strain over apples. Bake till tender, basting occasionally. If liked the syrup can be coloured with a little cochineal before straining over the apples. These apple rings are delicious served with cold pork or ham. Enough for 4.

MRS. LLOYD WILLIAMS, Tamale.

Banana Chutney.

Twelve bananas, 1 lb. tomatoes (green or ripe), ½ lb. onions, ½ lb. brown sugar, ½ lb. raisins (may be left out), ½ pint vinegar, 1 tablespoon salt, 1 or 2 peppers.

1. Cut up the bananas and tomatoes.
2. Chop the onions and raisins.
3. Put all the ingredients into a black native pot.
4. Bring slowly to the boil.
5. Boil gently until the consistency of jam, and all the ingredients suspended (about 4 to 2 hours).

N.B.—This quantity makes over 2 lbs. and will keep indefinitely.

ACHIMOTA.

Béchamel Sauce.

In a small saucepan put a little butter, then flour and mix well with wooden spoon, add a little milk to a smooth cream and salt to taste. Bring to boil.

ACHIMOTA.

Bouquet Garni.

1 sprig of parsley
½ teaspoon mixed herbs
1 bay leaf
A few peppercorns.
1 blade mace.
Tie all together in a piece of muslin.

MRS. BEACH JOHNSTONE, Accra,

Brandy Butter.

6 ozs. butter
1½ teaspoons vanilla essence
12 ozs. castor sugar
3 dessertspoons brandy.

Beat the butter until creamy. Add the sugar sieved, 1 teaspoon at a time, and beat well. Beat until the mixture is white. Add the flavouring and put on ice. To serve, stand dish in a larger dish surrounded with chopped ice. Sufficient for 16 persons.

MRS. KEAST, Accra.

Bread Sauce.

½ pint milk
2 ozs. breadcrumbs
1 oz. butter or margarine
1 blade mace
1 onion stuck with cloves
Seasoning.

1. Simmer onion and mace in the milk for ½ hour or until milk is well flavoured.
2. Strain and return to pan.
3. Add bread, butter and seasoning, stand aside half an hour, re-heat and serve.

MRS. BEACH JOHNSTONE, Accra.

Baking Powder.

Four tablespoons corn flour, 4 tablespoons carbonate soda, 3 tablespoons tartaric acid, mix all these together, then pass through a sieve twice and put into airtight tins.

LADY THOMAS.

Red Pickled Cabbage.

As it is sometimes possible to obtain red cabbage it can be pickled and kept in the Frigidaire. One small red cabbage, 1 lb. beetroot cooked, or tinned beetroot, 1 lb. Portugal onions, 1 quart spiced vinegar. Take any decayed and outside leaves from the cabbage. Cut it in quarters and remove the hard stick from the centre. Take each quarter and cut it across in fine shreds. Cut up in thin slices the beetroot and onions, and lay alternate slices of cabbage, beetroot and onions on a large dish with a liberal layer of coarse salt between each layer. Cover with another dish and put in Frigidaire for 24 hours. Strain off the liquid. Boil the vinegar and fill jars with pickle. Pour the vinegar into them and cover. If spiced vinegar is unobtainable, add a few peppercorns and 2 or 3 cloves to the vinegar before boiling. Should the pickle be a poor colour add a little carmine.

MRS. KEAST, Accra.

Date Chutney.

Half lb. stoned dates, 2 ozs. raisins or sultanas, 2 ozs. onions, 2 ozs. sugar, oz. salt, 3 peppers, pint vinegar. Stone and chop the dates. Clean sultanas, chop onions very fine, put all in a saucepan with the vinegar and gently simmer until soft. Add the sugar, salt and peppers. Bottle while hot. N.B.—Banana chutney is made in the same way.

MISS EVELYN BELLAMY, Cape Coast.

Date Nuts.

Two cups flour, 1 cup sugar, ½ lb. butter, 1 egg, 1 teaspoon soda, 2 teaspoonfuls cream of tartar, and enough milk to mix stiffly. Roll out, and cut in pieces large enough to roll a date in and bake in a moderate oven.

ACHIMOTA.

Devilled Groundnuts.

Skin some groundnuts. Make some salad oil very hot in a frying pan. (There should be blue smoke arising before the nuts are put in.) Fry a nice light brown, then strain off the oil, and throw them into a cloth which has been sprinkled with salt and cayenne pepper. Toss them about.

MRS. EMMETT, Accra.

Garri.[1]

Six eggs, garri—5d., lard—3d., tomatoes, onions, pepper, salt. Beat the eggs, add the ground tomatoes, pepper, salt, onions. Beat again and mix well. Heat the lard and pour in the mixture, and stir until well cooked. Pour water on the garri, add in salt and let it rise. Then add to the fried eggs and stir well until cooked. Turn into a dish and serve hot or cold.

SISTER ANGELE, Cape Coast.

---

[1] *Garri* or *gari* is a granular food made from cassava. DS

Gboma Detsi

One chicken, cabbage—3d., onions—1d., tomatoes—1d., pepper and salt. Cut and boil the chicken. Next remove from soup and fry meat lightly in hot lard or dripping. Add onions, tomatoes, pepper. When fairly cooked, pour soup over it and allow to simmer. Finally add the cooked cabbage and allow all to simmer for some minutes.

SISTER ANGELE, Cape Coast.

Groundnut Oil.

Six lbs. groundnuts, 2 buckets of cold water.

1. Pound raw groundnuts.
2. Grind it and divide into two buckets.
3. Mix gradually with water until bucket is full. Do the same to second bucket.
4. Allow to stand for 7 hours until oil rises to top.
5. Skim off oil.
6. Put into small saucepan, two tablespoons water, add oil.
7. Boil water and oil until the water evaporates and leaves the oil.
8. Pour oil into a bottle and cork it.

MISS SPEARS.

Horse-radish Sauce (Hot).

Half pint white sauce made with stock only, to which 1 teaspoon lemon juice has been added, 4 tablespoons grated horse-radish, 1 tablespoon vinegar, 2 tablespoons cream or milk.

1. Add horse-radish to sauce.
2. Add cream and vinegar, reheat and serve with roast beef.

Horse-radish Sauce (Cold).

4 tablespoons grated horseradish
1½ tablespoons vinegar

Pinch salt

1 gill whipped cream or 1 gill milk thickened with 1 teaspoon corn flour.

½ teaspoon dry mustard

½ teaspoon sugar

2 yolks of eggs.

1. Put the horse-radish in cold water until firm.
2. Scrub well, peel and grate finely.
3. Mix well together the mustard, sugar, yolks and salt.
4. Gradually add cream or vinegar and lastly horseradish.

MRS. BEACH JOHNSTONE, Accra.

Konkada.

Two grated coconuts, 1 packet sugar (3d.), 2 lime leaves, 1 breakfast cup rice or tapioca. Mix the grated coconut with a cup of water. Squeeze, strain, and put aside to be used lastly. Mix the coconut again with 3 cups of warm water and strain. Add the sugar and the lime leaves to the milk and bring to the boil. Add the rice or tapioca, and bring to the boil for 20 minutes stirring it occasionally. Add the first cup of coconut milk, and let it boil for 20 minutes. Simmer for 5 minutes and serve hot or cold.

SISTER ANGELE, Cape Coast.

Millet Porridge.

Fresh millet, little salt. Grind the millet into fine powder. Steep in cold water and add boiling water and pinch of salt. Let it cook very slowly until done, stirring frequently to prevent burning.

MRS. STEELE, Tamale.

Green Mango Chutney.

Green mangoes, 1 pint vinegar, 1 lb. sugar, ½ lb. stoned raisins, ½ lb. currants, 6 oz. green ginger, ½ teaspoonful of cinnamon, ½ teaspoonful of nutmeg, 4 ozs. salt. Peel and slice the mangoes thinly, sprinkle over them the salt, let them remain 24 hours, then drain well.

Make a syrup by boiling ½ lb. vinegar and sugar together. Put the remainder of the vinegar into a preserving pan, add the mangoes, boil up, simmer gently for about 10 minutes, then add the raisins, currants, ginger, cinnamon and nutmeg. Cook very slowly for half an hour, add the syrup gradually stir and boil the mixture until the greater part of the syrup is absorbed and then bottle and cork immediately to exclude the air.

MRS. MILNE, Winneba.

Mango Chutney.

Thirty green mangoes, 2 lbs. of sugar. ½ lb. of salt, 2 lbs. of stoned raisins, 2 ozs. of green ginger, 2 ozs. of onions, 2 ozs. of peppers, 1½ pints of vinegar.

Peel and slice the mangoes and put them with the raisins, peppers, ginger and onions through the mincing machine. Then add the sugar and salt to the vinegar. Bring to the boil and let it become cold and then mix the mangoes, etc., into the vinegar. Turn into bottles and cork tightly. Let them stand in the sun for 4 days—when they are ready for use or to store.

MRS. FIELDGATE, Koforidua.

Mango Chutney.

One pint vinegar, 1 lb. moist sugar, 1 lb. raisins or currants, 1 lb. sultanas, ¼ lb. salt, 4 lb. green mangoes (cut into dice), 2 ozs. powdered (or lump) ginger, 1 oz. garlic (if possible), ½ teaspoonful cayenne.

Put vinegar and sugar to boil, then add the other ingredients, boil all gently until the mango and garlic are quite tender. The raisins should be cut roughly and the garlic* into small pieces.

This is a very good recipe.

MRS. DIXON, Salaga.

Mayonnaise Sauce.

1 yolk of egg
½ teaspoon castor sugar
¼ pint salad oil
2 teaspoons Tarragon vinegar
1 teaspoon dry mustard
2 teaspoon of vinegar
1 tablespoon cream or milk
Salt and pepper.

1. Mix dry ingredients and yolk of egg.
2. Whisk in, drop by drop, the oil and vinegar.
3. Add milk or cream at the last and very gradually. One dessertspoonful of boiling water, added at the end, is an improvement.

N.B.—When adding oil and vinegar, measure into an empty bottle, cork the bottle with a cork in which you have made two holes, place bottle on its side on box or tin so that the oil will drip into the basin slowly, then both hands are free to beat the mixture.

MRS. BEACH JOHNSTONE, Accra.

To whip Ideal Milk.

One tablespoonful of gelatine (¼ oz.), 3 tablespoonfuls of hot water, 1 teaspoonful of sugar, teaspoonful vanilla essence, I large tin of Ideal milk. Dissolve gelatine in hot water, add sugar and vanilla. Pour slowly into milk, which should have previously been slightly warmed. Whip well and leave to set in a cool place. Before serving, well whip again.

MRS. SINCLAIR, Kumasi.

---

* If no garlic, use a little onion instead.

Mint Sauce.

1 tablespoon chopped mint
¼ pint vinegar.
1 tablespoon sugar.

1. Dissolve sugar in water.
2. Add vinegar and mint and stand aside for 1 hour.

MRS. BEACH JOHNSTONE, Accra.

Native Batter.

Twopence corn, 2d. rice, 3d. sugar and plantain, palm oil, a pinch of salt.

1. Grind corn and rice together. Add water and a pinch of salt. Mix to a paste. Allow to stand for hour.

2. Grind the plantain, add to paste with sugar. Add more water if paste is too thick.

3. Heat a little palm oil in a frying pan and pour in a little of the batter at a time, just enough to cover the bottom of the frying pan. Fry till nicely browned, turn and fry the other side. Time 15 minutes.

SISTER ANTONIA, Keta.

Norwegian Open Sandwiches.

Cut brown or white bread and butter and trim into neat rounds. Take eating apples, core and slice them into thin rings. Dip each slice into lemon juice which has been squeezed on to a plate. (Lemon keeps the apple from turning brown.) Lay an apple ring on each slice of bread and fill the hole in the middle with a spoonful of jam—for instance a berry of strawberry jam—both to sweeten and decorate the sandwich. It is not necessary to peel the apples. This recipe is suitable for a buffet supper.

MRS. LLOYD WILLIAMS, Tamale.

Orange Cheese.

Four eggs, 1 orange rind and juice, 1 lime (juice only), 2 ozs. butter, ½ lb. sugar, (lump.)

294

1. Rub off orange rind on to lumps of sugar.
2. Squeeze out juice of lime and orange.
3. Beat eggs.
4. Put all into basin, steam in boiling water, until thick.
5. Put into hot, dry jars and tie down.

MISS. SPEARS.

Palm Cabbage Cheese.

Palm cabbage boiled in the ordinary way, and served with a cheese sauce poured over and baked in the oven for a few minutes, is equally as good as cauliflower cheese.

MISS. BARCHI, Sekondi.

Palm Wine Bread.

Twenty-four tablespoons flour, 1 teaspoon sugar, 1 teaspoon salt, 2 teaspoons baking powder, 1d. palm wine (soda water bottleful). Sieve all dry ingredients into a basin, make a hole in the centre and put in the palm wine warmed slightly, mix with the hands till smooth, then knead for hour adding more flour if necessary, put into greased tins and leave to rise for 3 hours, bake in a moderate oven for 1 hour.

MISS. BARCHI, Sekondi.

Pap.

One lb. corn dough, 4 ozs. sugar. Put water on fire and bring to the boil. Blend and sieve dough and pour into boiling water. Keep stirring until cooked which generally takes 10 minutes. Serve hot or cold (add sugar to taste).

SISTER ANGELE, Cape Coast.

Pickled Onions.

Native onion (shallots)
Vinegar
Salt
Red peppers and vinegar.

Skin and wash onions, put on to boil with salt, and pepper for 5 minutes, put into hot, dry jars, tie down, keep for 1 month before use.

MISS SPEARS.

Potato Gnocchi.

One kilo (2½ lbs.) cold potatoes mashed, 3 handfuls flour, 1 egg, salt. Mix ingredients very well together, roll into long rolls—cut up and roll into pieces about this size:

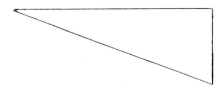

Put into salted boiling water, when the water boils up again they are cooked, pour a jug of cold water into the pan, sift out the gnocchi very carefully, they are very brittle, and put into a fireproof dish in which some baked breadcrumbs have been frying in lots of butter, sauté for a few minutes and serve in the same dish, about one-quarter quantity is enough for two people.

MRS. C. E. DE B. BIDEN.

Rice.

Half lb. rice, 4 pints water, teaspoon salt. Wash and pick any dark grains from the rice. Put it into boiling water (salted), cover and allow to boil until the water is dried up, do not stir. When a grain can be crushed easily between the fingers, leaving no grit or hard centre, it is done.

MRS. BECKETT, Accra.

Sandwich Mixtures.

1. Half lb. liver cut in small pieces, 2 ozs. fat bacon, 1 tablespoon chopped parsley, 1 teaspoon mixed herbs, 1 onion minced, ½ pint vegetable stock, ¼ lb. rice boiled very soft. Put the bacon into a frying pan over gentle heat and cook a little, remove from the pan and add the liver; brown each side, add the onion and brown slightly. Pour in the stock. Add the bacon, herbs, rice and parsley and simmer till all are tender and the mixture solid. Put three times through a sharp mincer, add salt and pepper and pound well. Make into sandwiches.

2. Two ozs. cheese, 1 teaspoon made mustard, pepper, 1 teaspoon vinegar, 1 teaspoon milk. Grate the cheese and mix with the other ingredients to a smooth paste.

With both of these mixtures, if extra butter is added after mixing, the fillings can be spread straight on to the bread which saves much time when many sandwiches have to be made.

MRS. NORTHCOTE, Accra.

Scotch Porridge (Breakfast Dish).

Four tablespoons oatmeal, 3 teacups water, teaspoon, salt. Put water in pot. Sprinkle in oatmeal slowly, stirring well all the time to keep from lumping. Add salt. Keep stirring till it boils. Boil slowly for hour, stirring frequently. Serve in plate with milk.

MRS. SWAN, Tamale.

Soda Bread

Two lbs. flour, 1 teaspoon carbonate soda, 1 teaspoon salt, mix these well together and then add enough sour milk or buttermilk to form an ordinary bread dough and turn it out of the bowl on to a floured board. Form it into a round cake about 4 inches deep, score it across and across with a knife dipped in flour, put it on to a flat floured baking tin and bake for an hour, let the oven be hot at first and when the cake has risen and begins to harden reduce the heat that it may cook through.

LADY THOMAS.

Sweet Potato Bread.

One cup mashed potatoes, 1 cup cornmeal, 1 cup flour, 1 egg, 2 teaspoons baking powder, ½ teaspoon salt.

1. Mix quickly into a dough with half milk and half water.
2. Make into small loaves or scones and bake in hot oven.

MISS SPEARS.

Sabayon Sauce.

One and a half wineglasses of sherry, 2 yolks of eggs, 1 tablespoon sugar. Put all in a pan and whisk over a gentle fire until a stiff froth. Do not allow to boil.

MRS. OAKLEY, Accra.

Sage and Onion Stuffing.

4 large onions
1 teaspoon chopped sage
Seasoning
1 oz. dripping or margarine
Milk or egg to bind.

1. Put onions into cold water, bring to boiling point and boil 5 minutes.
2. Strain, put into fresh water and boil till tender, add sage and cook for 5 minutes.
3. Drain off water, chop finely and mix with fat and seasoning.
4. Bind together with beaten egg or milk.

MRS. BEACH JOHNSTONE, Accra.

Salad Dressing.

Mix together and boil 1 teaspoon flour, 3 lbs. butter, 2 yolks of eggs, ¼ teaspoon salt, 1 lb. sugar, 1 teaspoon dry mustard, ½ cup vinegar, 1 cup sweet milk. Remove from the fire and mix in the beaten whites of the eggs.

ACHIMOTA.

Salad Dressing.

Take yolk of one hard boiled egg (using the white for garnishing), beat the yolk up fine, add 1 teaspoonful of fine sugar, ½ teaspoonful of dry mustard, pepper, salt, 1 tablespoonful of vinegar. Then mix together and add 2 tablespoonfuls of Ideal milk. Proved to be excellent.

MRS. SINCLAIR, Kumasi.

Salad Dressing that will keep.

Beat up an egg in a basin, add half a teaspoon of dry mustard and the same of pepper. Stir in a small tin of condensed milk, and, when thoroughly mixed, fill up the empty tin with vinegar and stir all together. Pour contents into a bottle.

MRS. PASSELLS, Accra.

A Simple Salad Dressing.

One teaspoon dry mustard, 2 teaspoons flour, 2 tablespoons sugar, 1 teaspoon salt, pinch of pepper, 1 egg, 1 teacup (small) vinegar, 1 teacup milk. Mix dry ingredients and put all in a double-lined pan, cook until thick, stir all the time, but do not boil.

MRS. WILKINS, Kumasi.

Salad Dressing without Oil and Vinegar.

Mix 1 tablespoonful flour, 1 tablespoonful butter, 1 tablespoonful sugar, 1 large teaspoonful mustard, 1 small teaspoonful salt. Add 2 well beaten eggs mixed with one large teacup milk, and ½ teacup of lemon juice, alternately. Beat to a smooth cream—place over a slow heat and stir until thick—Do not allow to boil.

MRS. C E. DR B. BIDEN.

Sauces.

Make sauces in the proportion of 1 oz. flour, 1 oz. butter or margarine, and pint warm milk. First melt the butter in a pan, and when hot add the flour gradually. Do not brown. Stir well with a wooden spoon and when thoroughly well mixed, add the milk a little at a time. Boil for 2 or 3 minutes stirring well. Season to taste either with sugar or pepper and salt. Beat well, strain, and before serving stir in a small piece of butter. Any of the following may be added after the sauce is cooked. Lime juice, vermouth, sherry, rum, or brandy, chopped hard-boiled eggs, parsley, oysters, chopped mushrooms, capers, or anchovy essence. To improve the colour of anchovy sauce add 2 or 3 drops of cochineal.

To make a richer sauce add some cream before serving. If by any chance the sauce has become lumpy put through a tammy cloth. To keep sauce warm stand the small saucepan containing it in a larger one with hot water. Pour the sauce with a lid to prevent a skin forming.

MRS. KEAST, Accra.

Gubbins Sauce.

½ oz. butter
1 tablespoon cream or milk
2 teaspoons made mustard
Salt
1 dessertspoon vinegar
Red or black pepper
1 teaspoon tarragon vinegar.

1. Put butter in basin over hot water and melt.
2. Add remainder of ingredients and stir till all very hot.

N.B.—This sauce is excellent for pouring over joints of turkey, chicken or game previously cooked and unused. They should be divided into neat pieces, scored with a knife and grilled or fried and served very hot with plenty of sauce to cover them.

MRS. BEACH JOHNSTONE, Accra.

Hard Brandy Sauce.

Two ozs. butter, 2 ozs. castor sugar, 1 sherry-glass of brandy, 1 sherry-glass of sherry. Mix butter and sugar. Add sherry drop by drop stirring all the time, add brandy the same way, beat until the mixture sets. Put on ice and serve cold.

MRS. SUTHERLAND, Koforidua.

Sauces.

(Proportions for thickening sauces.)
1. Coating consistency ...   1 oz. flour to ½ pint of liquid.
2. Pouring consistency ...   ½ oz. flour to ½ pint of liquid.
3. Thickened gravy ...   ¼ oz. flour to ½ pint of liquid.

White Sauce.

(Coating consistency.)
1 oz. margarine
I oz. flour
salt and pepper
½ pint liquid, i.e. milk or of milk, fish or meat stock, or water.

1. Melt margarine, add flour and cook for a few minutes, stirring little and not allowing the flour to discolour.

2. Remove from fire, add liquid slowly, stirring all the time.

3. Stir until boiling, cook for 5 minutes, add seasoning and use.

MRS. BEACH JOHNSTONE, Accra.

Stuffing or Forcemeat.

1 oz. breadcrumbs
¼ teaspoon mixed herbs
½ oz. finely chopped suet
A little grated lemon rind
Seasoning
1 teaspoon chopped parsley
Enough egg or milk to bind.

1. Mix all well together with the milk or egg.
2. Use for stuffing or form into coils, coat with egg and breadcrumbs and fry.
3. When required for fish, use margarine instead of suet.

MRS. BEACH JOHNSTONE, Accra.

Tapioca.

1. Grate cassava into pan of water.
2. Strain starch and water through muslin.
3. Allow to stand in the pan for one day for sediment to settle.
4. Pour off any water.
5. Break into small pieces and put into frying pan over a very low heat.
6. Stir about in pan until it becomes hard.
7. Bottle and keep ready for use.

MISS SPEARS.

Tomato Sauce.

Three slices bacon cut into small pieces, 1 slice chopped onion, 2 tablespoons flour, 1½ cups strained tomatoes, 1 tablespoon chopped green peppers, ½ teaspoon salt, few gratings nutmeg, cayenne. Put bacon into saucepan, add onion and brown slightly, add flour, heated tomatoes, and stir till thick and smooth, add seasoning and peppers.

MRS. SINCLAIR, Kumasi

Green Tomato Chutney.

To 2 lbs. sliced green tomatoes add 1 lb. sliced onions, 1 tablespoonful sugar or to taste. Tie in separate cloths 1 handful red peppers, 1 handful peppercorns and a few cloves, cover all with vinegar and boil slowly till vinegar is absorbed and chutney a dark brown colour, bottle; will keep indefinitely.

MRS. BARTON, Kumasi.

Tomato Ketchup.

4 onions
¼ pint vinegar
½ teaspoon ginger, or root ginger
¾ lb. sugar.

1. Wash ingredients requiring washing, cut up tomatoes, skin onions.
2. Boil all ingredients, excepting sugar.
3. When soft, rub through sieve, add sugar (and raisins, if liked).
4. Boil up and put in hot, dry jars, tie down.

MISS SPEARS.

Household Hints

Bath Powder.

Equal quantities of boracic powder, Fuller's earth, and orris-root powder. Sieve all separately and finally all together.

MRS. KEAST, Accra.

Boot Cream.

Half oz. Lux soap or finely-shredded soap, 1 oz. white wax, 1 small tablespoon turpentine. Pour the turpentine over the wax and soap, leave 24 hours, then add sufficient boiling water to make the consistency of cream. Keep in covered jar.

MISS SPEAR.

Brass (To Clean).

To keep brass ornaments and trays from getting that mildewed look when cleaned with metal polish try cleaning with fresh limes and sand, then rinse with cold water and when dry rub over with polishing cloth (chamois).

MRS. LOGAN, Accra.

Recipe for Brass Cleaning.

A small tin of globe paste, melt before the fire until liquid, pour into a bottle, add a double quantity of paraffin oil.

MRS. BROWNING, Cape Coast.

Brasso (To use.)

Brasso used by itself is inclined to leave white marks on any ornamentations or the brass. This can be prevented by mixing a little kerosene with the Brasso.

MRS. AUCHINLECK, Accra.

Cleaning Brass.

Brass which has become very stained with verdigris rub with the rind of a lime before cleaning in the ordinary way.

MRS. CRANSTON, Accra.

Brass and metal dish covers can be cleaned, if there happens to be no brass polish available, with a squeezed lemon or lime and a little whiting. Put a pinch of whiting on the articles to be cleaned and rub well in—using the lemon as sponge.

MRS. NICHOLSON, Accra Ice Co.

Candles (To last long).

Candles last double time if held by the wick and coated with varnish and dried. The varnish forms a cup which holds the grease which therefore does not run to waste.

MRS. FRASER, Achimota.

Damp Stains.

To remove damp stains from black material: rub gently with a clean cotton rag dipped in eau-de-cologne.

MRS. SHAW, Accra.

A Hint when Dyeing.

Put the powder into an old piece of linen, or any material and tie up like a blue bag, then there is no fear of small specks of undissolved powder being found on the garment when finished, also hang the garment straight out without wringing.

MRS. BUTLER.

Enamel Stains.

Stains and discolouration can be removed by a rag dipped first in lemon juice and then in kitchen salt. Rinse with warm water.

MRS. CRANSTON, Accra.

Face Lotions.

Face lotions will be found much more refreshing, if 3 placed in the Frigidaire for a short time before use.

MRS. SAMUEL, Accra.

Floor and Furniture Polish.

Shred ½ cake Sunlight soap very thinly and 2 oz. beeswax, place in a deep tin. Cover well with turpentine. Leave a day or two till soap and wax have dissolved then stir in 1 pint boiling water. Beat briskly till a thick cream when it is ready for use.

MRS. NORTHCOTE, Accra.

Palm Oil Furniture Polish.

Half pint palm oil, ½ pint turpentine, ½ pint methylated spirit, ¼ pint vinegar. Pour into a bottle, cork securely. Shake before use.

MISS SPEARS.

Furniture and Floor Polish.

(The ingredients for which are available in every Bush Station).
1 packet (12) ordinary wax candles as sold everywhere
2 bars red soap as sold everywhere
4 pints kerosene.

Pare soap and wax candles very finely and melt over hot stove or in brick oven. Stir in the kerosene being careful that the mixture does not boil or come into contact with flame, when thoroughly mixed put aside to cool. This will give a stiff paste mixture which can be let down with cold kerosene to required consistency for use. In use the mixture should not be a stiff paste but should flow freely from the bottle, as several liquid applications give a far better result than one or two paste applications.

MRS. CUTHBERT, Koforidua.

Furniture Polish.

Very thin engine oil rubbed on to furniture and then taken off, gives an excellent polish.

MRS. AUCHINLECK, Accra.

Furniture Polish.

Two tablespoons linseed oil boiled, 2 tablespoons methylated spirit, 2 tablespoons vinegar. Put in a bottle and shake well before using.

MRS. BROWNING, Cape Coast.

Gloy Substitute.

Take one tablespoon flour and mix with cold water to a thin paste (cream consistency), put into a saucepan and stir over a very low light until just boiling, if the paste thickens too much during the heating, add cold water gradually and beat in, add a few drops of oil of cloves to keep the paste from going bad quickly.—Cost 1½ d.

ACHIMOTA.

Grease Spots.

The best way to remove grease spots from light delicate materials is by using oil of eucalyptus. Dab the spot gently with a small quantity of the oil in a piece of cotton-wool. A second application may be necessary, put garment aside to dry. It leaves no mark on the material as so many other grease removers do, this I have tried and found good.

MRS. KELLY, Accra.

Grease Stains from Silks.

To remove grease stains from georgette or similar materials, rub gently till dry with a clean handkerchief or piece of cotton wool. If all the grease has not been absorbed, rub some powdered French chalk into the spots, leave overnight and brush out thoroughly the next morning. If the chalk is applied while the grease is moist it is apt to cake and dull the finish of the fabric.

MRS. SAMUEL, Accra.

Hair-wash.

One oz. tincture jaborandi, 1 oz. cantharides, 1 drachm tincture lavender, 8 ozs. water. To be rubbed well into the roots of the hair.

MRS. BROWNING, Cape Coast.

Lace (To wash).

A little sugar added to the water in which lace is rinsed after washing, stiffens it slightly. The unattractive shine which ironing sometimes produces on black lace can be avoided by protecting the lace with a thin piece of silk which has first been damped.

MRS. CRANSTON, Accra.

Lamp (To prevent from smoking).

One teaspoonful of vinegar in a lamp prevents it from smoking.

ACHIMOTA.

Leather bags which have become shabby are easily renovated by dipping a sponge into warm water in which a little oxalic acid has been dissolved and rubbing the soiled surface vigorously.

MRS. NICHOLSON, Accra.

Kumasi lilies will last much longer if arranged in vases with no water.

MRS. SAMUEL, Accra.

To Remove Mildew from Linen.

Mix soft soap with an equal quantity of powdered starch and half as much salt. Add the juice of a lemon or lime, blend all together. Lay the mixture on both sides of the stain with a brush. Put in the sun, leave out all night to get the dew and early sun. If the mildew is very bad, repeat the treatment several times, it will not harm the linen.

If you want your linen to wear well try this plan: instead of folding table cloths and sheets lengthways as is generally done, fold them the other way occasionally, as they last much longer if the folds are sometimes changed in this way than if always folded in the same place.

MRS. NICHOLSON, Accra.

Linen that has got a bad colour may be made whiter by soaping thoroughly and spreading in the sun. Do not allow the cloth to dry, but keep wet with soap suds.

MRS. BECKETT, Accra.

Polishing Mirrors.

Add a dash of vinegar to the water used for cleaning mirrors and glassware. This gives a brilliant polish.

MRS. CRANSTON, Accra.

Stubborn Nuts (To remove).

Heat the end of the spanner and place on the nut for a few seconds. This will expand the nut only and generally allow it to be removed without breaking the bolt.

MRS. CUTHBERT, Koforidua.

Razor Blades (To resuscitate).

When in the "Bush" and the last blade gives out it may be caused to give further service by being dipped for a few seconds into Scrubb's ammonia.

MRS. CUTHBERT, Koforidua.

Mayonnaise Sauce (Bottled)

Is improved if whites of eggs are beaten stiffly and added to it. Add also some champignons cut in half.

Pistachio Nuts.

When unobtainable, peel and chop brazil or walnuts, and colour with a small quantity of Marshall's vegetable green.

MRS. KEAST, Accra.

Sand-bags (Utility of).

A hot sandbag holds heat longer than a rubber hot bottle and is quickly heated on the top of the stove or in oven. Old flannel filled with dry sea sand with a detachable cotton or linen cover.

MRS. FRASER, Achimota.

Silk Sewing.

When machining georgette or any similar material, place a piece of tissue-paper underneath. This will prevent puckering and can be easily torn away.

MRS. SAMUEL, Accra.

Stains on Knives.

Unsightly stains on knives may be removed by means of a slice of raw potato dipped in brick-dust. Stained ivory knife handles should be rubbed with a cloth dipped in turpentine.

MRS. BARTLETT, Accra.

To Remove Gin Stains from a Decanter.

The white stain caused by gin in a glass decanter is very easily dissolved off by lime juice.

MRS. BECKETT, Accra.

Removal of Stains.

A simple method of removing stains or marks from light-coloured fabrics without using inflammable agents such as petrol or benzene, is by using borax water. Dissolve a teaspoonful of powdered borax in a pint of hot water and apply with absorbent cotton.

MRS. BROWNING, Cape Coast.

Ink Stains (To remove).

Mix ½ tin of milk with water and pour it slowly through the stained cloth. Continue to do this till the stain has disappeared and then wash well to remove milk. Do not leave the stained cloth to soak in the milk as this merely spreads the stain.

MRS. NORTHCOTE, Accra.

Ink Stains (To remove).

To take an ink stain out of a coloured cotton material, cover with mustard, and let stand for several hours, then wash in cold water.

ACHIMOTA.

For stains on leather chairs use a mixture of one part vinegar and two parts of boiled linseed oil—shake well. Apply sparingly and polish well with furniture polish.

MRS. NICHOLSON, Accra.

Homemade Stickfast.

1 tablespoon flour
1 tablespoon size
1 teaspoon alum
A few drops of oil of cloves

1. Mix flour and cold water to smooth paste, add boiling water and boil until a thick paste.
2. Dissolve size in a little hot water and add to paste.

3. Stir in the alum and cloves, this should keep fresh for months, if kept covered over.

MISS SPEAR.

Tussore Silk.

For best results, tussore silk should be quite dry before it is ironed, otherwise it will have a streaky appearance and lose its fine gloss.

MRS. CRANSTON, Accra.

Useful Measures.

Tablespoon   = 1 oz.
Dessertspoon = ½ oz.
Teaspoon   = ¼ oz.

Average teacup holds about a quarter of a lb. of flour and a breakfast cup half a pound.

MRS. BARTLETT, Accra.

Useful Hints.

Do not air clothes or linen on croton or adadsi bushes, if a leaf or branch get broken, the sap will leave a stain like mould which is impossible to get out.

MRS. MILNE, Winneba.

A glass rose-holder makes quite a nice and useful part to a dressing table for putting nail scissors, file, tweezers, iodine pen, thermometer, button hook, etc., all things that one needs handy.

Borax scattered in drawers, keeps roaches away.

MRS. BECKETT, Accra.

Polished furniture can be rubbed over with a little olive oil well rubbed in and then polished with a soft dry duster.

Windows and mirrors are much more easily cleaned with a metal polish (such as Brasso). This also prevents flies settling on them. The same method can be used for windscreens of cars. The boys in West Africa make a better job of windows cleaned this way instead of water and leathers.

MRS. HOLLAND, Oda.

To remove hot plate marks from polished tables.

Take some olive oil and put in a saucer and add a small quantity of salt to it and then apply to the marks and rub carefully. Several applications may be needed for bad marks.

To keep cockroaches away from drawers and cupboards.

Sprinkle powdered borax in the drawers and cupboards. This is very good indeed.

MRS. FIELDGATE, The Residency, Koforidua.

Veterinary Hint.

Two parts of olive oil and one part of kerosene shaken in a bottle and applied, as follows, will usually cure skin troubles on dogs and cats: Rub a little in every morning for three days. Wash the part with warm water and soap on the fourth day. Repeat after interval of three days if necessary.

MRS. KEAST, Accra.

Vim.

Equal quantities of silver-sand, whiting, soap powder. Mix all together very thoroughly.

MRS. HENDERSON, Accra.

When Vinegar is Useful.

Polished furniture will take on a much more brilliant shine if it has first been rubbed over with vinegar and water (of equal quantities).

MRS. HOLLAND, Oda.

314

Vinegar added to water in which fish is being boiled not only whitens the fish but keeps it firm.

MRS. NICHOLSON, Accra.

Warm vinegar takes stains, heat marks, etc., out of mahogany, rub well, it is also an excellent polish for lacquer, tables, and trays. Polish with a spot of paraffin very lightly.

MRS. NICHOLSON, Accra.

To Clean Windows.

Old newspapers used as polishing cloths are excellent and easy to use.

MRS. FIELDGATE, Koforidua.

Choosing Poultry.

When you choose poultry, see that the beak and claws of a fowl are soft, not stiff or horny—the bones of all young birds are soft and easily broken.

Tough Meat.

A spoonful of vinegar put into the water in which meat or fowls are boiled makes them tender.

Game (To keep sweet).

Ground coffee sprinkled freely amongst the fur or feathers of freshly-shot game will keep it sweet for a considerable time. It should always be treated in this way when packed for travelling.

When Boiling Rice.

Lemon juice added to the water will not only whiten the rice but separate the grains also,

Light Mashed Potatoes.

A teaspoonful of baking powder added to mashed potatoes with the milk before they are whipped will make them very light and flaky.

MRS. BARTLETT, Accra.

Baking Powder.

Half a pound ground rice, 3 ozs. tartaric acid, 5 ozs. carbonate of soda, mix together and bottle.

MRS. BROWNING, Cape Coast.

Coffee (Locally-grown).

Locally-grown coffee is excellent if roasted and ground at home, just sufficient should be roasted to last for not more than two days.

To roast: To ½ lb. coffee beans (raw), add one teaspoonful butter and one dessertspoonful sugar, stir over good fire till butter and sugar are melted, then roast, stirring frequently.

MRS. BARTON, Kumasi.

Fire lighting.

Dry orange and lime skins in sun. They start the cook's fire quicker and more safely than kerosene.

MRS. FRASER, Achimota.

Rice for Curry.

To separate the grains, pour some cold water into the pan of rice. Strain and dry on sieve in cool oven with door open.

MRS. KEAST, Accra.

Leaking Casseroles.

Make a mixture of pea-flour and water, and let it stew all day in the casserole by the fire, the pea-flour will get into the crack and stop the leak in nine cases out of ten. This is useful to know of in a country where these articles cannot be mended and people are puzzled to know what to do with cracked, casseroles.

MRS. KELLY.

Eggs for Salad.

Eggs which have been boiled hard ready for salad-making should be put immediately under running cold water. This prevents them from becoming discoloured.

New baking-tins will never rust if they are rubbed all over with lard and then baked in a warm oven for about half an hour.

Add a little sugar to the water in which potatoes are boiling and this will help to keep them white and whole.

A quick and simple way to remove the smell of onions from a pan is to boil some used tea leaves in it.

Tough Chicken.

Add a little pure malt vinegar to the water in which a chicken is boiled. This will ensure tenderness, even if the bird is old.

Lemon juice sprinkled over bananas will keep them from becoming discoloured.

MRS. LYNCH, Cape Coast.

Cold Storage Beetroot.

Should be boiled for 24 hours and when cold covered with vinegar coloured with carmine.

MRS. KEAST, Accra.

When preparing pawpaw, do not remove all the seeds. They are not only of an agreeable flavour, resembling that of nasturtium-leaves but a few, well masticated, are an aid to digestion.

MRS. SAMUEL, Accra.

Lettuces (To keep fresh).

Cut off the top two inches of the outside leaves and stand, roots up, in about an inch of water.

MRS. MOOR, Koforidua.

Miscellaneous.

Lettuce which is tired can be revived by placing the stems in soda water, the gas in the water having restorative powers.

MRS. NICHOLSON.

Eggs (To preserve).

Grease all over as soon as laid. They will keep for weeks.

Eggs (To determine Sex).

Pullets are smooth and cockerels rough at the ends.

MRS. MOOR, Koforidua.

Meat.

Boiled salt beef or boiled ham to be eaten cold, if left in the water it is boiled in, will be more tender.

When frying sausages, sprinkle salt in the pan, and the fat will not splash.

Hang frozen meat under a fly-proof cover all day in the sun, and rub well with vinegar just before roasting.

To make a chicken tender, kill it at 10 a.m. Let it hang all day, undressed, in the shade before roasting for dinner. If wanted for lunch, kill late evening before, and hang all night. Dress and clean bird early next morning and put in ice chest until wanted.

Choose a turkey with black legs, and preferably a cock for roasting.

Slices of bacon fat tied on to the breast of any bird will help to make it tender. Baste continually.

Soup.

To take fat off cold soup or stock, dip iron spoon in hot water. Before serving hot soup, draw paper over to remove any grease. For very greasy soup, strain through a cloth wrung out in cold water and heat again. For over-salted soup, add one or two potatoes, or a little coarse sugar.

Fish.

Put a little bicarbonate of soda to boiling salmon to make it a good pink colour.

When frying fish, season the breadcrumbs with pepper and salt.

Tinned Goods.

Test tinned fish, meat and fruits by placing tin in basin of water deep enough to well cover it. Should bubbles rise, the tin is unfit for use.

Tinned beetroot is improved if it is coloured with Marshall's carmine or cochineal. Similarly loganberries, raspberries and strawberries.

MRS. KEAST, Accra.

Vegetables.

1. Bread tied in muslin and boiled with vegetables such as onions or cabbage will prevent unpleasant smell; or a pan of boiling vinegar near the vegetable pan will be equally effective.
2. When frying tomatoes, to keep them from becoming pulpy after slicing, dip them in vinegar.

3. For boiled ham and cabbage, boil the ham with the cabbage.

Stewed Fruit.

First prepare a syrup in the proportion of ½ lb. sugar to ½ pint water. Bring it to the boil and then lay the fruit in and simmer gently. The same syrup, bottled, is useful for making lime drinks. Should the fruit be sweet, less sugar may be added.

Puddings.

1. Tinned Christmas puddings are greatly improved if they are re-mixed with eggs beaten up in brandy enough to make the puddings moist.

2. When using suet for boiled or steamed puddings, or for making a suet crust, add some fine white breadcrumbs to the mixture before adding the liquid, in the proportion of 1 dessertspoon of crumbs to 3 oz. suet. Similarly, if dripping is used.

3. Cover a boiled or steamed pudding with grease-proof paper before tying on the pudding cloth.

MRS. KEAST, Accra.

BIBLIOGRAPHY

British Red Cross Society (Gold Coast branch), (1933). *The Gold Coast Cookery Book*, Government Printing Office, Accra.

Brown, A. Samler (ed) (1922). *The South and East African Year Book and Guide, 1922*, Sampson Low, Marston & Co., London.

De Santis, E., (2005). *Major Sydney Banks Keast, O.B.E., M.C.*, 'Ubique' web site, http://members.aol.com/reubique/major.htm

Ghana Catholic Bishops' Conference, (2006). *Historical Dates*, Ghana Catholic Bishops' Conference web site, http://www.ghanacbc.org/historical_dates.html

Irvine, D.S., (1954). 'Review of *Gold Coast Cookery and Nutrition*', *African Affairs*, Vol. 53, No. 212. (Jul.1954).

Kelly's Directories, Ltd. (1940). *Kelly's Handbook to the Titled, Landed and Official Classes, 1940*, Kelly's Directories Ltd, London.

Simpson, D., (1995). 'Aggrey and Fraser: An Unique Photograph', *African Affairs*, Vol. 94, No. 374. (Jan., 1995).

Whitakers (1931). *Whitaker's Almanack, 1931*, Joseph Whitaker, London.

Also available from Jeppestown Press:

Where the Lion Roars: An 1890 African
Colonial Cookbook
Mrs A. R. Barnes

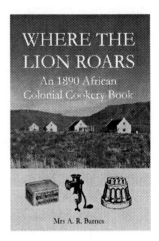

A reprint of one of Africa's earliest English-language cookery books, dating from 1890. Mrs Barnes' recipes for translucent, aromatic melon and ginger konfyt; fiery curries; and sweet peach chutney are as delicious now as they were a century ago; while instructions for making a canvas water cooler, and for treating snake-bite or fever, offer a fascinating insight into the domestic lives of southern Africa's Victorian colonists. ISBN: 0-9553936-1-2

For full details of our inventory, or to order direct, view our web
site at www.jeppestown.com

JEPPESTOWN

The Bulawayo Cookery Book and Household Guide
Edited by Mrs N. Chataway

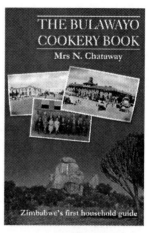

This reprint of Zimbabwe's earliest cookery book is packed with recipes for Edwardian African delicacies: garnet-coloured tomato jam; fiery, home-made ginger beer and spicy bobotie. Packed with contemporary advertisements for companies like Puzey and Payne, Philpott and Collins and Haddon and Sly, the book even contains a section on veld cookery, contributed by Colonel Robert 'Boomerang' Gordon, D.S.O., O.B.E., who went on to raise and command the Northern Rhodesia Rifles at the outbreak of the First World War. ISBN: 0-9553936-2-0

For full details of our inventory, or to order direct, view our web site at www.jeppestown.com

JEPPESTOWN

The Anglo-African Who's Who 1907
Walter H. Wills (ed.)

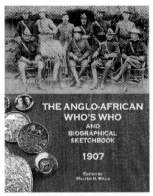

A reprint of Walter Wills' quirky colonial reference book, containing the details of nearly 2,000 prominent men and women of Edwardian Africa. This astonishing work includes biographies of settlers, soldiers, explorers, politicians and traditional leaders from every corner of the continent. Invaluable for genealogists, historians, military researchers and medal enthusiasts, it offers details of over 1,200 separate medal awards, together with fascinating biographical sketches of colonial African celebrities—many of whom were known personally to the editor. ISBN: 0-9553936-3-9

For full details of our inventory, or to order direct, view our web site at www.jeppestown.com

JEPPESTOWN

The Rhodesia Medal Roll
David Saffery (ed)

Containing the names of over 12,000
recipients and revealing 2,300 previously
unpublished decorations, this definitive
book is the ultimate compendium of
Rhodesian military and civilian honours
and awards gazetted between 1970 and
1981. Fully indexed by surname, it is
perfect for medal collectors and dealers,
historians and genealogists—and a brilliant heirloom souvenir for
recipients and their families. ISBN: 0-9553936-0-4

Rhodesia Medal Roll
Honours and Decorations of the
Rhodesian Conflict 1970-1981
David Saffery

For full details of our inventory, or to order direct, view our web
site at **www.jeppestown.com**

JEPPESTOWN

Matabeleland and the Victoria Falls
C. G. Oates (ed)

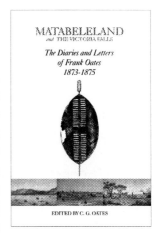

This book draws on the original diaries, letters, paintings and sketches of Frank Oates to paint a vivid picture of the Victorian exploration of Central Africa. It documents his encounters with legendary rulers such as King Lobengula of the Ndebele and larger-than-life characters like the ivory hunter Frederick Selous, and records Oates' final, fatal trek through the Zambezi Valley towards Victoria Falls. ISBN: 978-0-9553936-4-8

For full details of our inventory, or to order direct, view our web site at www.jeppestown.com

JEPPESTOWN

With Captain Stairs to Katanga
Joseph A. Moloney

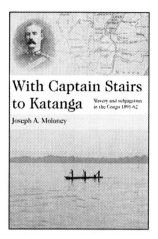

While British and Belgian companies greedily eyed the mineral riches of central Africa, a group of Victorian mercenaries marched nearly 1,000 miles through the bush to confront Msiri, the most powerful ruler in Katanga, and annex his kingdom. First published in 1893, this fascinating narrative will transport you to a world of cannibals, missionaries and slave traders; of a provocative military invasion and its bloody climax; and of the mercenaries' nightmarish return march—wracked by starvation and fever—back to the coast of East Africa. Containing a lively and detailed first-hand account of the 'scramble for Africa', this book is essential reading for anyone curious about the motivation and processes of European conquest in Africa. ISBN: 0-9553936-5-5

For full details of our inventory, or to order direct, view our web site at **www.jeppestown.com**

J E P P E S T O W N

10% discount! ORDER FORM

Use this form to order any of our books by post to addresses in the United Kingdom. For overseas orders please use the web site www.jeppestown.com.

Title	Price	Quantity	Total
Where the Lion Roars: An 1890 African Colonial Cookbook	~~£12.95~~ £11.66		
The Bulawayo Cookery Book and Household Guide	~~£12.95~~ £11.66		
The Ghana Cookery Book	~~£12.95~~ £11.66		
The Anglo-African Who's Who 1907	~~£18.95~~ £17.06		
The Rhodesia Medal Roll	~~£17.95~~ £16.16		
Matabeleland and the Victoria Falls	~~£12.95~~ £11.66		
With Captain Stairs in Katanga	~~£12.95~~ £11.66		
Postage and packing within the UK			add £2.80
Total			

To order, send a cheque or postal order for the total amount (made payable to **Jeppestown Press**) to Jeppestown Press, 10A Scawfell St, London, E2 8NG.

Delivery details:

Name:

Address:

Telephone number (in case of query):